Conference Proceedings of the Society for Experimental Mechanics Series

Series Editor

Kristin B. Zimmerman
Society for Experimental Mechanics, Inc.,
Bethel, USA

The Conference Proceedings of the Society for Experimental Mechanics Series presents early findings and case studies from a wide range of fundamental and applied work across the broad range of fields that comprise Experimental Mechanics. Series volumes follow the principle tracks or focus topics featured in each of the Society's two annual conferences: IMAC, A Conference and Exposition on Structural Dynamics, and the Society's Annual Conference & Exposition and will address critical areas of interest to researchers and design engineers working in all areas of Structural Dynamics, Solid Mechanics and Materials Research.

Brian Damiano · Babak Moaveni · Antonio De Luca · Keith Worden
Editors

Structural Health Monitoring & Machine Learning, Vol. 12

Proceedings of the 43rd IMAC, A Conference and Exposition on Structural Dynamics 2025

River Publishers

Published, sold and distributed by:

River Publishers
Broagervej 10
9260 Gistrup
Denmark

www.riverpublishers.com

ISBN 97887-438-0157-3 (Hardback)

ISBN 97887-438-0169-6 (eBook)

https://doi.org/10.13052/97887-438-0157-3

Conference Proceedings of the Society for Experimental Mechanics

An imprint of River Publishers

Preface

Structural Health Monitoring & Machine Learning represents one of twelve volumes of technical papers presented at the *43rd* IMAC, A Conference and Exposition on Structural Dynamics, organized by the Society for Experimental Mechanics, and held February 10-13, 2025. The full proceedings also include volumes on Nonlinear Structures & Systems; Model Validation and Uncertainty Quantification; Dynamic Substructuring & Transfer Path Analysis; Special Topics in Structural Dynamics & Experimental Techniques; Computer Vision & Laser Vibrometry; Dynamic Environments Testing; Sensors & Instrumentation and Aircraft/Aerospace Testing Techniques; Topics in Modal Analysis & Parameter Identification I&II; and Data Science in Engineering.

Each collection presents early findings from analytical, experimental and computational investigations on an important area within Structural Dynamics. Structural Health Monitoring is one of these areas which cover topics of interest of several disciplines in engineering and science.

Structural Health Monitoring & Machine Learning are specific subject areas within the SEM umbrella of technical divisions, namely the Dynamics of Civil Structures including other technical activities devoted to structural analysis, testing, monitoring, and assessment. This volume covers a variety of topics including Bayesian Inference Methods, and Structural Health Monitoring with Digital Twinning.

The organizers would like to thank the authors, presenters, session organizers, and session chairs for their participation in this track.

Editor:
Brian Damiano, *Oak Ridge National Laboratory, Oak Ridge, TN, USA*; Babak Moaveni, *Tufts University, Medford, MA, USA*; Antonio De Luca, *Thornton Tomasetti, Ft. Lauderdale, FL, USA*; Keith Worden, *University of Sheffield, Sheffield, UK.*

Contents

Chapter 1
Theoretical Foundations and Practical Applications of Damage Detection Using Autocovariance Functions

Jyrki Kullaa

Abstract Autocovariance functions (ACFs) can be utilized as damage-sensitive features in structural health monitoring. They have several advantages: they include the necessary information about the dynamic characteristics of the structure for damage detection, they are easy to estimate, they contain many data points, their accuracy can be controlled, and they are spatiotemporally correlated. Damage detection is performed in the time domain. ACFs have the same form as a free decay of the system for a stationary random process. A major issue of ACFs is that the free decay at a natural frequency includes cross-terms also from other modes. Therefore, the data lie in a high-dimensional space. For spatial correlation, the required number of sensors therefore increases considerably with an increasing number of active modes. Fortunately, the number of sensors can be reduced if temporal correlation is also utilized. Using spatiotemporal correlation, it is possible to detect changes in both natural frequencies and mode shapes. The objective is to pursue data redundancy, so that damage can be detected in the noise space. A simple and useful formula is presented, relating the number of active modes, the number of sensors, and the model order for damage detection. The conditions are also given for the design parameters limiting detection to frequency changes only or mode shape changes only. It is also shown that the variability of the excitation characteristics between measurements has no effect on damage detection. Numerical experiments were performed to validate the theoretical considerations.

Keywords Autocovariance function · Spatiotemporal correlation · Damage detection · Data redundancy · Model order

Introduction

Structural health monitoring (SHM) aims at receiving an early warning about structural damage or failure. Damage detection is based on vibration data measured from the structure during normal operation. Therefore, the excitation cannot be controlled or measured, and it may also vary between measurements. If the changes of the dynamic characteristics of the structure are statistically significant, it is an indication of damage. Training data are first acquired under different environmental or operational conditions to distinguish changes due to damage from changes due to environmental or operational variability.

Damage detection in the time domain is an attractive alternative to parameter-based methods, because time domain data include more data points and system identification is not needed. Covariance functions have been used in damage detection [3–12]. In this study, autocovariance functions (ACFs) are used as damage-sensitive features. They have been shown to work with numerical and experimental data [11].

In this paper, the applicability of ACFs for damage detection is theoretically investigated. More specifically, a relationship between the number of active modes, the number of sensors, and the model order in the data analysis is explored. Additionally, the effect of the variability of the excitation characteristics is studied (operational variability).

The objective of the proposed SHM system design is to make the measurement data redundant. Then, some variables can be computed using the remaining variables. For a redundant system, the data space can be divided into two subspaces, the signal space and the noise space. The signal space contains useful information of the vibration and the environmental or operational effects. The noise space consists mostly of measurement error. This was also discussed in [12]. Once damage appears, the new data are assumed to appear also in the noise space of the training data, which is easier to detect, because the variance is assumably much smaller in the noise space than in the signal space. It should be noted, however, that the

Jyrki Kullaa
Department of Automotive and Mechanical Engineering, Metropolia University of Applied Sciences, Leiritie 1, 01600 Vantaa, Finland
e-mail: jyrki.kullaa@metropolia.fi

Brian Damiano et al. (eds.), *Structural Health Monitoring & Machine Learning, Vol. 12*, Conference Proceedings of the Society for Experimental Mechanics Series, https://doi.org/10.13052/9788743801573-1

existence of the noise space does not guarantee that the data from the damaged structure enters the noise space. Therefore, the degree of redundancy should be increased if possible so that the dimension of the noise space is greater than one.

The paper is organized as follows. The autocovariance functions are introduced in the next section, in which important formulas are given for the SHM system design. The proposed damage detection and localization algorithm in the time domain follows. A numerical experiment is performed to validate the theoretical consideration. Finally, concluding remarks are given.

Autocovariance Functions for Damage Detection

If the excitation is stationary random, the autocovariance functions of the structural responses (e.g. acceleration, velocity, displacement, strain) have the same form as a free decay of the system, which is also the foundation of operational modal analysis (OMA) [13].

The autocovariance function of a zero-mean random process $\{y(t)\}$ is

$$R_{yy}(\tau) = E\left[y(t)y(t+\tau)\right] \tag{1}$$

where $E[\cdot]$ is the expectation operator and τ is the time lag. Using modal superposition of linear structures, the displacement response $\mathbf{y}(t)$ at time t can be written as

$$\mathbf{y}(t) = \sum_{r=1}^{n} \boldsymbol{\phi}_r q_r(t) \tag{2}$$

where n is the number of active modes, $\boldsymbol{\phi}_r$ is the mode shape vector of mode r, and $q_r(t)$ is the modal coordinate of mode r. If we denote ϕ_{ir} as the ith component of vector $\boldsymbol{\phi}_r$, the autocovariance function of the displacement degree-of-freedom (DOF) $\{y_i(t)\}$ is

$$R_{ii}(\tau) = E\left[\sum_r \phi_{ir} q_r(t) \sum_s \phi_{is} q_s(t+\tau)\right] = \sum_r \sum_s \phi_{ir}\phi_{is} E\left[q_r(t)q_s(t+\tau)\right] \tag{3}$$

For a stationary random process with white noise excitation, the ACF can be derived [13, 14, 5]:

$$R_{ii}(\tau) = \sum_{s=1}^{n} \left[A_{is}\cos\left(\omega_{ds}\tau\right) + B_{is}\sin\left(\omega_{ds}\tau\right)\right] e^{-\zeta_s\omega_s} \tag{4}$$

where

$$A_{is} = \sum_{r=1}^{n} F_{rs}\phi_{ir}\phi_{is}\boldsymbol{\phi}_r^T \mathbf{BQB}^T \boldsymbol{\phi}_s \tag{5}$$

and

$$B_{is} = \sum_{r=1}^{n} G_{rs}\phi_{ir}\phi_{is}\boldsymbol{\phi}_r^T \mathbf{BQB}^T \boldsymbol{\phi}_s \tag{6}$$

where

$$F_{rs} = \frac{1}{2m_r\omega_{dr}m_s\omega_{ds}}\left[\frac{-\zeta_r\omega_r - \zeta_s\omega_s}{\left(\zeta_r\omega_r+\zeta_s\omega_s\right)^2 + \left(\omega_{dr}+\omega_{ds}\right)^2} + \frac{\zeta_r\omega_r + \zeta_s\omega_s}{\left(\zeta_r\omega_r+\zeta_s\omega_s\right)^2 + \left(\omega_{dr}-\omega_{ds}\right)^2}\right] \tag{7}$$

and

$$G_{rs} = \frac{1}{2m_r\omega_{dr}m_s\omega_{ds}}\left[\frac{\omega_{dr}+\omega_{ds}}{\left(\zeta_r\omega_r+\zeta_s\omega_s\right)^2 + \left(\omega_{dr}+\omega_{ds}\right)^2} + \frac{\omega_{dr}-\omega_{ds}}{\left(\zeta_r\omega_r+\zeta_s\omega_s\right)^2 + \left(\omega_{dr}-\omega_{ds}\right)^2}\right] \tag{8}$$

where m_r, ω_r, ω_{dr}, ζ_r are, respectively, the modal mass, the undamped natural circular frequency, the damped natural circular frequency, and damping ratio of the mode r. Matrix $\mathbf{B}$ is the load distribution matrix, and $\mathbf{Q}$ is a diagonal matrix where the diagonal entries are the spectral densities of the independent loads. $\mathbf{B}$ is assumed to be constant during a single measurement. An example of an ACF with 300 lags is shown in Fig. 1, when the number of modes is 7.

From Equation (4), it can be seen that the ACF has the same form as a free decay of the system. However, the decay at natural frequency ω_{ds} includes also cross-terms from other modes, as seen in Equations (5) and (6). This can make damage detection challenging, because the modal amplitudes ratios between sensors (A_{is}/A_{js} and B_{is}/B_{js}) may be different in each measurement.

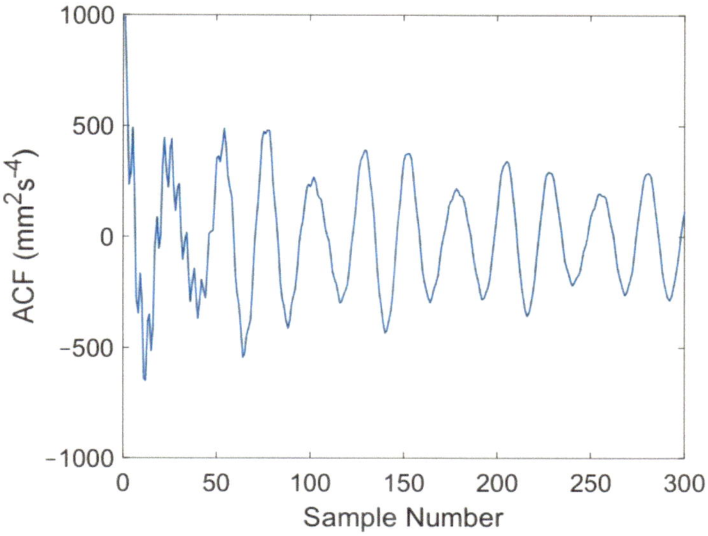

Fig. 1 Autocovariance function with 7 active modes

In the design of an SHM system, three parameters are important for damage detection: the number of active modes n, the number of sensors p, and the model order m used in the data analysis. The number of active modes cannot be controlled, but it affects the selection of the other two parameters. If the number of active modes is too large, filtering could be applied to remove the contribution of some modes. Once n is known, the number of sensors can be determined. This decision influences the hardware and maintenance costs and should be kept to a minimum. Optimal sensor placement is beyond the scope of this study but should also be considered. If changes in both the mode shapes and frequencies must be detected, this number must be at least equal to n. Once the first two parameters are fixed, the model order can be determined. It only affects the duration of the data analysis and the memory usage without additional hardware costs.

The selection of design parameters is based on redundancy of the ACF data. The redundancy can be spatial, temporal, or spatiotemporal. The results are only presented here without lengthy derivations.

Spatial correlation ($m = 0$) detects only changes in the mode shapes. The required number of sensors p is

$$p>\frac{1}{2}n\,(n+1) \tag{9}$$

For many real structures, this condition may yield too large a sensor network and high costs.

Temporal correlation ($1 \leq p \leq n$) detects only changes in the natural frequencies or modal damping. The model order used in the analysis must be

$$m>2n \tag{10}$$

Spatiotemporal correlation ($p \geq n$) can detect both changes in the frequencies, damping, and mode shapes. The model order m must be

$$m>\frac{2n^2}{p}-1 \tag{11}$$

These formulas, especially Eq. (11) can be applied to the design of an SHM system. Note that environmental influences were not considered in the formulas. Their contribution can be taken into account by increasing the number of sensors p and the model order m.

Damage Detection Algorithm

The damage detection algorithm is briefly introduced. More details can be found in [15]. For each data set and for each sensor separately, the ACFs are estimated. The user has to determine the number of lags in the ACFs. The training data are comprised of the ACFs from the undamaged structure under different environmental or operational conditions. The data are copied and shifted m times for spatiotemporal correlation. The model order m is determined by the user with the help of

Eqs. (10) or (11). A covariance matrix of the time-shifted training data is estimated. The covariance matrix is subjected to a whitening transformation for data normalization. When new data (ACFs) arrive, the same whitening transformation is applied to these data. If the dynamic characteristics of the structure have changed, the new data are assumed to appear in the noise space and thus outside the hypersphere (for Gaussian data). This can be detected by applying principal component analysis to all data. The first principal component is now dictated by the data points outside the hypersphere. The first principal component scores are only retained, reducing the data dimensionality to one. Extreme value statistics (EVS) distributions [16] are identified for the scores of the training data by dividing the data into equal sized subgroups. The extreme values of each subgroup are plotted on a control chart with control limits determined from the probability of a false alarm [17]. If the data points of the test data are outside the control limits, an alarm is raised.

Numerical Experiment

The structure being monitored was a bridge deck with a concrete slab and steel stiffeners (Fig. 2). A detailed description of the model can be found in [18]. The first 7 modes were active, having natural frequencies of 3.95 Hz, 5.35 Hz, 13.7 Hz, 15.4 Hz, 17.9 Hz, 24.1 Hz, and 24.8 Hz. The corresponding damping ratios were 0.01, 0.01, 0.02, 0.02, 0.03, 0.03, and 0.03.

The sampling interval was $\Delta t = 0.01$ s and the measurement period was almost 44 min including $2^{18} = 262144$ samples. A long measurement period is necessary to provide accurate ACF estimates [19].

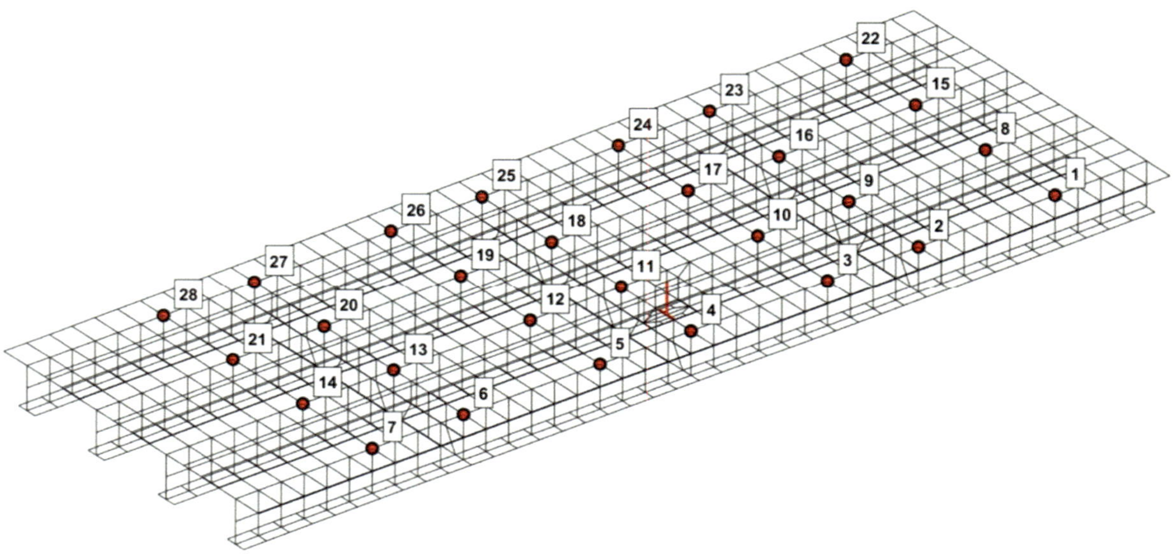

Fig. 2 Finite element model of the bridge deck with labeled sensor positions. Damage location is close to sensor 11

Because environmental influences were not considered in this study, the excitation was the primary cause of varying the ACFs (operational variability). Some variability came from the measurement noise, which was also different in each measurement. The number of independent excitations varied randomly between 1 and 3. Furthermore, the excitation points were randomly selected from all nodes at the joints between the steel webs and flanges. The load histories were generated in the frequency domain between 0 and 25 Hz. Each measurement had different load functions with random amplitudes and phases at each frequency pin. In addition, it was randomly determined if a loading had zero contribution at a randomly located 5 Hz interval. This simulated measurements in which some modes were not excited.

The FE analysis was performed in the frequency domain [20]. Measurement noise was simulated by adding Gaussian noise to each sensor. The average signal-to-noise ratio (SNR) was 30 dB. The ACFs were estimated from the long response time histories at lags τ between 0 and 3 s, resulting in a length of 300 data points in each measurement (Fig. 4a).

In the data analysis for damage detection, the ACFs were concatenated to form a long data matrix (Fig. 4b). To remove discontinuities between measurements, m data points had to be removed from each data set.

The first 100 data sets were from the undamaged structure and the next 36 data sets from the damaged structure with an increasing crack length (Fig. 3). The number of different crack lengths was 6, and each damage level was monitored with 6 simulations. The first 70 data sets were used as training data.

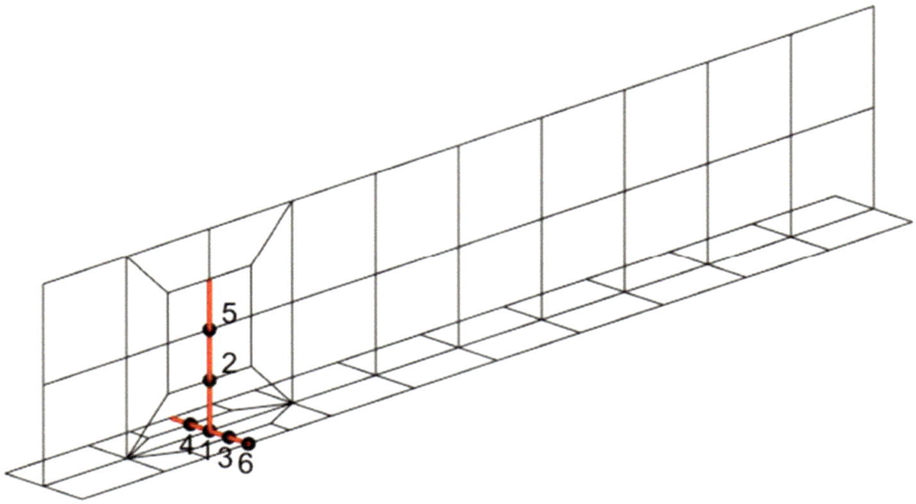

Fig. 3 A detail of the steel girder with a sequence of crack propagation [18]

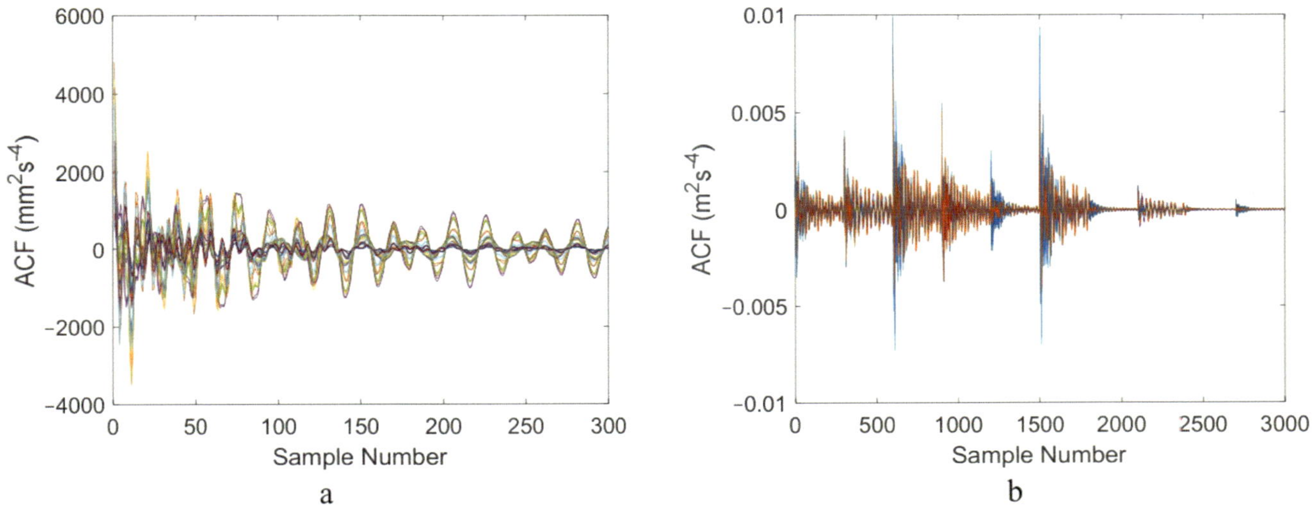

Fig. 4 a) Autocovariance functions of 28 accelerometers from measurement 1. b) Autocovariance functions of 9 accelerometers [2:3:28] from measurements 1 to 10

The whitening matrix was identified using the training data, but principal component analysis was applied to all data. The first principal component scores were only retained and divided into subgroups each consisting of all data from a single measurement. The minimum and maximum of each subgroup were used for damage detection by identifying extreme value distributions for the training data and determining the probability of a false alarm equal to 0.001 to compute the control limits. Finally, a control chart for the extreme values was plotted.

Damage localization was based on the projection of the first principal component on the sensor coordinates and selecting the largest length, which was supposed to reveal the sensor closest to damage.

SHM systems for damage detection for different sensor arrays were designed. The number of active modes was assumed known ($n = 7$).

In the first case, spatial correlation ($m = 0$) was only considered. According to Eq. (9), the number of sensors had to be greater than 28. If all 28 accelerometers were used, the control chart in Fig. 5a resulted. Damage detection was successful even if the number of sensors was not sufficient. This is probably because distant modes had only a small contribution to the ACFs. Damage was localized to sensor 12 (Fig. 5b). Sensor 11 also had a high damage index. Because the crack was located between sensors 11 and 12, damage localization was considered successful. Note that with spatial correlation, changes in the mode shapes could only be detected.

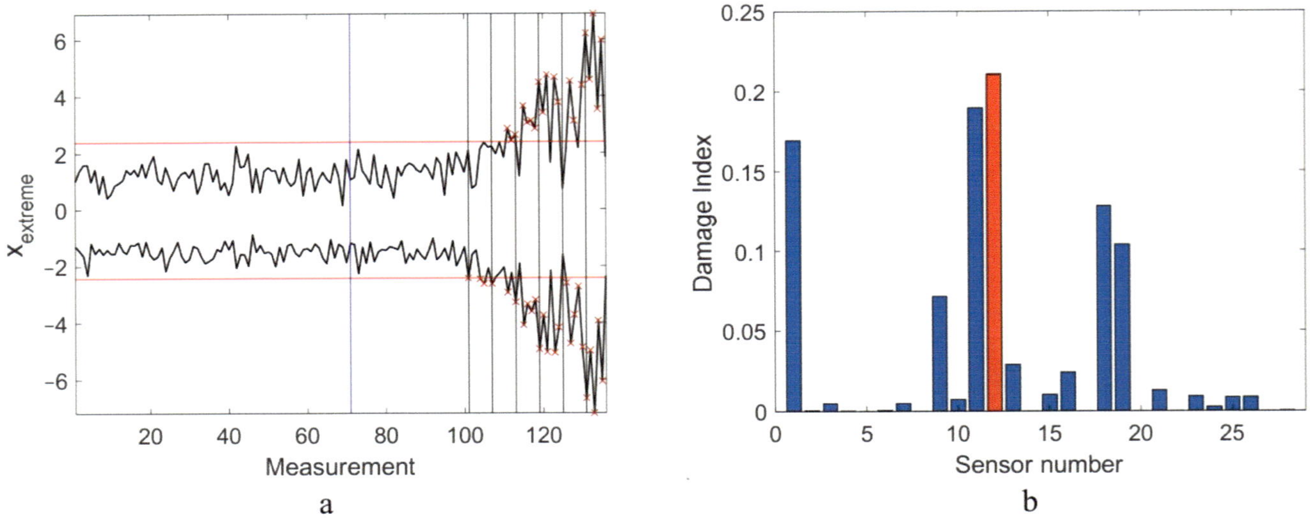

Fig. 5 a) EVS control chart for 28 accelerometers and spatial correlation ($m = 0$). Data on the left side of the leftmost vertical line were used as the training data, and the other vertical lines indicate the six damage levels with increasing crack lengths. Logarithmic scaling was applied to the extreme values. b) Damage localization

The second system had 14 accelerometers (sensors 2:2:28). If spatial correlation was used, damage detection failed (Fig. 6). Using Eq. (11), the condition for the model order was $m > 6$. For the model order equal to $m = 10$, the control chart in Fig. 7a was plotted. Damage was successfully detected with occasional false positives. Damage was incorrectly localized to sensor 16 (Fig. 7b).

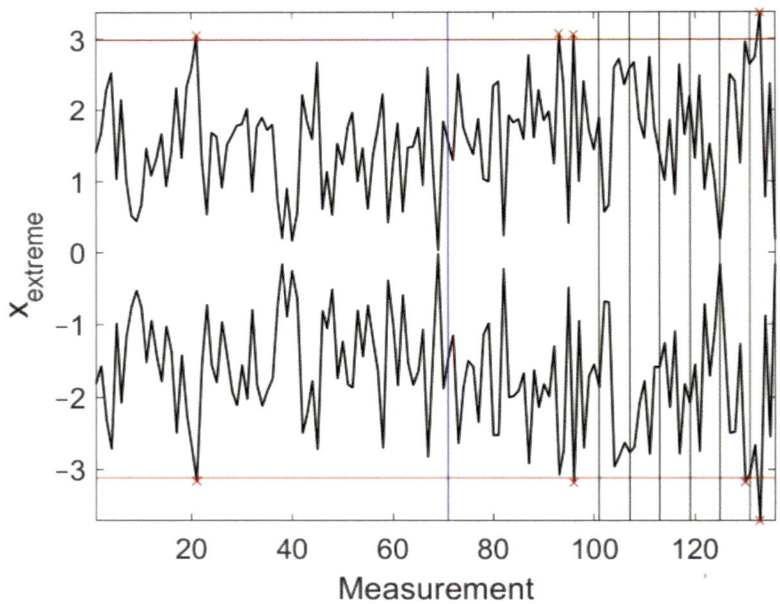

Fig. 6 EVS control chart for 14 accelerometers [2:2:28] and spatial correlation ($m = 0$)

For the third system, hardware costs were further reduced by installing only 9 accelerometers (sensors 2:3:28). Now, the model order in the data analysis had to be increased ($m > 9.9$). If the model order equal to $m = 16$ was used, the result was the control chart in Fig. 8a showing successful detection, but incorrect damage localization to sensor 8 (Fig. 8b). On the other hand, if too small a model order was used ($m = 4$), damage could not be detected (Fig. 9a).

The fourth system had only three accelerometers (sensors 2, 11, and 20), implying that temporal correlation was only possible. According to Eq. 10, the model order had to be greater than 14. Using $m = 20$ resulted in the control chart in

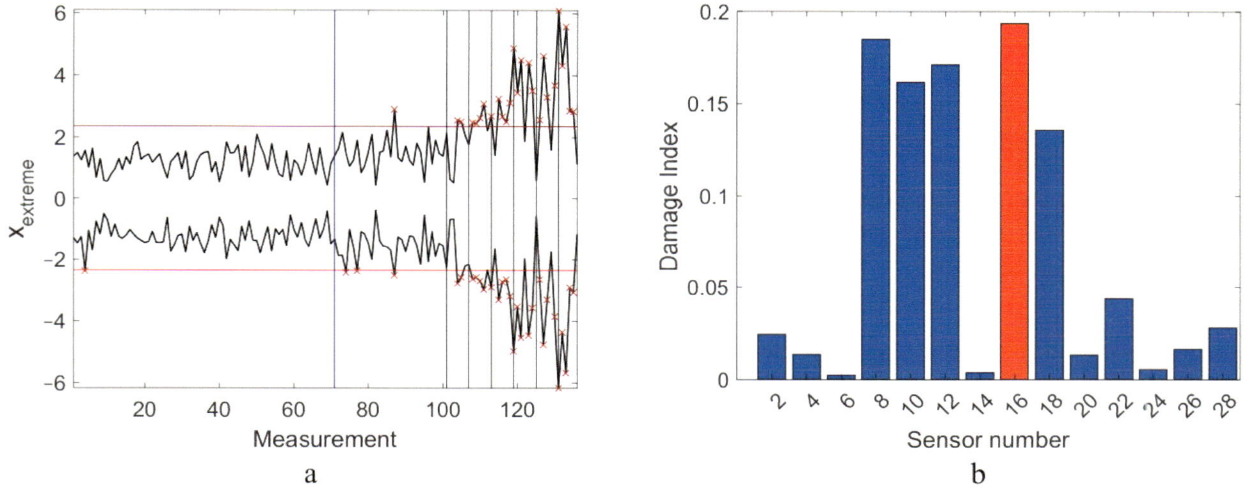

Fig. 7 a) EVS control chart for 14 accelerometers [2:2:28] and spatiotemporal correlation ($m = 10$). b) Damage localization

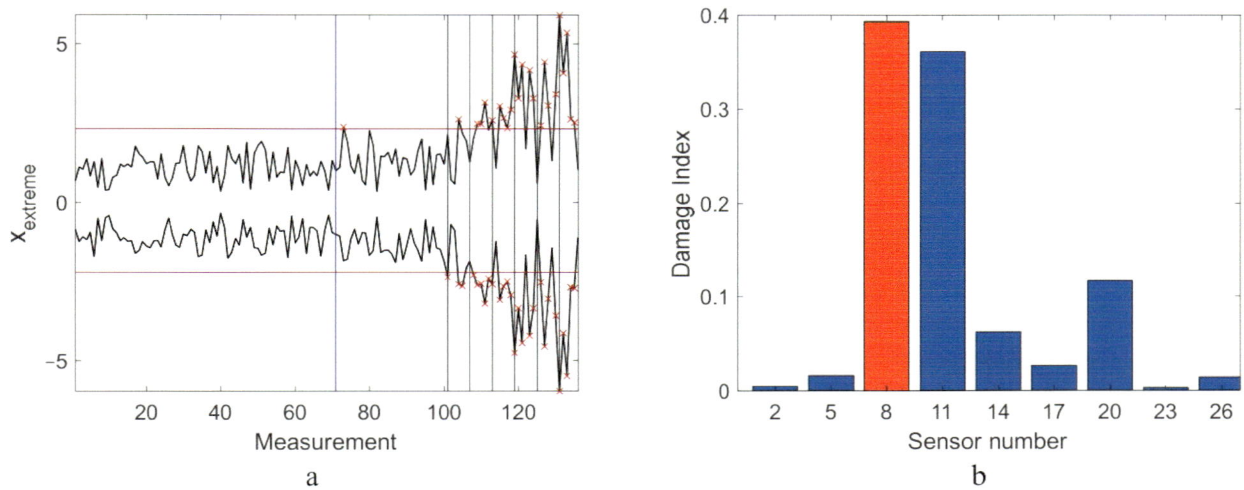

Fig. 8 a) EVS control chart for 9 accelerometers [2:3:28] and spatiotemporal correlation ($m = 16$). b) Damage localization

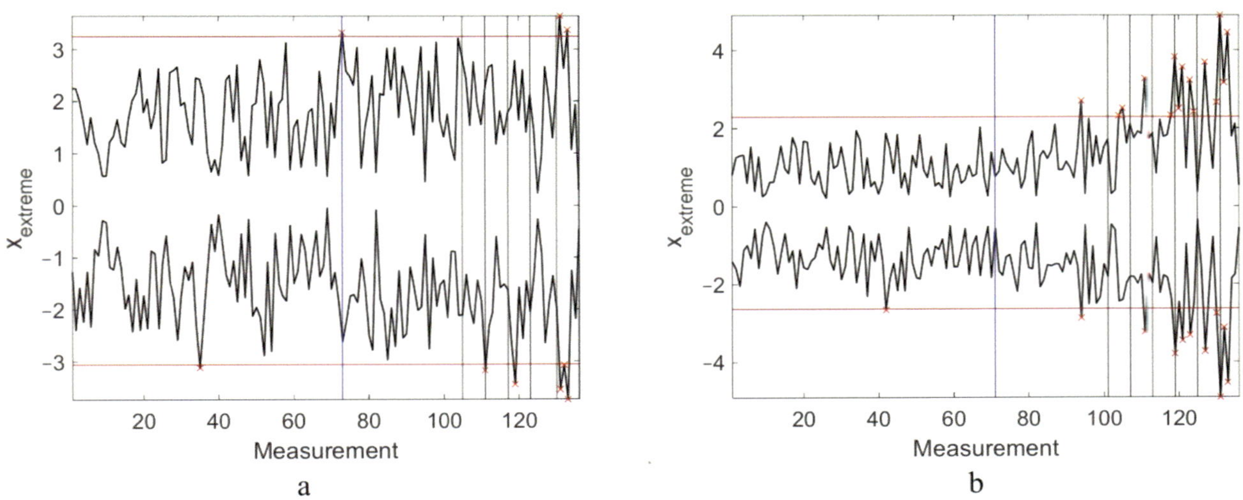

Fig. 9 a) EVS control chart for 9 accelerometers [2:3:28] and spatiotemporal correlation ($m = 4$). b) EVS control chart for 3 accelerometers [2, 11, 20] and temporal correlation ($m = 20$)

Fig. 9b with reasonable damage detection capability. Detection of natural frequency changes was only possible. Damage was correctly localized to sensor 11 having the largest damage index (not shown).

For systems 2–4, it was observed that the theoretical minimum for the model order m was not optimal, but a slightly larger number yielded better results. The reason was probably an increased dimensionality of the noise space, increasing the probability of the test data to appear in that space. In addition, systems 2–3 with spatiotemporal correlation were able to detect changes in both frequencies, damping, and mode shapes.

Damage localization was correct only when using spatial or temporal correlation. With spatiotemporal correlation, localization failed. On the other hand, the sensor closest to damage also had a high damage index in all cases.

Conclusion

Autocovariance functions are promising damage-sensitive features in the time domain. Their usage was theoretically and numerically explored. Practical formulas for the design parameters were given for the design of an SHM system. If the number of active modes is known, the minimum number of sensors can be computed. Once the number of sensors is determined, the required model order used in the data analysis can be computed.

The main conclusions are:

1. To detect both frequency and mode shape changes, the number of sensors must be at least equal to the number of active modes. The required model order can then be computed. This spatiotemporal correlation model is suggested for most cases.
2. If the number of sensors is less than the number of modes, only changes in frequencies and damping can be detected but not changes in mode shapes.
3. For spatial correlation, changes of mode shapes can only be detected. A large number of sensors is necessary, which is impractical in many cases.
4. In spatiotemporal correlation analyses, a slightly greater model order than the required minimum was found to yield optimal results.
5. The excitation variability has no effect on damage detection, provided the process is stationary random and the design parameters fulfil the given conditions.
6. The proposed method yielded incorrect damage localization in some cases, but a large damage index resulted also for the sensor closest to damage.

Acknowledgments This research has been supported by Metropolia University of Applied Sciences.

References

1. Li, X.Y., Law, S.S., Matrix of the covariance of covariance of acceleration responses for damage detection from ambient vibration measurements. Mechanical Systems and Signal Processing, 24(4), 945–956, 2010.
2. Zhang, M., and Schmidt, R., Sensitivity analysis of an auto-correlation-function-based damage index and its application in structural damage detection. Journal of Sound and Vibration, 333(26), 7352–7363, 2014.
3. Zhang, M., and Schmidt, R., Study on an auto-correlation-function-based damage index: Sensitivity analysis and structural damage detection. Journal of Sound and Vibration, 359, 195–214, 2015.
4. Li, W., Huang, Y., A method for damage detection of a jacket platform under random wave excitations using cross correlation analysis and PCA-based method. Ocean Engineering, 214, 107734, 2020.
5. Yang, Z., Wang, L., Wang, H., Ding, Y., Dang, X., Damage detection in composite structures using vibration response under stochastic excitation. Journal of Sound and Vibration, 325(4–5), 755–768, 2009.
6. Wang, L., Yang, Z., Waters, T.P., Structural damage detection using cross correlation functions of vibration response. Journal of Sound and Vibration, 329(24), 5070–5086, 2010.
7. Trendafilova, I., A method for vibration-based structural interrogation and health monitoring based on signal cross-correlation. Journal of Physics Conference Series, 305(1), 012005, 2011.
8. Huo, L.-S., Li, X., Yang, Y.-B., Li, H.-N., Damage detection of structures for ambient loading based on cross correlation function amplitude and SVM. Shock and Vibration, 2016, 3989743, 2016.
9. Döhler, M., Mevel, L., Hille, F., Subspace-based damage detection under changes in the ambient excitation statistics. Mechanical Systems and Signal Processing, 45(1), 207–224, 2014.
10. Li, M., Huang, T., Structural damage detection based on quadratic correlation function of strain responses. Latin American Journal of Solids and Structures, 21(1), 2024.

11. Kullaa, J., Jonscher, C., Liesecke, L., Rolfes, R., Damage detection with closely spaced modes using autocovariance functions. In: Proceedings of the 10th International Operational Modal Analysis Conference (IOMAC 2024), Vol. 2, Springer, 87–94, 2024.
12. Yan, A.-M., Golinval, J.-C., Null subspace-based damage detection of structures using vibration measurements. Mechanical Systems and Signal Processing, 20(3), 611–626, 2006.
13. Brincker R., Ventura, C., Introduction to operational modal analysis. Chichester, West Sussex: Wiley, 2015.
14. James III, G.H., Carne, T.G., Lauffer, J.P., The natural excitation technique (NExT) for modal parameter extraction from operating structures. Modal Analysis: The International Journal of Analytical and Experimental Modal Analysis, 10(4), 260–277, 1995.
15. Kullaa, J., Damage detection and localization under variable environmental conditions using compressed and reconstructed Bayesian virtual sensor data. Sensors, 22(1), 306, 2022.
16. Coles, S., An introduction to statistical modeling of extreme values. Bristol, UK: Springer, 2001.
17. Montgomery, D.C., Introduction to statistical quality control. 3rd edition. New York: Wiley, 1997.
18. Kullaa, J., Robust damage detection using Bayesian virtual sensors. Mechanical Systems and Signal Processing, 135, 106384 2020.
19. Bendat, J.S., Piersol, A.G., Random data: Analysis and measurement procedures. 4th edition. Blackwell, Hoboken, N.J., USA: Wiley, 2010.
20. Clough, R.W., Penzien, J., Dynamics of structures. 2nd edition. New York: McGraw-Hill, 1993.

Chapter 2
On the Real Time Tightness Measurement of Complex Shaped Flanges

Wolfgang Witteveen, Simon Desch, and Lukas Koller

Abstract The tightness of a flange is a time-varying variable and depends on the current state of the structure. For obvious reasons, this could be a critical and important information. It would be desirable to get such information in real-time.

In this extended abstract, an example of a flange with 12 bores is used to give a numerical proof that this may be possible in principle. With the help of special trial vectors for a small sliding contact area, so-called contact modes, the tightness state of a joint can be reconstructed based on strain measurements. This is possible within a fraction of a second. This offers the possibility for corrective actions when a critical condition regarding tightness is detected.

Keywords Flange tightness · State monitoring · Virtual sensor

Introduction

Loads and vibrations cause deformations in the contact area of flanges and these deformations obviously affect the tightness. In the worst case, the tightness is no longer guaranteed and the system leaks. The possibility of monitoring leak tightness of flanges in real-time can therefore be a significant improvement to such systems. Through numerical simulation and experimental studies, it is well documented in the literature that the gap and pressure distribution in a contact area are complex functions of the state, see for example [1] and [2]. The existing options for assessing tightness are only moderately suitable for dynamically loaded structures. Static pressure films can be clamped between the contacting surfaces. After the pressure has been applied, the bolts must be loosened again, the film is removed, and the color change is evaluated because it is a measure of the pressure. These films are suitable for assessing the tightness according to the pre-tensioned bolt, but not for permanent monitoring. In [2], a foil is used that must be clamped between the contact surfaces. The sensor is based on a material whose electrical properties are pressure dependent. The foil is divided into cells and the contact pressure can be determined for each individual cell. This technology seems suitable in principle for contact and leak monitoring, but there are some disadvantages: (1) Since the foil must be clamped, the behavior of the joint changes. (2) It is questionable how pressure and heat resistant the foil is - important questions for practical use. (3) Another question is whether such films can be used for very large flanges, such as those required for pipes with a diameter of 1m and more.

In this project it was numerically investigated whether it might be possible to compute the gap distribution with a few strains outside the flange contact area. The magnitude of the strains must be within a measurable range and the result must not be too sensitive to noise.

This extended abstract is organized as follows: The first section gives an idea about the theory which is applied in the following section to a flange contact with 12 bores. The results are investigated with respect to the strain magnitudes and its sensitivity with respect to noise. The full paper can be found in [3].

Wolfgang Witteveen
University of Applied Sciences Upper Austria, Degree Program Mechanical Engineering, 4600 Wels, Austria
e-mail: wolfgang.witteveen@fh-wels.at

Simon Desch · Lukas Koller
FH OOE Research and Development GmbH, 4600 Wels, Austria
e-mail: simon.desch@fh-wels.at; lukas.koller@fh-wels.at

Brian Damiano et al. (eds.), *Structural Health Monitoring & Machine Learning, Vol. 12*, Conference Proceedings of the Society for Experimental Mechanics Series, https://doi.org/10.13052/9788743801573-2

Brief Outline of the Theory

Only the idea of the theory is outlined below. The detailed derivation can be found in [3]. It is assumed that a usable FE model of the structure including the flange area is available. With the use of proper trial vectors (commonly called "modes"), the normal displacement (= gap) between the two contact surfaces can be computed in the form of

$$\mathbf{g} = \mathbf{\Phi}_g \mathbf{q} \tag{1}$$

where the $(C \times 1)$ vector $\mathbf{g}$ holds the normal distance of all node-to-node contact pairs which form the contact area. The $(C \times Q)$ matrix $\mathbf{\Phi}_g$ holds in its columns the portion of the modes which belong to the gap area and the $(Q \times 1)$ vector $\mathbf{q}$ holds the scaling factors (commonly called "modal coordinates") of the modes. It is obvious that the mode base must be able to capture global structural deformations like vibrations and very local ones like the deformations in the contact area. This can be ensured by extending proven mode bases with so-called contact modes. This allows both types of deformation to be represented with sufficient accuracy. For more information on contact modes, the interested reader is referred to [4]. Regarding linear strains, the relation

$$\varepsilon = \mathbf{\Phi}_\varepsilon \mathbf{q} \tag{2}$$

also apply where the $(E \times 1)$ vector ε holds all potential strain measurements at E positions on the structure. The $(E \times Q)$ matrix $\mathbf{\Phi}_\varepsilon$ maps the modal coordinates to the strains. By the use of the pseudo inverse equation (2) can be rearranged and plugged into (1) so that

$$\mathbf{g} = \mathbf{G}\varepsilon \tag{3}$$

with the $(C \times E)$ matrix

$$\mathbf{G} = \mathbf{\Phi}_g \mathbf{\Phi}_\varepsilon{}^\dagger \tag{4}$$

is obtained. Relation (3) is not useful because it holds all potential strain gauges which is far too much for practical use. Training data is used to reduce the number of strain gauges. We assume that, for example through simulation, T training data ε_1 to ε_T are available. They are arranged column by column in the $(E \times T)$ matrix $\mathbf{E}_T$. In a next step Proper Orthogonal Decomposition (POD, see exemplarily [5]) is used to extract a S dimensional subspace which optimally approximates all T training data in an Euclidian sense. The S vectors which span the subspace are arranged column wise in a $(E \times S)$ matrix $\mathbf{E}_S$. Now the Discrete Empirical Interpolation Method (DEIM, see exemplarily [6]) can be used for a somehow optimal extraction of S sensor positions out of E potential ones. The application of DEIM to $\mathbf{E}_S$ gives a $(S \times E)$ matrix $\mathbf{B}^T$ and a $(E \times S)$ matrix $\mathbf{E}_D$ with the properties

$$\varepsilon_D = \mathbf{B}^T \varepsilon \tag{5}$$

and

$$\varepsilon = \mathbf{E}_D \varepsilon_D. \tag{6}$$

Note, that in relation (5) the $(S \times E)$ vector ε_D holds a S dimensional subset of the entries in ε. Consequently, $\mathbf{B}^T$ selects the actual used sensors out of all potential ones. The matrix $\mathbf{E}_D$ in relation (6) is used to computed all potential strains on the base of the selected subset stored in ε_D. When (6) is plugged into (3) the final relation

$$\mathbf{g} = \mathbf{G}_D \varepsilon_D \tag{7}$$

with the time invariant $(C \times S)$ matrix

$$\mathbf{G}_D = \mathbf{G}\mathbf{E}_D \tag{8}$$

is obtained. Relation (7) can be used to compute the gap distribution $\mathbf{g}$ based on the strain measurements in ε_D.

Numerical Example

The proposed method is tested on a purely numerical example. The aim is to give a kind of numerical prove that the deformation state of a joint, and thus the tightness, can be determined using just a few strain gauge measurements. As shown in Fig. 1, two pipes are connected with a flange. The dimensions and all other relevant parameters can be found in [3]. The two flange rings are connected via 12 bores (M20 screws). The entire structure is rigidly mounted on one side and 3 forces are applied on the other side (F_x, F_y and F_z). The FE model consists of 131040 linear hexahedron elements and 179162 nodes. The contact surfaces of the flange are congruently meshed with 7944 (= C) node pairs. The contact pressures and the friction forces are computed by nonlinear penalty laws which can be found [3].

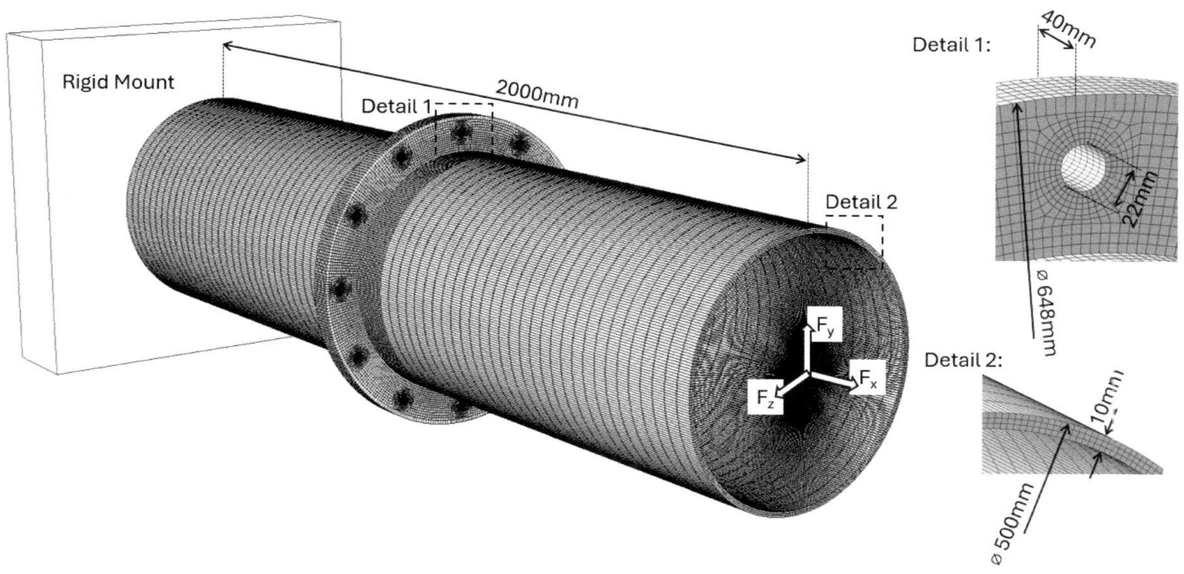

Fig. 1 Pipe structure with flange

Fig. 2 shows the positions of all potential strain measurements. The labeling of each position with two directions is intended to indicate that the strains in these two directions can be measured. The bolts are also fitted with a strain gauge so that the bolt strain can be measured in the longitudinal direction. In sum, this are 156 ($= E$) potential sensor positions.

The potential of the presented method is numerically tested based on non-linear computations which serve as reference solutions. The results of these non-linear computations are the normal distances in the contact area ($=$ gap) as well as the strains at the sensor positions. Based on these strains, the gap in the joint is then reconstructed using the proposed method and then compared with the actual gap from the reference computation. The details of the nonlinear computation can be found in [3]. For the sake of testing 120 load cases are constructed using random numbers for the forces F_x, F_y and F_z. A constant bolt load is acting in all cases. For the construction of $\mathbf{E}_T$, 600 training load cases have been created via the same procedure. For more details on the test and training sets, see [3].

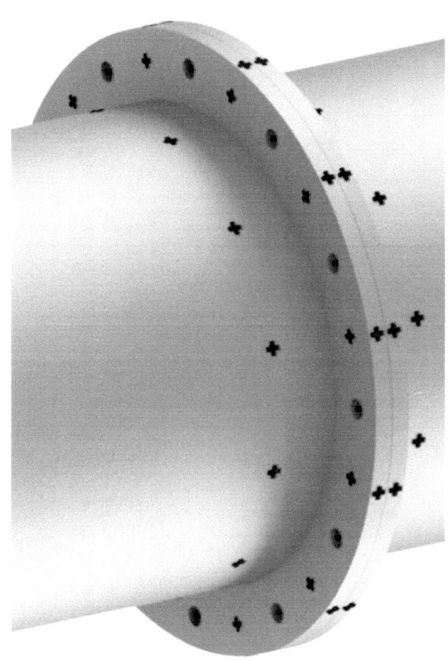

Fig. 2 Potential strain measurement locations

Results

The application of the former procedure leads to the selection of 10 strain measurements which are depicted in Fig. 3. Two of them are strain gauges in the bolts and 8 more on both flange rings measuring the strains in tangential direction.

The result of all 120 test cases is of satisfying accuracy. The test case with the worst approximation is given in Fig. 4. The red color indicates areas of critical gapping. The reconstructed gap distribution is quite similar as the reference. In summary it can be stated that the gap distribution can be reconstructed based on a few (= 10) strain measurements.

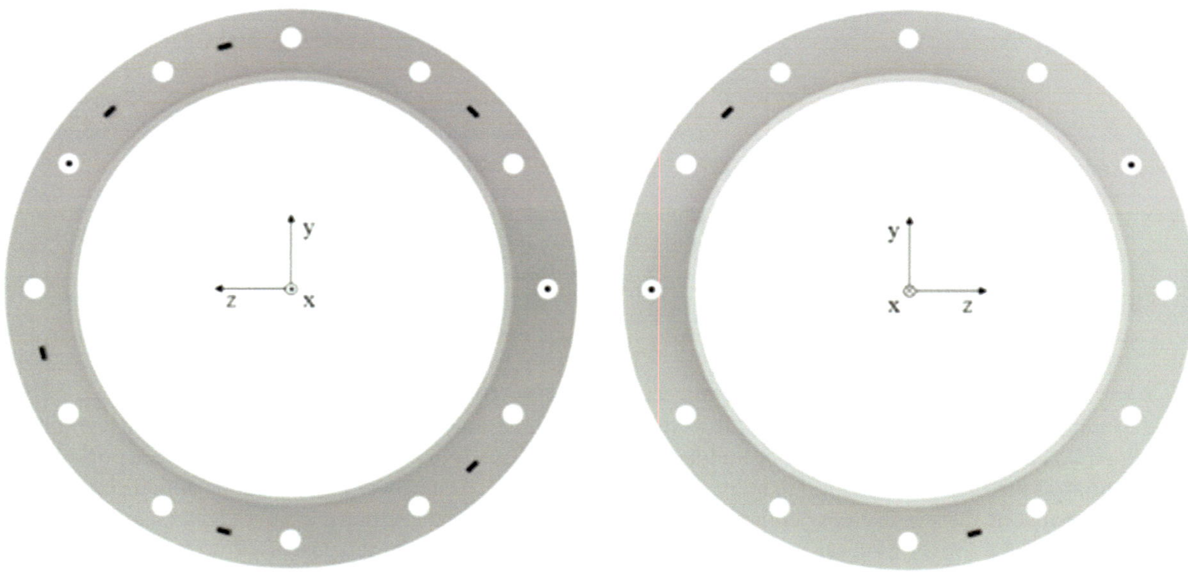

Fig. 3 Selected strain measurements

Fig. 4 Strain based gap (right) vs. reference computation (left). The red color indicates a critical opening in the contact area

Comments on the Measurability of the Strains

An important criterion for feasibility is the magnitude of the strains that occur. Very small strains do not lead to any problems in the simulation but are not measurable with real sensors. A look on the strain data reveals that in case of critical loads (like Fig. 4), the strains are in a good measurable range. This is not necessarily the case for low loads, but the flange is then not in a critical state.

Comments on the Sensitivity to Noisy Data

To get a first impression of the sensitivity to noise, the strains were artificially polluted by random numbers. It turns out that test sets with critical loads react very robustly to noise.

Comments on the Real-Time Capability

Real-time capability requires that in an actual realization, the transformation of the strain measurements into the gap distribution by the matrix-vector multiplication (7) is faster than the sampling time of the data acquisition system. Corresponding investigations have shown that this takes less than one millisecond with 10 sensors and almost 8000 entries in the gap vector $\mathbf{g}$.

Conclusion

The numerical investigation presented suggests that the gap distribution inside a flange contact can be reconstructed via a model based virtual sensor with few strain measurements. This could be used to assess the tightness, for example. It turns out that the result has a certain robustness against noise and the strains are in a range that is good to measure, at least for critical load situations. The arithmetic operation that converts the strains into the gap distribution takes less than a millisecond.

The reconstruction of the gap distribution presented here is actually a kind of worst case in terms of effort. Simpler questions such as ‘Is the gap uncritical or not?’ would probably be more relevant. It is conceivable, for example, to train a neural network for this question without reconstructing the entire gap distribution.

References

1. Witteveen, W., Kuts, M., Koller, L., 2023, “Can transient simulation efficiently reproduce well known nonlinear effects of jointed structures?”, Mechanical Systems and Signal Processing, 190, doi:10.1016/j.ymssp.2023.110111.
2. Dreher, T., Brake, M., R., W., Seeger, B., Krack, M., 2021, “In situ, real-time measurements of contact pressure internal to jointed interfaces during dynamic excitation of an assembled structure”, Mechanical Systems and Signal Processing, 160, doi:10.1016/j.ymssp.2021.107859.
3. Witteveen, W., Desch, S., Koller, L., “Can real-time flange tightness monitoring be possible with strains? A numerical pre-study.”, Journal of Structural Dynamics [En ligne], Special issue on Tribomechadynamics, under review
4. Pichler, F., Witteveen, W., Fischer, P., 2017, “A complete strategy for efficient and accurate multibody dynamics of flexible structures with large lap joints considering contact and friction”, Multibody System Dynamics, 40(4):407–436, doi:10.1007/s11044-016-9555-2.370
5. Chatterjee, A., “An introduction to the proper orthogonal decomposition”, SIAM Journal on Scientific Computing, 78(7):808–817, URL http://www.jstor.org/stable/24103957.
6. Chaturantabut, S., Sorensen. D., C., 2010, “Nonlinear model reduction via discrete empirical interpolation”, SIAM Journal on Scientific Computing, 32(5):2737–2764, doi:10.1137/090766498.

Chapter 3
Parameter Rejection in Sensitivity-based Model Updating using Output Feedback Eigenstructure Assignment

Martin D. Ulriksen and Dionisio Bernal

Abstract Model updating involves a parameter estimation problem, in which a set of model parameters is adjusted to minimize the discrepancy between identified system features and the associated model predictions. To promote uniqueness in the estimation problem, the number of included parameters must be no larger than the number of features. This often results in the model updating being cast with a (proper) subset of the uncertain parameters, whereby the errors induced by treating the omitted parameters at their nominal values are accepted. In this paper, we review a scheme that attempts to mitigate the noted issue by minimizing the sensitivity of the parameter estimation to fluctuations of the omitted parameters around their nominal values. Control over the sensitivities is realized by adjusting output feedback gains in a closed-loop setting, which, given that the operation is offline, can be implemented through processing of open-loop input-output data. The scheme is tested in the context of a numerical example with a truss system.

Keywords Model updating · parameter estimation · parameter rejection · output feedback · eigenstructure assignment

Introduction

The parameter estimation in model updating constitutes a minimization problem, wherein the objective function is some measure of the discrepancy between identified system features and the corresponding model predictions. A common setting, which is also chosen in this study, is to let modal data comprise the features and to let the updating parameters relate to the system's mass and/or stiffness [1]. In the widely used sensitivity method, which is the one of interest here, the updating parameters are adjusted by iteratively solving a Taylor linearization [2]. The parameter estimation problem in each iteration proves ill-posed when the number of updating parameters exceeds the number of identifiable system features, which is often encountered in vibration analysis [2].

The standard procedure for mitigating the noted posedness issue in the sensitivity method is to treat some of the uncertain parameters at their nominal values and omit them from the updating. Yet, such deselection may distort the parameter estimation, so, somewhat inspired by the work on disturbance rejection in control engineering [3], we propose a parameter rejection scheme that can be directly included in the sensitivity method to (theoretically) nullify the effect of the discarded parameters. To be specific, the proposed scheme concerns design and use of closed-loop features that allow for discarding some uncertain parameters from the model updating while still rejecting their influence in the parameter estimation. This parameter rejection is attained by rendering the closed-loop features invariant to the discarded parameters by use of output feedback eigenstructure assignment [4]. The proposed scheme also allows for designing multiple closed-loop systems to increase the number of features, but since this part has already been covered in details in the literature [5], we will focus on the parameter rejection.

In most vibration applications, it suffices to cast the model updating in an offline setting instead of operating online in real time. Consequently, the output feedback that enables the eigenstructure assignment for parameter rejection can be realized *virtually* through processing of measured open-loop input-output data [6]. This virtual implementation, which is formulated

Martin D. Ulriksen
Department of Mechanical and Production Engineering, Aarhus University, 8200 Aarhus, Denmark
e-mail: mdu@mpe.au.dk

Dionisio Bernal
Department of Civil and Environmental Engineering, Northeastern University, Boston, MA 02115, USA
e-mail: D.Bernal@northeastern.edu

Brian Damiano et al. (eds.), *Structural Health Monitoring & Machine Learning, Vol. 12*, Conference Proceedings of the Society for Experimental Mechanics Series, https://doi.org/10.13052/9788743801573-3

under the assumption that the considered system is linear and time-invariant (LTI) during the open-loop data collection, has several noteworthy merits. Two immediate ones are that it eliminates the practical overhead associated with utilizing physical controllers [7], and that it allows for computing several closed-loop systems—and hereby eigenstructures—based on a single open-loop input-output data realization.

Background Theory and Problem Statement

We consider a physical system $\mathcal{S}$ with known inputs $u(t) \in \mathbb{R}^r$ and outputs $y(t) \in \mathbb{R}^m$. The physics-based model representation of system $\mathcal{S}$ is an LTI state-space formulation of order $n \in 2\mathbb{N}$, namely,

$$\dot{z}(t) = Az(t) + Bu(t), \tag{1a}$$

$$y(t) = Cz(t), \tag{1b}$$

with the state vector $z(t) \in \mathbb{R}^n$ and the matrices $A \in \mathbb{R}^{n\times n}$, $B \in \mathbb{R}^{n\times r}$, and $C \in \mathbb{R}^{m\times n}$. We note that model (1) is formulated under the assumption that the direct transmission is zero or already subtracted from the outputs in (1b), which is chosen, without any loss of generality, to simplify the developments later in the paper.

Now, let the model parameters to be updated be $\theta \in \Theta \subset \mathbb{R}^p$, which, with respect to (1), implies that $A = A(\theta) \in \mathbb{R}^{n\times n}$, $B = B(\theta) \in \mathbb{R}^{n\times r}$, and $C = C(\theta) \in \mathbb{R}^{m\times n}$. These matrices follow as

$$A = \begin{bmatrix} 0 & I \\ -M^{-1}K & -M^{-1}D \end{bmatrix}, \qquad B = \begin{bmatrix} 0 \\ M^{-1}B_2 \end{bmatrix}, \qquad C = \begin{bmatrix} C_{\mathrm{d}} - C_{\mathrm{a}}M^{-1}K & C_{\mathrm{v}} - C_{\mathrm{a}}M^{-1}D \end{bmatrix}, \tag{2}$$

with the mass, damping, and stiffness matrices $M = M(\theta)$, $D = D(\theta)$, $K = K(\theta) \in \mathbb{R}^{\frac{n}{2}\times\frac{n}{2}}$, the input-distribution matrix $B_2 \in \mathbb{R}^{\frac{n}{2}\times r}$, and the output-selection matrices C_{d}, C_{v}, $C_{\mathrm{a}} \in \mathbb{R}^{m\times\frac{n}{2}}$ for displacement (d), velocity (v), and acceleration (a) outputs.

Assumption 1 *For all $\theta \in \Theta$, model* (1) *is observable and controllable with $M = M^\top \succ 0$, $D = D^\top \succ 0$, and $K = K^\top \succ 0$.*

With the chosen model parametrization, we assume that system $\mathcal{S}$ is in the *unknown* configuration $\theta_* \in \Theta$. The aim is to estimate θ_* by minimizing the discrepancy between the system features and the model predictions and then adjust model (1) accordingly. Let $f_{\mathcal{S}} \in \mathbb{C}^q$ be the identified system features and $f_{\mathcal{M}(\theta)} \in \mathbb{C}^q$ the corresponding model predictions, then

$$\theta_* \approx \hat{\theta}_* = \underset{\theta\,\in\,\Theta}{\arg\min}\; \mathcal{H}(\theta), \tag{3}$$

where $\mathcal{H}$ is the objective function that expresses the selected discrepancy measure. Minimization problem (3) is generally nonlinear and is, by means of the sensitivity method, solved iteratively through the Taylor linearization

$$f_{\mathcal{S}} - f_{\mathcal{M}(\theta_k)} = \mathcal{J}_{\theta_k}\big(\theta_{k+1} - \theta_k\big). \tag{4}$$

Here, we have introduced the counter $k \in \mathbb{N}_0$ along with the Jacobian matrix $\mathcal{J}_{\theta_k} \in \mathbb{C}^{q\times p}$, which is evaluated at $\theta_k \in \Theta$ using model (1). Formulation (4), which is initialized at $k = 0$ with a *known* θ_0, constitutes an inverse problem for the unknown parameter vector θ_{k+1}. It is solved in an ℓ_2-norm sense, whereby it is assumed that $\mathrm{rank}(\mathcal{J}_{\theta_k}) = p$. A necessary condition for satisfying $\mathrm{rank}(\mathcal{J}_{\theta_k}) = p$ is obviously that $q \geq p$, and since we choose to use the imaginary part of an eigenvalue subset as features, p is bounded from above by the number of identifiable eigenvalues of system $\mathcal{S}$. Some parameters that are actually unknown and uncertain must typically be discarded in the updating to satisfy $q \geq p$. Let these parameters be gathered in $\mu \in \mathbb{R}^h$, then we seek to pose (4) such that the influence of μ is rejected without including μ explicitly in (4).

Eigenstructure Assignment for Parameter Rejection

The influence of μ is rejected in the estimation of θ after (4) if the features in f are invariant to changes in μ. Let us return to model (1) under Assumption 1 and extend it with some *fictive* inputs, $\tau(t)$, that are spatially distributed like $u(t)$ and comply with the static output feedback law

$$\tau(t) = Gy(t). \tag{5}$$

Here, $G \in \mathbb{C}^{r \times m}$ is a gain matrix, which can be complex-valued since the feedback is realized virtually. By adding the fictive inputs to model (1), we attain the resulting virtual closed-loop model

$$\dot{z}(t) = Wz(t) + Bu(t), \tag{6a}$$
$$y(t) = Cz(t), \tag{6b}$$

with the closed-loop state matrix

$$W = W(\theta) \triangleq A + BGC \in \mathbb{C}^{n \times n}. \tag{7}$$

The eigendecomposition of the closed-loop state matrix is written as $W = \Psi\Lambda\Phi$, with the jth right eigenvector $\psi_j \in \mathbb{C}^n$, the jth left eigenvector $\phi_j \in \mathbb{C}^{1 \times n}$, and the jth eigenvalue $\lambda_j \in \mathbb{C}$ for $j = 1, \ldots, n$. It thus follows that $\phi_j (A + BGC - \lambda_j I) = 0$, which can be written in the partitioned form

$$\begin{bmatrix} A^\top - \lambda_j I & C^\top \end{bmatrix} \begin{bmatrix} \phi_j^\top \\ \gamma_j \end{bmatrix} = 0, \tag{8}$$

where we, for notational convenience, have introduced $\gamma_j \triangleq G^\top B^\top \phi_j^\top \in \mathbb{C}^m$. With respect to (8), it is opportune to note that Assumption 1 yields null$[A^\top - \lambda_j I \quad C^\top] \subset \mathbb{C}^{(n+m) \times m}$, where null denotes (right) null space. As previously outlined, the scope of the eigenstructure assignment is to render some of the closed-loop eigenvalues, λ_j, invariant to changes in μ. Lemma 1 provides some basic insight to address this scope.

Lemma 1 *Let $\lambda(W)$ be the eigenspectrum of W, let δW be a perturbation of W, and let $(\tilde{\lambda}_j, \tilde{\phi}_j)$ be a left eigenpair of $W + \delta W$. Then, $\tilde{\lambda}_j \in \lambda(W)$ if $\tilde{\phi}_j^\top \in$ null$(\delta W^\top)$.*

Now, let δW_μ and δW_θ denote the perturbations of W induced by the perturbations $\delta\mu$ and $\delta\theta$, respectively. We then seek to design closed-loop model (6) such that $\phi_j^\top \in$ null$(\delta W_\mu^\top)$ for some j. To this end, we return to (8) under Assumption 1 and let a basis for null$[A^\top - \lambda_j I \quad C^\top]$ be $\mathcal{Z}_j = [\mathcal{X}_j^\top \; \mathcal{Y}_j^\top]^\top$, with $\mathcal{X}_j \in \mathbb{C}^{n \times m}$ and $\mathcal{Y}_j \in \mathbb{C}^{m \times m}$. Hereby,

$$\phi_j^\top = \mathcal{X}_j \alpha_j, \tag{9}$$

where $\alpha_j \in \mathbb{C}^m$. If $\phi_j^\top \in$ null$(\delta W_\mu^\top)$, then pre-multiplying (9) by $\delta W_\mu^\top$ yields

$$\delta W_\mu^\top \mathcal{X}_j \alpha_j = 0, \tag{10}$$

so a sufficient condition for the existence of an α_j that satisfies relation (10) is rank$(\delta W_\mu) < m$. Let δA_μ, δB_μ, and δC_μ be the perturbations of A, B, and C induced by $\delta\mu$. Then, $\delta W_\mu = \delta A_\mu + (B + \delta B_\mu)G(C + \delta C_\mu) - BGC$, which, when plugged into (10), results in

$$\Big(\delta A_\mu^\top + (C + \delta C_\mu)^\top G^\top (B + \delta B_\mu)^\top - C^\top G^\top B^\top\Big)\phi_j^\top = 0. \tag{11}$$

By introducing $\tilde{\gamma}_j \triangleq G^\top \big(B + \delta B_\mu\big)^\top \phi_j^\top$ and assuming that rank$\big(\delta W_\mu\big) < m$, we can combine (8) and (11) to attain the augmented system of homogeneous equations

$$\begin{bmatrix} A^\top - \lambda_j I & C^\top & 0 \\ \delta A_\mu^\top & -C^\top & C^\top + \delta C_\mu^\top \end{bmatrix} \begin{bmatrix} \phi_j^\top \\ \gamma_j \\ \tilde{\gamma}_j \end{bmatrix} = 0, \tag{12}$$

which is the eigenstructure assignment formulation for parameter rejection. As (12) implies, the spatial distribution but not the magnitude of $\delta\mu$ enters the formulation if the magnitude parameterization in μ is linear.

We consider g closed-loop eigenvalues and their associated left eigenvectors and order them as $\big(\lambda_j, \phi_j\big)$ for $j = 1, \ldots, g$. To this end, let $\Omega \triangleq B^\top \big[\phi_1^\top \; \ldots \; \phi_g^\top\big] \in \mathbb{C}^{r \times g}$ and $\Gamma \triangleq \big[\gamma_1 \; \ldots \; \gamma_g\big] \in \mathbb{C}^{m \times g}$, then we attain the identity

$$\Omega^\top G = \Gamma^\top, \tag{13}$$

which is an inverse problem for the unknown G. In the overdetermined case of $g > r$, formulation (13) will, as demonstrated in [5], typically be inconsistent, hence we confine the discussion to $g = r$.

Theorem 1 *Assume that Ω in* (13) *has full rank with $g = r$. Then, r eigenvalues of closed-loop model* (6) *can be assigned invariant to δW_μ for* rank$(\delta W_\mu) < m$.

Implementation of the Scheme

The model updating is formulated with features that are composed of the imaginary parts of q closed-loop eigenvalues assigned using (12). According to theorem 1, r eigenvalues of closed-loop model (6) can be assigned invariant to $\delta\mu$ if $\text{rank}(\delta W_\mu) < m$, but we often encounter $p > r$, where it is recalled that p is the number of parameters in θ. In such cases, we must therefore design multiple closed-loop models to satisfy $q \geq p$.

Let d be the number of closed-loop models, which must be selected such that it satisfies $q \geq p$. For $l = 1, \ldots, d$, the gain matrix $G^{(l)}$ is designed using the physics-based model in parameter configuration θ_k and with the magnitudes in $\delta\mu$ being user-defined. Hereby, (7) yields the closed-loop state matrix $W^{(l)}$, with the assigned eigenvalues $\lambda_j^{(l)}$ and left eigenvectors $\phi_j^{(l)}$ for $j = 1, \ldots, r$. The imaginary parts of the assigned eigenvalues for all d realizations, which amount to $q = dr$, are gathered to constitute the model-based feature vector, $f_{\mathcal{M}(\theta_k)}$.

For the physical system, $\mathcal{S}$, which is in parameter configuration θ_*, the state matrix estimate $\hat{A}_\mathcal{S}$, the input matrix estimate $\hat{B}_\mathcal{S}$, and the output matrix estimate $\hat{C}_\mathcal{S}$ are inferred from system identification. Subsequently, the matrix triplet is used to form the experimental closed-loop state matrix estimate

$$\hat{W}_\mathcal{S}^{(l)} = \hat{A}_\mathcal{S} + \hat{B}_\mathcal{S} G^{(l)} \hat{C}_\mathcal{S} \tag{14}$$

for each of the d gain matrices. The experimental feature vector, $f_\mathcal{S}$, is populated with the imaginary parts of the eigenvalues of the q closed-loop eigenmodes that correspond to the model-based ones.

The proposed model updating scheme, which follows formulation (4), is terminated when/if convergence is attained according to the simple criterion

$$\epsilon_f \geq \max\left|f_\mathcal{S} - f_{\mathcal{M}(\theta_k)}\right|, \tag{15}$$

where ϵ_f is a user-defined threshold, which must satisfy $0 < \epsilon_f < \max\left|f_\mathcal{S} - f_{\mathcal{M}(\theta_0)}\right|$. It is opportune to note that the gain design must be conducted in each iteration to satisfy the invariance property in the features.

Numerical Example

We consider the two-dimensional finite-element truss system depicted in Fig. 1, with known inputs at both degrees of freedom (DOF) in node 8 and known displacement outputs at both DOF in nodes 4, 9, and 11. We let θ be composed of mass perturbations in nodes 2, 4, and 6 and let μ be the spring stiffnesses k_1 and k_2. The term *nominal model* refers to the updating model and *truth model* to the model replacing the physical system, $\mathcal{S}$. In the nominal model, the bars have a cross-sectional area of 10^{-4} m^2, a modulus of elasticity of 200 GPa, and a mass density of $8,000$ kg/m^3, so the mass of the truss is approximately 300 kg. The nominal model is classically damped with 2 % damping in each eigenmode, and both springs have the stiffness 100 kN/m. The mass matrix of the truth model is taken as the mass matrix of the nominal model with the addition of mass perturbations of 5 kg in node 2, 8 kg in node 4, and 3 kg in node 6. The springs in the truth model have the stiffnesses $k_1 = 70$ kN/m and $k_2 = 150$ kN/m, and the moduli of elasticity in the truth model are assigned random

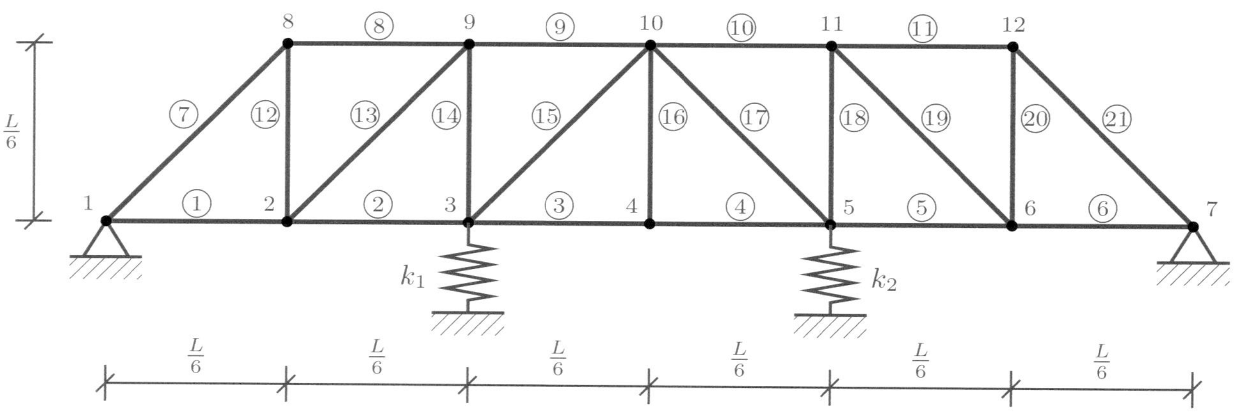

Fig. 1 Finite-element truss system with node and element numbering

perturbations that allow for ± 1 % deviation with respect to the nominal value. The truth model has the same damping matrix as the nominal model.

The truth model is simulated in a Monte Carlo setting with 500 realizations, where the inputs excite the first four eigenmodes of the model, which have the damped eigenfrequencies $\{10.34, 17.47, 19.50, 24.29\}$ Hz. The inputs and outputs are temporally discretized with a sampling frequency of 200 Hz for 100,000 samples and subsequently contaminated with 5 % additive white Gaussian noise. The open-loop estimates $\hat{A}_S$, $\hat{B}_S$, and $\hat{C}_S$ are inferred via a data-driven subspace identification algorithm [8] with a model order of 20. The identified matrices are subsequently modally truncated to contain only the first four eigenmodes and their complex conjugates.

The setting $r = 2$ and $m = 6$ allows for designing gain matrices that each assigns two eigenvalues invariant to a perturbation of rank 5 or less, and we note that $\text{rank}(\delta W_\mu) = 2$. With three unknown parameters to be estimated and four open-loop eigenmodes that are identifiable, we choose to operate with two different gain matrices and assign two eigenvalues with each of them. The first gain matrix assigns the first and second closed-loop eigenvalues at 0.95 times the first and second open-loop eigenvalues of the nominal model, while the second gain matrix assigns the third and fourth closed-loop eigenvalues at 0.95 times the third and fourth open-loop eigenvalues of the nominal model.

The parameter estimation is initialized with $\theta_0 = \begin{bmatrix}0 & 0 & 0\end{bmatrix}^\top$, and we recall that the true configuration is $\theta_* = \begin{bmatrix}5 & 8 & 3\end{bmatrix}^\top$. Fig. 2 depicts the Monte Carlo simulation-based probability density functions (PDFs) attained for the parameter estimates $\hat{\theta}_*$ with and without parameter rejection. Evidently, the rejection of μ improves the estimation accuracy, with the means of $\hat{\theta}_*^{(1)}$, $\hat{\theta}_*^{(2)}$, and $\hat{\theta}_*^{(3)}$ deviating, respectively, 0.2 %, 0.63 %, and 2.33 % from the true values. The corresponding errors without the parameter rejection are 18 %, 9 %, and 36.67 %. It can also be seen that the parameter rejection reduces the estimation precision, which is expected since the scheme without rejection employs only $\hat{A}_S$ (and the associated errors) from the truth model.

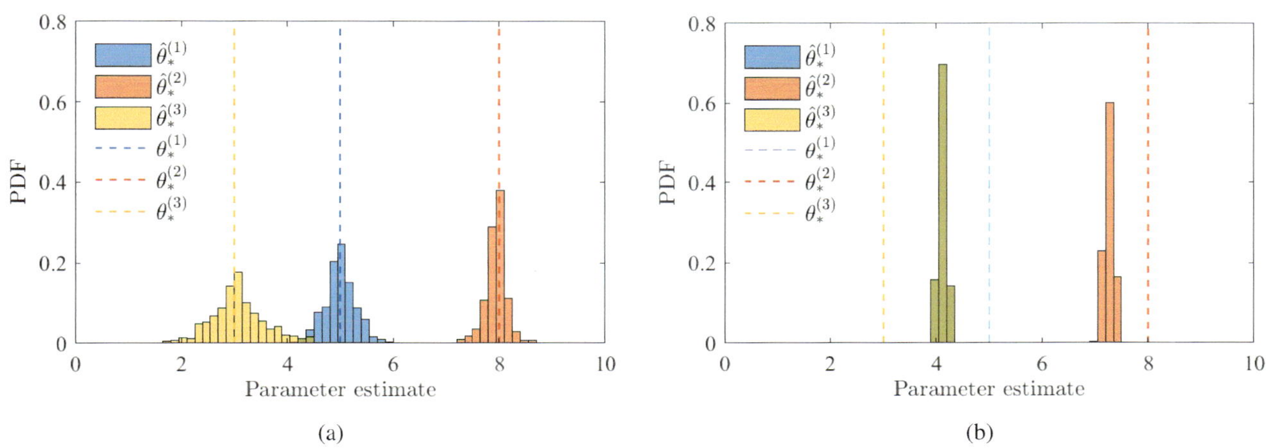

Fig. 2 PDFs for the parameter estimates $\hat{\theta}_*^{(1)}$, $\hat{\theta}_*^{(2)}$, and $\hat{\theta}_*^{(3)}$ based on 500 realizations; (a) with parameter rejection and (b) without parameter rejection (where $\hat{\theta}_*^{(1)}$ and $\hat{\theta}_*^{(3)}$ are equal).

Closing Remarks

The paper reviews a scheme that facilitates parameter rejection in sensitivity-based updating of LTI models by means of eigenstructure assignment. The premise of the scheme is to conduct the updating with closed-loop eigenvalue features that are assigned theoretically invariant to the parameters to be rejected. The invariance formulation calls for the spatial distribution of the parameters in question but not the associated magnitudes. Each gain allows for rendering r eigenvalue features invariant to parameters that induce perturbations in the resulting closed-loop state matrix of rank $m-1$ or less, where r and m are the number of inputs and the number of outputs. Compared to sensitivity-based model updating without parameter rejection, the proposed scheme comes with the price of added computational complexity due to the required eigenstructure assignment.

Acknowledgments The work conveyed in this paper was conducted by the authors during the second author's Otto Moensted Visiting Professorship at Aarhus University, Denmark. The financial support from the Otto Moensted Foundation is gratefully acknowledged.

References

1. Friswell, M.I. and Mottershead, J.E. *Finite element model updating in structural dynamics*. Kluwer Academic Publishers, Dordrecht, 1st edition (1995).
2. Mottershead, J.E., Link, M., and Friswell, M.I. "The sensitivity method in finite element model updating: A tutorial". *Mechanical Systems and Signal Processing*, 25(7):2275–2296 (2011).
3. Wu, Z.H., Zhou, H.C., Guo, B.Z., and Deng, F. "Review and new theoretical perspectives on active disturbance rejection control for uncertain finite-dimensional and infinite-dimensional systems". *Nonlinear Dynamics*, 101:935–959 (2020).
4. Liu, G.P. and Patton, R.J. *Eigenstructure assignment for control system design*. John Wiley & Sons, Inc. (1998).
5. Bernal, D. and Ulriksen, M.D. "Output feedback in the design of eigenstructures for enhanced sensitivity". *Mechanical Systems and Signal Processing*, 112:22–30 (2018).
6. Bernal, D. "Virtual output feedback in parameter estimation". *Mechanical Systems and Signal Processing*, 142:106786 (2020).
7. Pedersen, S. and Ulriksen, M.D. "Closed-loop experimental testing framework for structural control applications". *Structural Control and Health Monitoring*, 28(8):e2765 (2021).
8. van Overschee, P. and De Moor, B. *Subspace identification for linear systems: Theory - implementation - applications*. Kluwer Academic Publishers, 1st edition (1996).

Chapter 4
Structural Health Monitoring of a Ferry Quay: Instrumentation and Impact of Tidal Levels on Modal Parameters

Luigi Sibille, Torodd Skjerve Nord, Ba Tung Le, Bartosz Siedziako, and Alice Cicirello

Abstract This study investigates the influence of environmental factors on the modal parameters of linkspans, one of the two main structures of ferry quays, focusing specifically on tidal level variations. The Structural Health Monitoring (SHM) system implemented on the Magerholm ferry quay, part of a collaboration between Møre og Romsdal County and the Norwegian University of Science and Technology (NTNU), was used to collect acceleration responses over a six-month period. An Automated Operational Modal Analysis (AOMA) algorithm was performed to identify the modal parameters of the structure considering a 20 second window for each day of the monitoring campaign. Tidal levels were monitored independently, and for each day, a strong correlation between tidal levels and the identified first natural frequency of the linkspan was distinguished. To explicitly quantify and remove the majority of the tidal level effects, a well-established Blind Source Separation (BSS) technique, the so-called Principal Component Analysis (PCA) was carried out directly on the first natural frequency and tidal levels. Despite the fact that the assumptions of the AOMA were violated due to the non-white noise conditions caused by tidal levels and operational loads, this preliminary investigation demonstrates, for the first time, the strong correlation between tidal level fluctuations and modal parameters of linkspans.

Keywords Marine Structures · Ferry Quay · Structural Health Monitoring · Automated Operational Modal Analysis · Environmental effects

Introduction

Ferry quays operate in challenging environments that significantly influence their structural integrity and longevity. Subjected to harsh weather conditions, including strong winds, heavy rainfall, and fluctuating temperatures, these structures face continuous exposure to harsh conditions that accelerate wear and degradation [1, 2]. The marine environment poses additional challenges, with saltwater exposure leading to the corrosion of steel components and the deterioration of concrete. Furthermore, operational factors, such as the repeated impacts from ferries and the vibrations caused by vehicle traffic, increase the mechanical stresses experienced by these quays [3].

Despite being designed for a service life of approximately 50 years, many ferry quays experience deterioration earlier than expected, necessitating more frequent repairs or even premature replacement. Inspections, such as the annual and five-year protocols established by the Norwegian Public Roads Administration (NPRA), aim to monitor the condition of these structures [4]. However, these inspections are often insufficient to detect all potential issues, as structural damage can go unnoticed until the next scheduled inspection, increasing the risk of costly repairs or even structural failure. Structural Health Monitoring (SHM) systems can complement these inspection protocols by providing continuous, real-time data on the structural condition of ferry quays. SHM techniques enable asset owners to monitor changes in structural parameters, providing valuable information for maintenance planning and decision-making [5].

The influence of environmental conditions, such as tidal level variations, plays a significant role in the structural behavior of ferry quays and, consequently, in the application of SHM techniques [6]. Tidal levels affect the dynamic characteristics,

Luigi Sibille (✉) · Torodd Skjerve Nord · Ba Tung Le · Bartosz Siedziako
Department of Ocean Operations and Civil Engineering, Norwegian University of Science and Technology, Larsgardsvegen 2, 6009 Ålesund, Norway
e-mail: luigi.sibille@ntnu.no; torodd.nord@ntnu.no; batung.le@ntnu.no; bartosz.siedziako@ntnu.no

Alice Cicirello
Department of Engineering University of Cambridge, Trumpington Street, Cambridge, UK
e-mail: ac685@cam.ac.uk

Brian Damiano et al. (eds.), *Structural Health Monitoring & Machine Learning, Vol. 12*, Conference Proceedings of the Society for Experimental Mechanics Series, https://doi.org/10.13052/9788743801573-4

including their modal parameters, such as natural frequencies and mode shapes. These modal parameters are essential indicators of a structure's health and are often used to detect changes in stiffness, mass distribution, or boundary conditions [7, 8]. Therefore, the assessment of the health of the structure requires filtering out environmental effects, particularly if they are expected to have a significant influence [9]. SHM techniques should consider these environmental influences [10] and apply appropriate filtering to ensure that variations in modal parameters reflect the structural condition rather than external environmental factors. However, the methodologies employed for system identification and environmental effect filtering must respect certain conditions. If modal parameters are found to be dependent on environmental effects, such as the periodic nature of tidal variations, or operational loads, such as the adjusting position maneuvers of linkspans of ferry quays, the assumptions for performing common System Identification (SI) algorithms, such as the Stochastic Subspace Identification (SSI) method, may no longer be valid. In such cases, it is better to use SI algorithms that do not require respecting the white noise condition, allowing for a more accurate identification of modal parameters.

To explore this challenge, the Magerholm ferry quay was instrumented with an SHM system in 2023, transforming it into the Magerholm Research Quay (MQR). The monitoring system, implemented in collaboration with Møre og Romsdal County and the Norwegian University of Science and Technology (NTNU), consists of 22 accelerometers, 2 GPS antennas for synchronization, and 1 thermometer for evaluating thermal effects. The system aims to provide insights into how ferry quays are influenced by EOVs and tools for hazard alarming and damage detection.

This paper is a preliminary study that aims to evaluate the correlation between tidal levels and the modal parameters, particularly the first natural frequency, of linkspans for the first time. It gives an overview of the monitoring system that has been set up at the Magerholm Research Quay. It describes its design, sensor layout, and data acquisition system. Additionally, it presents a detailed analysis of time histories of the acceleration responses recorded on the linkspan. An Automated Operational Modal Analysis (AOMA) algorithm based on the SSI method was applied to 20-second-long recordings collected daily over a six-month period. Next, the correlation between tidal levels and the first identified natural frequency of the structure was investigated by performing Least Squares Regression. Additionally, Principal Component Analysis (PCA) was performed to explore the temporal fluctuations of the principal components and separate the tidal effects from the natural frequency.

The Magerholm Research Quay

The MRQ is a collaborative project between Møre og Romsdal County and NTNU. The project aims to use real-time data collected from the structure to investigate quays' structural behavior and optimize maintenance practices. Situated along Route 60, the Magerholm ferry quay serves as a critical link between Magerholm and Sykkylven. This quay transports around 950,000 vehicles annually, making it the fifth most utilized quay in Norway for vehicle traffic. The quay, along with its main components, is illustrated in Fig 1.

The quay consists of two primary structures: a reinforced concrete pier and a steel linkspan. Originally constructed in 1997, it underwent a major renovation in 2015 to handle larger ferries, including a 25-meter extension of the concrete pier and modifications to the linkspan.

The pier now spans 110 meters and is supported by end-bearing circular steel piles filled with C45 concrete, used for both the deck and the piles. Thirteen fenders are distributed across the quay to absorb ferry-induced impacts. In response to the upgrade to electric ferries, a charging station has been installed on the pier. A vacuum anchoring system provides stability, minimizing sway during loading and unloading operations. The steel linkspan, measuring approximately 15 meters in length and 9 meters in width, facilitates vehicle and passenger transfers. It incorporates longitudinal beams made from S355 steel and cross beams of S235 steel, with a front beam made of Hardox400 steel to resist the powerful ferry impacts. The linkspan is supported vertically by a concrete abutment and two lifting towers. The lifting towers, operated by a ferry operator, adjust the linkspan's position to account for water-level changes such as tides and waves. Four conical fenders, positioned between the linkspan and the concrete foundation, absorb longitudinal movements in the surge direction.

The monitoring system comprises 22 accelerometers, 2 GPS antennas, and 1 thermometer. The SHM system is illustrated in Fig 2. On the pier, 5 submersible uni-axial (Dytran 3211B2) sensors, 3 uni-axial (DY3055D3) sensors, and 4 tri-axial (DY3233A) sensors from Dytran, with sensitivities of 100 mV/g, 500 mV/g, and 1000 mV/g, respectively, are installed. Additionally, 10 submersible uni-axial (Dytran 3211B2) sensors are positioned on the linkspan, where they are exposed to waves during high tide and are partially submerged during storm surges.

The sensors on the pier are labelled with "P", while those on the linkspan are labelled with "L". Uni-axial sensors are identified by "T" for transversal (sway direction), "L" for longitudinal (surge), and "V" for vertical (heave) orientations, while tri-axial sensors are marked with "A" as the final letter. All the sensors deployed are Integrated Electronic

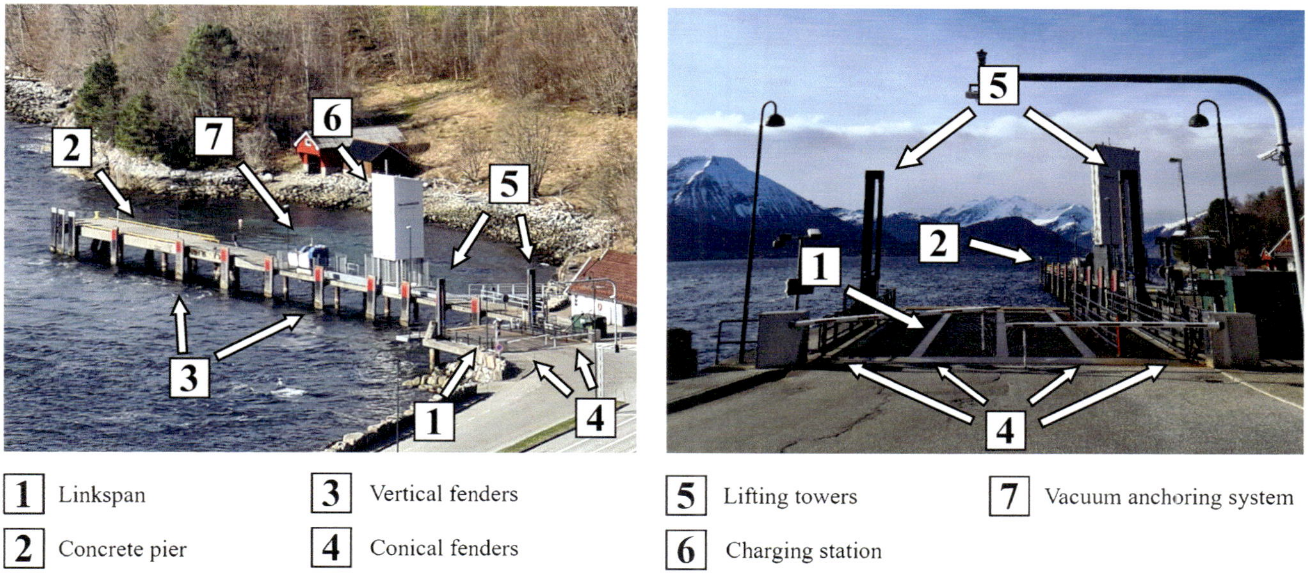

Fig. 1 The Magerholm Research Quay and its main components

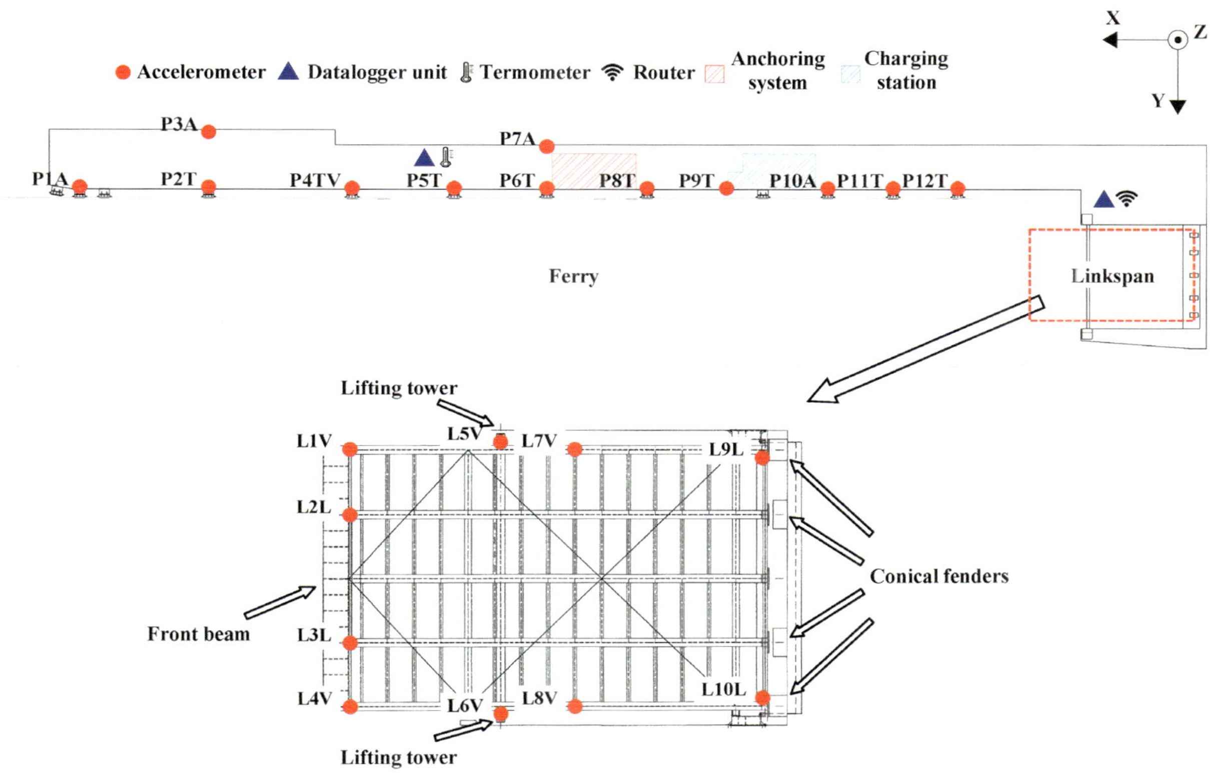

Fig. 2 Position of sensors on the Magerholm Research Quay

Piezo-Electric (IEPE) using AC coupling. The sampling frequency is adjustable up to 2560 Hz, and is typically set at 512 Hz for efficient data processing and storage. A scheme of the monitoring system is depicted in Fig 3. The sensors are connected to data logger units through waterproof wires, while a MAX BR1 LTE router ensures seamless 4G+ data transfer to a server. The data acquisition system is controlled by a cRIO 9035, integrating sound and vibration, GPS, and temperature modules. Synchronization with the server occurs twice per hour, with local storage on two 4TB hard drives for redundancy. The data logger units are programmed to be controlled via the Internet.

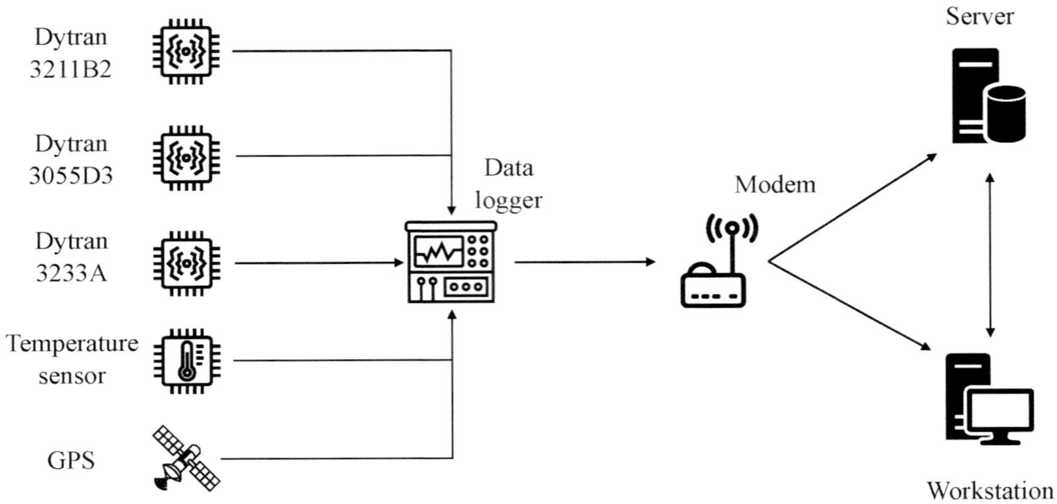

Fig. 3 Scheme of the monitoring system

Analysis of the Time Histories

In what follows, while both the concrete pier and linkspan have been described to provide a more comprehensive understanding of the sensor instrumentation, this paper focuses exclusively on the data recorded from sensors positioned on the linkspan. Of the 10 sensors installed on the linkspan, only 4 are utilized in this study, as the remaining sensors were damaged during the storm "Ingunn" in February 2024, which led to the collapse of the linkspan. Specifically, data from sensors L5V, L6V, L7V, and L8V (refer to Fig 2b) collected over a six-month period from March to August 2024, are analyzed. The selected accelerometers recorded accelerations only in the vertical direction. To illustrate typical daily time histories, accelerations recorded over a 24-hour period, starting at midnight, from accelerometer L5V are presented in Fig 4. Acceleration peaks generally correspond to ferry impacts on the linkspan. The variation in acceleration response across different impacts highlights the influence of operational and environmental factors on the dynamic of the quay. The duration of the docked state varies, ranging from 8 minutes during peak hours to up to 2 hours at night. On the depicted day in Fig 4, a total of 55 impacts are identifiable from the time history, aligning with the ferry schedule [11].

Figure 5 illustrates the acceleration response during a complete ferry docking event. Initially, small variations in acceleration are observed as the linkspan aligns to ensure that the impact occurs at a precise location on the ferry. The clearance of the ferry changes based on the tidal level, requiring the linkspan to be aligned before each impact. This is followed by the ferry impact, marked by a significant spike in acceleration as the ferry contacts the quay, representing the peak forces during

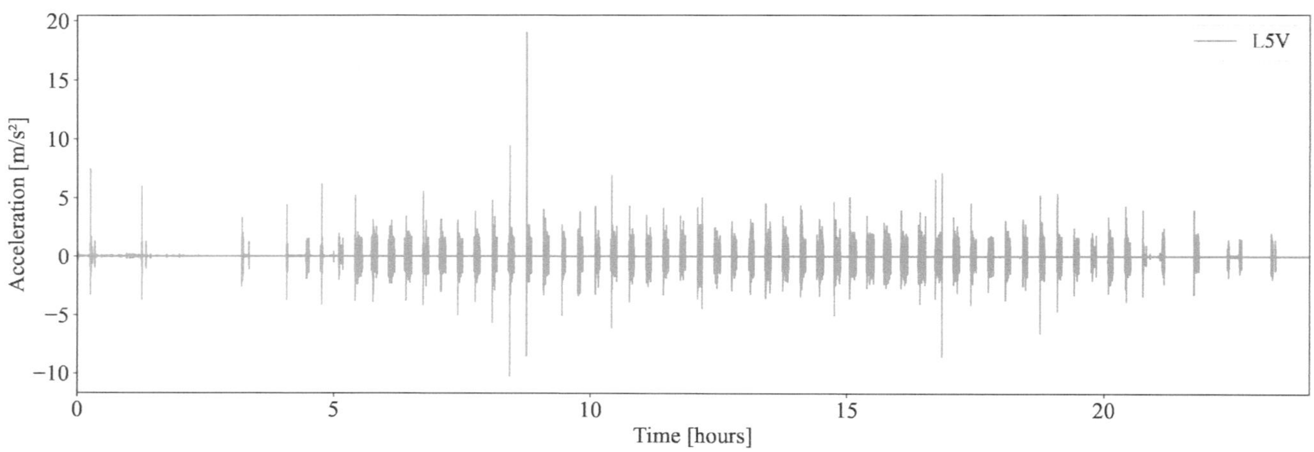

Fig. 4 Time history recorded over 24 hours from midnight from sensor L5V

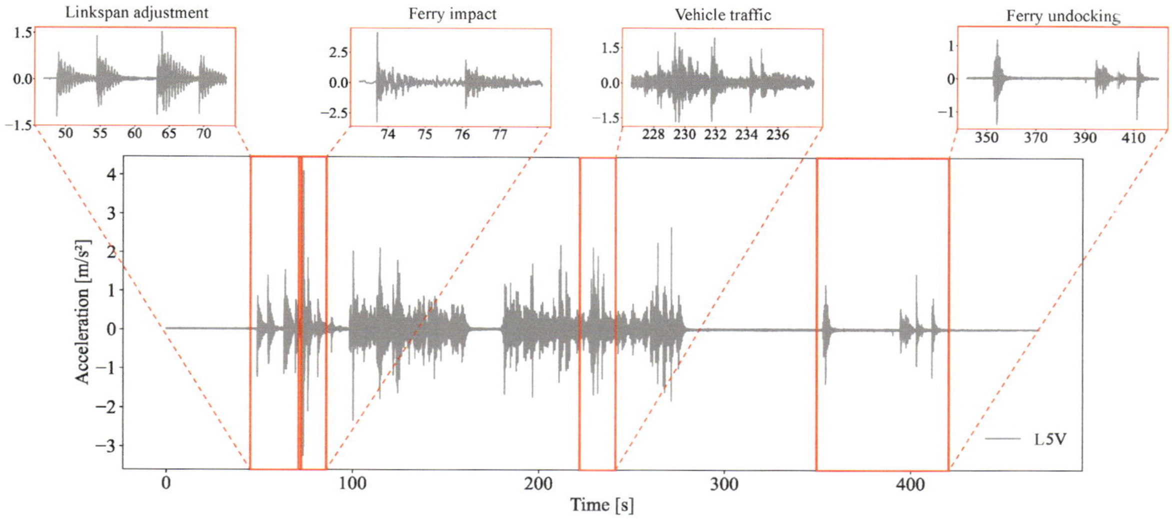

Fig. 5 Time history and main events of one docking recorded from sensor L5V

the event. After the impact, moderate vibrations are recorded as vehicles disembark and board the ferry. Finally, smaller fluctuations in acceleration are observed as the ferry undocks, indicating the departure of the ferry and the structure's return to its resting state.

Tital Level Variations and Modal Analysis

The tide fluctuations are obtained by the Norwegian Mapping Authority. Figure 6a shows the tidal level fluctuations over 6 months of data. The reference point 0 corresponds to the Chart Datum or Lowest Astronomical Tide levels. One measurement is taken per day at 10 a.m. Notably, the tides result in continuous fluctuations driven by lunar cycles and climatic factors. The tidal levels capture both short-term daily tidal fluctuations and long-term season variations. Local environmental factors, such as wind, atmospheric pressure, and coastal geography, can also contribute to deviations from the regular tidal cycle.

A previous operational modal analysis of the Magerholm ferry quay was conducted using a covariance-driven SSI algorithm by Ba Tung et al. [12]. This modal analysis was validated against a Finite Element Model (FEM) of the structure, which shows that the first bending mode has a natural frequency of 2.48 Hz. However, for the sake of conciseness, the mode shapes identified in Ba Tung's analysis, as well as those calculated by the FEM model are not reported in this paper. In our study, an AOMA method, based on the covariance-driven SSI algorithm, was applied, with the Density-Based Spatial Clustering of Applications with Noise (DBSCAN) algorithm automatically filtering and selecting stable poles in the stabilization diagram. The AOMA was performed on time histories recorded at approximately 10 a.m. each day over a 6-month period to automatically identify the modal parameters of the linkspan. This AOMA method has demonstrated its robust performance across various applications, including a reinforced concrete (RC) road bridge [13], a long suspension bridge [14], and a helicopter blade [15]. The time window used for modal analysis corresponded to the 20-second period before the ferry impact, during the adjustment phase of the linkspan. This period was selected because the level of ambient excitation in other time windows was insufficient for reliable modal identification. The SSI was performed with a band-pass filter set between 0.5 and 20 Hz. The lower cutoff frequency of 0.5 Hz corresponded to the low-frequency limit of the sensors, while frequencies above 20 Hz were excluded as they were beyond the range of interest for the modal analysis. The number of orders in the SSI varied from 10 to 130, and the number of block rows was set to 100. Additionally, the modal analysis was conducted using only four accelerometers positioned relatively close to one another. This limited spatial coverage made it challenging to consistently identify many modes of the structure. It is important to note that the SSI was applied during the adjustment of the linkspan, a period when multiple operational loads, such as short-duration forces exerted from the lifting towers, were applied. This means that the white noise assumption was not fully respected. Despite this, the approach was still sufficient to investigate the fluctuation of the tidal level. However, in order to properly identify the modal properties of the structure, more suitable system identification algorithms should be considered to handle non-white noise conditions.

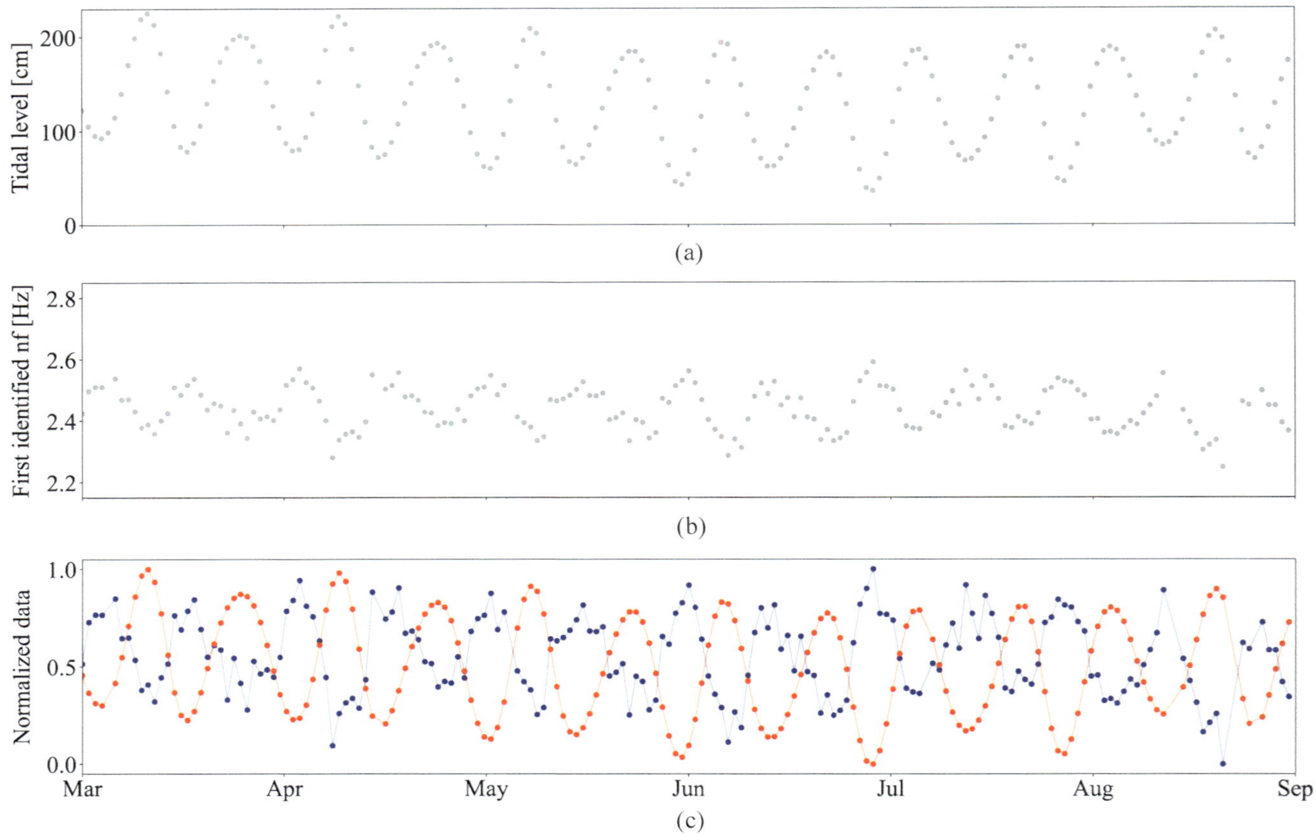

Fig. 6 Six months of data recorded once a day at approximately 10 a.m.: (a) Tidal level; (b) First identified natural frequency; (c) Normalized data: tidal level (red) and first identified natural frequency (blue), where the dots correspond to measurements, and the curves are obtained by interpolation for clarity

The investigation focused primarily on the first bending mode which natural frequency identified over the 6 months is shown in Fig 6b. The natural frequency fluctuates between approximately 2.25 Hz and 2.58 Hz, closely matching the FEM-calculated frequency of 2.48 Hz. The first identified natural frequency and tidal levels are normalized in order to compare their trends and are shown in Fig 6c. The dots represent the actual measurements taken once per day, while the curves are interpolations added to clarify trends in the data. A clear inverse relationship is observed between the two parameters: when the tidal level rises (red dots and line), the natural frequency drops (blue dots and line). This suggests that the boundary conditions of the structure are influenced by the tidal levels, with higher tidal levels likely changing the stiffness of the quay, leading to lower natural frequencies. This behavior is likely related to changes in the stiffness of the lifting towers, as they are hydraulic, or of the conical fenders, which vary depending on their inclination.

Correlation between Tidal Levels and Natural Frequency

Figure 7a shows the cross-correlation coefficient between the two parameters as a function of lag, with the lag on the x-axis representing the number of days the two parameters are shifted relative to each other. The y-axis represents the Pearson correlation coefficient, which ranges from -1 (perfect inverse correlation) to +1 (perfect direct correlation). At a lag of 0 days, the cross-correlation coefficient is approximately -0.83, indicating a strong inverse correlation between the first natural frequency and the tidal level when no shift is applied. This coefficient demonstrates that the two parameters are strongly and inversely correlated. The periodic oscillations in the cross-correlation plot suggest that the relationship between the two parameters is cyclical, likely driven by the regular tidal cycles. Peaks and troughs in the cross-correlation correspond to the natural periodicity of tidal variations, reinforcing the idea that tidal levels show a regular, predictable influence on the dynamic behavior of the structure.

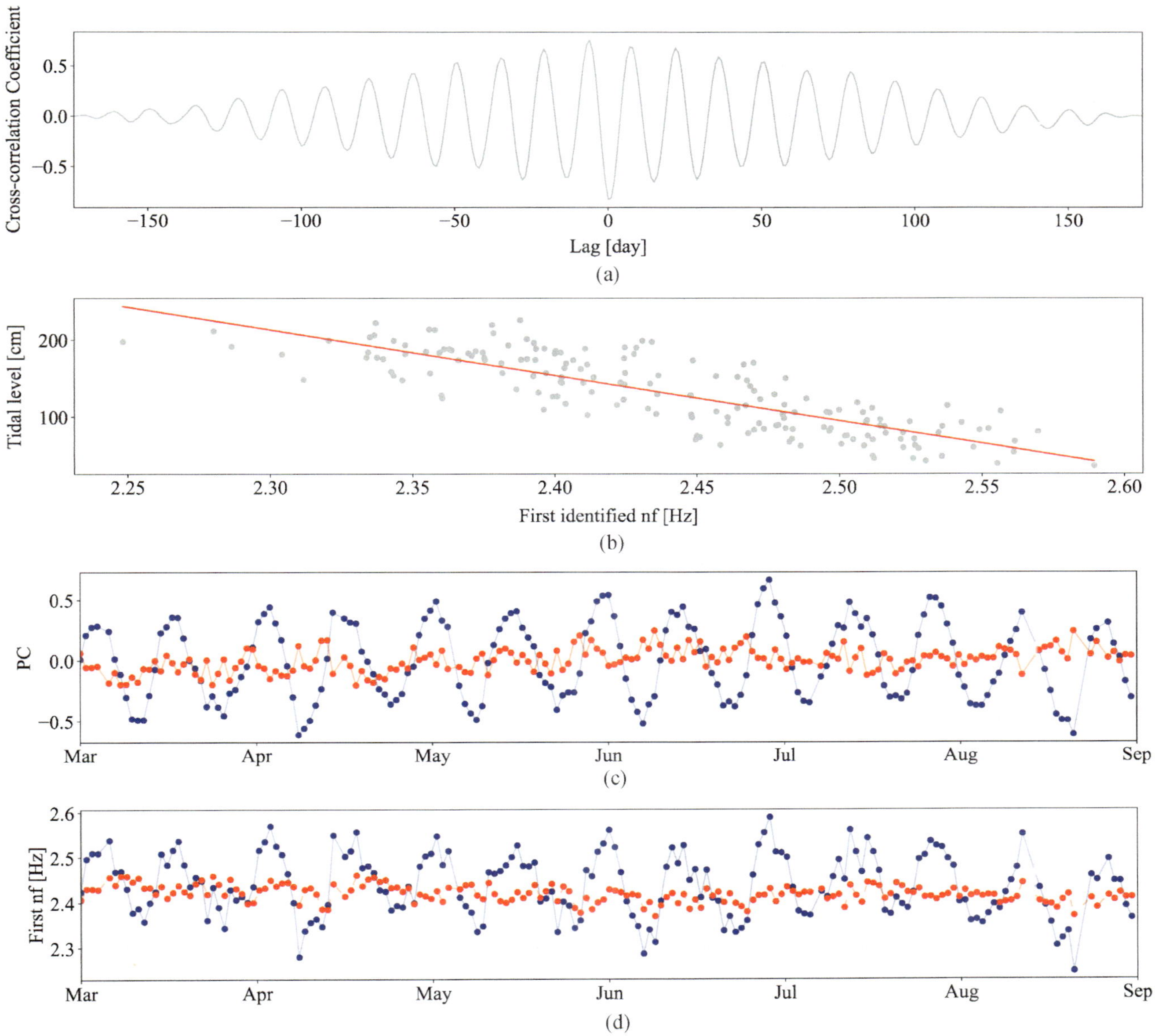

Fig. 7 a) Cross-correlation coefficient between tidal levels and the first natural frequency as a function of lag; b) Scatter plot of tidal level versus first natural frequency with least squares regression line; c) First (blue) and second (red) principal component of tidal levels and first identified natural frequency; d) First natural frequency before (blue) and after (red) the removal of the principal component

Figure 7b further supports this finding by showing the scatter plot of the first identified natural frequency of the linkspan and the tidal level. The scatter plot shows a strong correlation between the data, with points distributed within a relatively narrow band. The red line, obtained via least-squares regression, provides a linear approximation of the overall trend, clearly indicating that as the natural frequency increases, the tidal level decreases. This suggests that higher water levels reduce the stiffness of the dock structure, subsequently lowering its natural frequency.

In addition to the least-squares regression, the correlation between tidal levels and the first identified natural frequency is further investigated using PCA. PCA is a well-established "Blind Source Separation" technique. It enables to separate a set of source signals from a mixed signal without (or with little) info about the source and mixing process. PCA can be used for two temporal signals that are highly correlated with each other to evaluate the independent set of principal components. The principal components are the eigenvectors of the data's covariance matrix, and they are orthogonal to each other. The PCA representation is an optimal linear dimension reduction technique in the mean-square sense. Usually the last principal component is the one mostly due to noise. The results obtained by applying PCA to the first natural frequency and tidal levels are shown in Fig. 7c. It is observed that the largest variability represented by the the first principal component (blue dots and line in Fig 7c), is primarily due to the tidal fluctuations. The Pearson correlation coefficient between the tidal level and the first principal component is -0.98, confirming the very high inverse correlation between the two.

Finally, Fig 7d presents a comparison between the first identified natural frequency (blue dots and line) and the adjusted natural frequency (red dots and line) after removing the first principal component. From the plot, it is evident that the first identified natural frequency fluctuates between approximately 2.3 Hz and 2.6 Hz. After the adjustment, the natural frequency stabilizes, fluctuating in a narrower range around 2.45 Hz, which is close to the natural frequency of the FEM model. The reduction in fluctuation indicates that the tidal effects have been largely removed, and the adjusted natural frequency is now predominantly influenced by other operational and environmental variabilities, such as temperature, wind, and wave height.

It is worth clarifying that this analysis is based on the assumptions that: the different sensors used are affected by the same noise; the signal can be decomposed as a combination of linear independent set of principal components; the first one is mainly due to the tidal effect.

Conclusions

This paper presents the SHM system implemented at the Magerholm ferry quay, developed as part of a collaboration between Møre og Romsdal County and NTNU. The SHM system comprises 22 accelerometers, 2 GPS antennas, and 1 thermometer, all connected through wires to two logger units and a router for data transmission. An AOMA algorithm was used to identify the daily variation of the modal parameters of the linkspan over a six-month period. The environmental effects on the first natural frequency of the linkspan were investigated, with a particular focus on tidal levels.

The analysis revealed a significant inverse linear relationship between tidal levels and the first natural frequency, with a Pearson correlation coefficient of -0.83. Least Squares Regression was applied to quantify this relationship. Additionally, PCA was applied to the first natural frequency and tidal levels, showing that the first principal component is mainly caused by the tidal levels. After removing the first principal component, the resulting adjusted natural frequency displays fluctuations. These fluctuations are likely caused by changes in stiffness due to varying boundary conditions, specifically related to the hydraulic lifting towers and conical fenders, which change their mechanical properties based on the inclination of the linkspan. Additionally, other environmental and operational factors may also contribute.

Even though the AOMA might have resulted in inaccurate estimates of the modal properties, as the assumption of uncorrelated white noise excitation across the structure was violated by tidal levels and operational loads during the linkspan's adjustment phase, this is a preliminary study aimed at exploring the influence of tidal levels on the structure. Further analysis should focus on applying SI techniques capable of handling non-white noise assumptions to improve the accuracy of modal parameter identification under these complex environmental and operational conditions.

This preliminary analysis lays the groundwork for the application of more advanced techniques, such as the Hybrid Operational Modal Analysis [16] and Multivariate Nonlinear or Metric Learning approaches [17], to a broader dataset that includes additional environmental variabilities such as temperature, wind, and waves. These advanced techniques can help further filter out the environmental effects, improving the accuracy of the modal parameter identification and enhance structural analysis including FEM Updating, SI, and Damage Detection.

Acknowledgments The study was conducted with support from the Research Council of Norway through the Norwegian Regional Research fund in Møre og Romsdal county (SHMBru project 331578 and SARTORIUS project 353029). The authors gratefully acknowledge the Møre og Romsdal fylke for financing the research and for helping during the planning and execution of instrumentation and measurements.

References

1. Siedziako, B., Fenerci, A., and Nord, T.S. "Experimental vibration analysis on the rykkjem ferry dock during ferry berthing". In *Society for Experimental Mechanics Annual Conference and Exposition*, pages 103–111. Springer (2023).
2. Siedziako, B., Nord, T., and Fenerci, A. "Finite element model updating of a ferry dock bridge". *Journal of Physics: Conference Series*, 2647:182001 (2024).
3. Sibille, L., Nord, T.S., Siedziako, B., and Fenerci, A. "Impact force identification on a ferry dock bridge". *Journal of Physics: Conference Series*, 2647(18):182012 (2024).
4. Vegvesen, S. "Brutus - management system for bridges, ferry quays and other load-bearing structures in norway" (2023).
5. Olivieri, C., Fortunato, A., and DeJong, M. "A new membrane equilibrium solution for masonry railway bridges: the case study of marsh lane bridge". *International Journal of Masonry Research and Innovation*, 6(4):446–471 (2021).

6. Steenackers, G. and Guillaume, P. "Structural health monitoring of the z24 bridge in presence of environmental changes using modal analysis". In *Proceedings of IMAC*, volume 23 (2005).
7. Martucci, D., Civera, M., and Surace, C. "Bridge monitoring: Application of the extreme function theory for damage detection on the i-40 case study". *Engineering Structures*, 279:115573 (2023).
8. Farrar, C.R. and Worden, K. *Structural health monitoring: a machine learning perspective*. John Wiley & Sons (2012).
9. Magalhães, F., Cunha, Á., and Caetano, E. "Vibration based structural health monitoring of an arch bridge: From automated oma to damage detection". *Mechanical Systems and signal processing*, 28:212–228 (2012).
10. Peeters, B. and De Roeck, G. "One-year monitoring of the z24-bridge: environmental effects versus damage events". *Earthquake engineering & structural dynamics*, 30(2):149–171 (2001).
11. Fjord1. "Sykkelven-magerholm, ferry schedule" (2023).
12. Le, B.T., Siedziako, B., Nord, T.S., and Sibille, L. "Outcomes from field measurements on the magerholm ferry dock bridge: System identification, finite element model updating and sensitivity analysis". *Society for Experimental Mechanics Annual Conference and Exposition* (2025).
13. Civera, M., Sibille, L., Fragonara, L.Z., and Ceravolo, R. "A dbscan-based automated operational modal analysis algorithm for bridge monitoring". *Measurement*, 208:112451 (2023).
14. Civera, M., Rosso, M.M., Marano, G.C., and Chiaia, B. "Validation and comparison of two aoma approaches for the ambient vibration testing of long suspension bridges under strong wind loads". In *International Operational Modal Analysis Conference*, pages 475–484. Springer (2024).
15. Sibille, L., Civera, M., Zanotti Fragonara, L., and Ceravolo, R. "Automated operational modal analysis of a helicopter blade with a density-based cluster algorithm". *AIAA Journal*, 61(3):1411–1427 (2023).
16. ter Meulen, D.W.B., Cabboi, A., and Antonini, A. "Hybrid operational modal analysis of an operative two-bladed offshore wind turbine". *Mechanical Systems and Signal Processing*, 223:111822 (2025).
17. García Cava, D., Avendaño-Valencia, L.D., Movsessian, A., Roberts, C., and Tcherniak, D. "On explicit and implicit procedures to mitigate environmental and operational variabilities in data-driven structural health monitoring". *Structural Health Monitoring Based on Data Science Techniques*, pages 309–330 (2022).

Chapter 5
Outcomes from Field Measurements on the Magerholm Ferry Quay: System Identification, Finite Element Model Updating and Sensitivity Analysis

Ba Tung Le, Bartosz Siedziako, Torodd Skjerve Nord, and Luigi Sibille

Abstract Structural health monitoring (SHM) has become an essential practice in the research community due to the necessity of maintaining the longevity and safety of critical infrastructure. The Magerholm ferry quay examined in this study is an example of coastal infrastructure exposed to harsh environmental conditions and complex operational loads. As an important part of the region's transportation network, the quay accommodates significant daily traffic, including both local commuters and commercial vehicles. Despite that, previous SHM research has mainly focused on traditional bridge structures, leaving a considerable gap in our understanding of the health and performance of these equally vital maritime structures. This study explores various aspects of structural health monitoring for a linkspan (ferry docking bridge) using field measurements, system identification, finite element model updating (FEMU), and sensitivity analysis of the Magerholm linkspan.

Keywords Structural Health Monitoring · Link-span · System Identification · Finite Element Model Updating · Sensitivity Analysis

Introduction

The development of human society is linked to infrastructure development. As more and more structures near or exceed their design life, monitoring and maintenance have become increasingly challenging and expensive [1–3]. This issue is exacerbated by the increasingly harsh weather conditions attributed to global warming, particularly accelerating the deterioration of coastal infrastructure. To address this, researchers have been developing innovative techniques for asset condition monitoring, maintenance optimization, and life prediction [4–7].

Ferry terminals and their supporting infrastructure, for example linkspans, are critical components of the economies of coastal and island nations like Norway. These structures are subjected to harsh marine conditions and the excessively repeated impact of docking ferries [8], leading to structural damages [9]. One such damage example is the reduction of support provided by the lifting tower (Fig. 1), a critical component of a linkspan that supports the docking platform vertically and houses the jack used to adjust the bridge's height to accommodate varying tidal levels. Excessive operation can compromise the structural integrity of these towers. Despite their significance, our understanding of the behavior of lifting towers remains limited. It is clear that there is a need for further research on linkspans, with a particular focus on the behavior and health of lifting towers.

This study investigates the dynamic behavior of Magerholm linkspan through a combination of field experiments, system identification, and finite element modeling. Firstly, FEMU is also applied to accurately determine the actual condition of the lifting tower through the stiffness of the springs representing it. Afterwards, a sensitivity analysis was conducted to evaluate the influence of lifting tower stiffness on the dynamic behavior of ferry docks, with the aim of determining whether such damage could be easily detected. The results demonstrate that the natural frequencies of ferry docks are highly sensitive to lifting tower stiffness, particularly the first bending and first torsion modes.

B. T. Le (✉) · Bartosz Siedziako · Torodd Skjerve Nord · Luigi Sibille
Department of Ocean Operations and Civil Engineering, Norwegian University of Science and Technology, Larsgårdsvegen 2, 6009 Ålesund, Norway
e-mail: batung.le@ntnu.no; bartosz.siedziako@ntnu.no; torodd.nord@ntnu.no; luigisi@ntnu.no

Brian Damiano et al. (eds.), *Structural Health Monitoring & Machine Learning, Vol. 12*, Conference Proceedings of the Society for Experimental Mechanics Series, https://doi.org/10.13052/9788743801573-5

Field measurement

Magerholm Ferry Dock

The Magerholm ferry quay is part of Route 60, which connects Magerholm and Sykkylven. This route plays a vital role in the transportation system of the Møre og Romsdal area, with an average daily traffic of up to 2,500 vehicles [10]. This structure is composed of two main components: the steel docking bridge or so called linkspan and the side support quay (concrete bridge), as illustrated in Figs. 1 and 2. The linkspan is 16m long, 7m wide and constructed of steel. The bridge deck consisting of main longitudinal beams connected by cross beams and diagonal braces for structural stabilization. Since the structure is used for ferry docking, it must accommodate varying tide heights by adjusting the height of the ferry quay to match the ferry. To achieve this, lifting towers are employed; they are connected to a lifting beam located beneath the deck, serving as the support for the docking bridge. The other support is provided by the abutment, which includes conical fenders

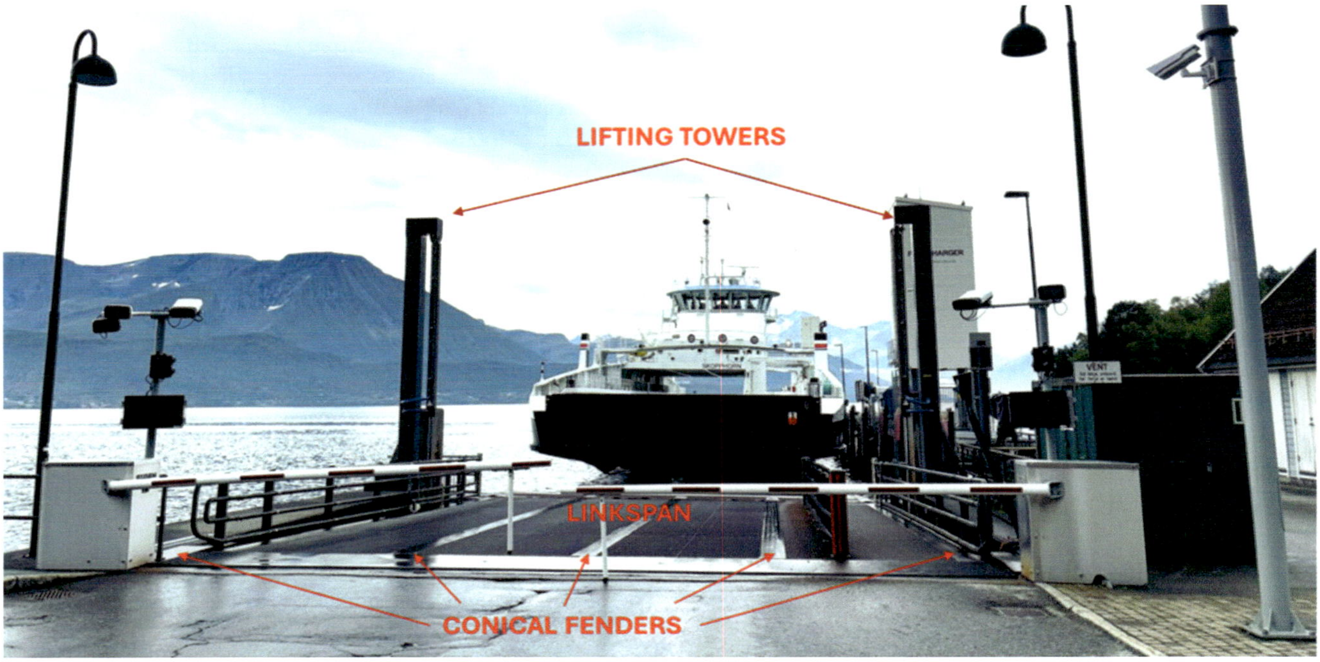

Fig. 1 Magerholm ferry quay with its structural components

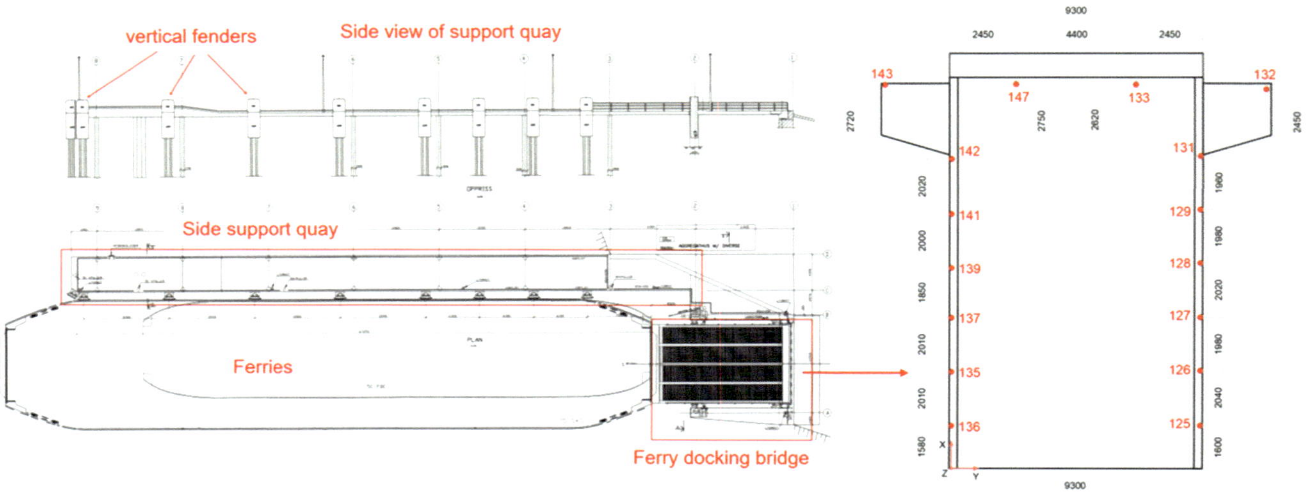

Fig. 2 Magerholm ferry dock sensor layout

beneath the main beam to absorb the impact from docking ferries. Above these components, steel grating are installed to accommodate movement of vehicles and passengers. It should be noticed that when the ferry is successfully docked, the lifting towers then release the jacks and the new support to the dock is the ferry itself. Field experiments presented in this studies were conducted in the "free state" when ferry dock bridge was supported by the lifting towers.

Field Measurement Setup

The installation and measurement of sensors on the ferry dock were conducted on May 31, 2022. For this measurement, G-Link 200 wireless sensors from MicroStrain were utilized, offering significant convenience compared to the conventional wired sensors. The use of wireless sensors allows for a rapid and flexible layout on the ferry dock without disrupting its operating schedule. A total of 16 G-Link 200 3-axis sensors with waterproof covers were deployed. These sensors transmit data to a WSDA-2000 gateway, which is capable of communicating with a computer equipped with software from the sensor provider. The sampling frequency was set to 128 Hz, and the accelerometer's range was adjusted to the lowest possible setting of ±2 g to enhance noise density, which the supplier specifies as 25 $\mu g/\sqrt{Hz}$. The sensors are mounted directly to the steel deck using magnetic plates from the sensors. The sensor layout is shown in Fig. 2.

System Identification

Modal Analysis

Acceleration time series graphs from the field measurement are illustrated in Fig. 3. It is possible to recognize notable events when the ferry docks, such as the adjustment of the lifting towers to allow the ferry to dock and leave, or the movement from vehicles on the docking bridge. After the ferry was undocked from the docking bridge, walking excitation was performed to simulate ambient noise, a crucial input for operational modal analysis.

The acceleration recorded from walking excitation has been used to perform modal analysis. Before applying covariance driven stochastic subspace identification (SSI) algorithm to identify modal information, the data was high-passed filtered

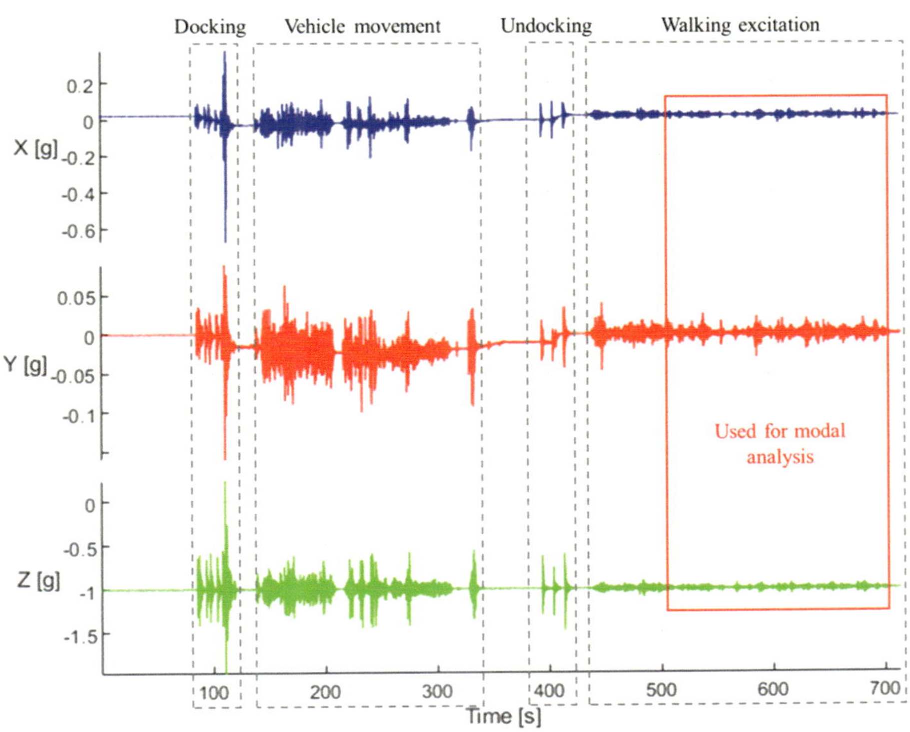

Fig. 3 Time series of accelerometer 147 during docking event of a Ferry. Direction X, Y and Z refer to longitudinal, transverse and vertical direction of the ferry dock

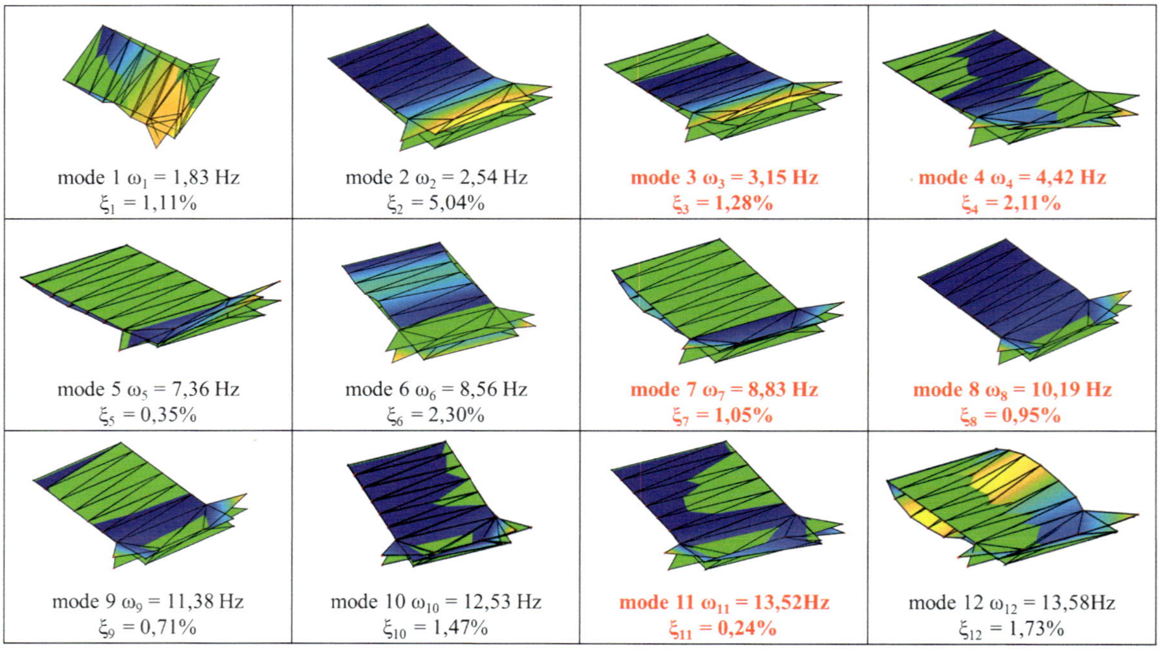

Fig. 4 Modal information from SSI: mode shapes, eigenfrequencies and damping in free state operation. Five modes noted in bold red color are chosen for the updating process

with a cut-off frequency of 0.5 Hz. The following parameters were used for SSI procedure: the number of orders was set to 200, number of blockrows was set to 100 and the number of blocks for covariance of the subspace matrix was set to 20. Finally, the mode shapes and natural frequencies are summarized in Fig. 4.

Figure 4 shows that, aside from the translation mode (mode 1), both bending and torsion modes have been identified. Modes 2, 3, 5, 6, and 7 correspond to the first and second bending modes of the entire bridge, while modes 8 to 11 indicate bending in the transverse direction of the bridge's tip. Torsional behavior is observed in modes 4 and 12. In some cases, two modes exhibit similar mode shapes, making it difficult to distinguish between them. The reason for this is believed to be the stiffness of the lifting towers. Since these towers lift the bridge using jacks, their stiffness is not stable, leading to similar mode shapes with different natural frequencies. It is important to note that modes 5, 10, and 12 exhibit unsymmetrical behavior. Given that the main structural elements are symmetric, this unsymmetrical behavior could indicate a change in the bridge's stiffness on one side over time. Five modes noted in bold red color in Fig. 4 are chosen for the updating process.

Finite Element Model Updating

Finite Element Model

An Finite element (FE) model, shown in Fig. 5, was constructed using ABAQUS [11] based on the existing drawings provided by the municipality [12]. However, some information regarding the side balconies was missing and therefore thicknesses were based on field measurements. The following cross sections were assigned to the main structural components: main beam: HE550B; cross beam: IPE240, HE240A, and UNP220; lifting beam: HE450B; diagonal bracing (L-shape): 200x200x16; and various plates with thicknesses ranging from 10 mm to 45 mm. These parts are constructed from St52-3N or RSt-37-2 steel, which have mechanical properties equivalent to the S235 and S275 steel types, respectively. Quadrilateral finite membrane-strain shell elements with reduced integration (S4R) were selected for the FE model. A mesh size sensitivity analysis for the ferry quay was conducted in [13], revealing that a mesh size between 50 mm and 100 mm is optimal. In this study, a mesh size of 50 mm was selected.

Only the structural components were modeled in ABAQUS. To accurately simulate the total mass of the docking bridge, non-structural mass was introduced to account for elements such as railings and steel gratings. The weight information for these parts was obtained from the existing drawings. The steel gratings were modeled at 90 kg/m², the large railings at approximately 81 kg/m, and the small railings at 19.25 kg/m. Ultimately, the entire structure weighed 53.64 tons.

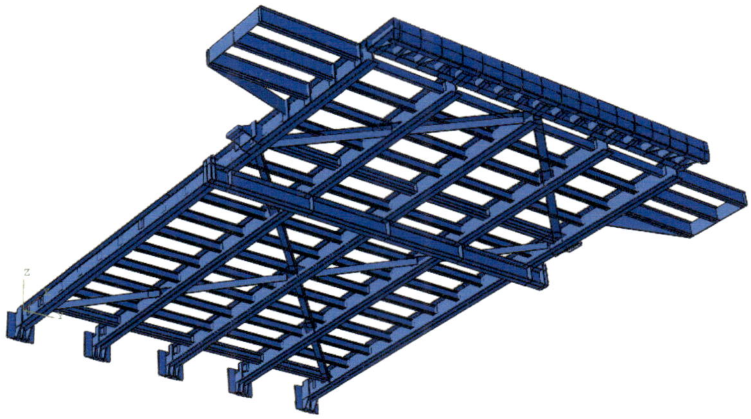

Fig. 5 Finite element model of Magerholm ferry dock in ABAQUS

As described in section 2.1, the docking bridge is supported by the abutment and lifting towers in its free state. Consequently, constraints in the transverse and vertical directions are introduced at the abutment. Springs with a stiffness of 2000 kN/m (as specified by the provider) are modeled in the longitudinal direction at the positions of the conical fenders. The lifting towers, which support the bridge vertically, are represented by vertical springs. The initial stiffness of these springs was set at 10 000 kN/m, as the exact value is unknown and will be updated later. The mode shapes extracted from FE model are depicted in Fig. 6.

Model Updating Methodology

In this study, Mottershead's sensitivity method [14] is applied to update the finite element model. This process is similar to an optimization problem, where the goal is to minimize the error between the FE model's output and the field measurement results, thereby improving the approximation of the computer model to the actual state of the structure. The output used for comparison in this study is the natural frequency of the linkspan. To align the model output as closely as possible with the measured data, the input parameters θ of the FE model—such as material density, Young's modulus, cross-sectional

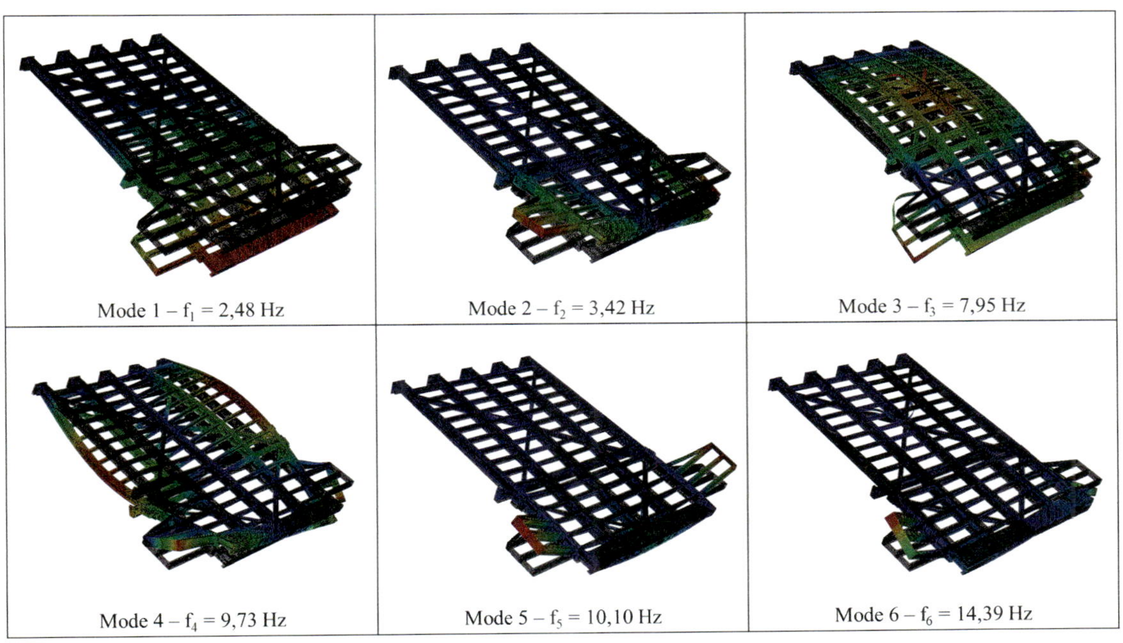

Fig. 6 First six modes of FE model

properties, etc—are systematically adjusted. This adjustment is represented by $\Delta\theta$, where $\Delta\theta_i = \theta - \theta_i$. These parameters are iteratively modified, until this quantity gradually approaches an acceptable small value:

$$J(\Delta\theta) = \epsilon_z^T W \epsilon_z \tag{1}$$

Here, W is a weighting matrix that accounts for the importance of different terms in the vector ϵ_z. It is defined as a diagonal matrix with diagonal values equal to $1/f_i^2$, where f_i are the measured frequencies in Hertz (Hz). The vector ϵ_z represents the difference between the FE model-calculated results $z(\theta)$ and the measured results z_m:

$$\epsilon_z = z_m - z(\theta) \tag{2}$$

In the iterative process, this difference can be expressed as $r_i = z_m - z(\theta_i)$. To minimize the error in each iteration, ϵ_z is updated by linearizing the non-linear relationship between θ and $z(\theta)$ as follows:

$$\epsilon_z \approx r_i - G_i \Delta\theta_i \tag{3}$$

G_i is the sensitivity matrix computed by

$$G_i = \left[\frac{\partial z_j}{\partial \theta_k}\right]_{\theta=\theta_i} \tag{4}$$

To avoid matrix singularity and ill-conditioning problem, it should be noted that all mentioned vectors and matrices should be normalized as presented in [15]. Replacing ϵ_z in Eq. (1) by (3) one can define the objective function:

$$J(\Delta\theta_i) = \|-W^{1/2} G_i \Delta\theta_i + W_i^{1/2} r_i\| \tag{5}$$

When Eq. (5) is applied in this study, with natural frequency as the quantity of interest, it is transformed as follows:

$$J(\Delta\theta_i)^* = \sum_{j=1}^{5} [W]_{j,j} \left(\frac{f_{m,j} - f_{n,j}}{f_{0,j}}\right)^2 \tag{6}$$

Here $f_{m,j}$ and $f_{n,j}$ are the jth measured and numerical frequencies respectively while $f_{0,j}$ is the jth initial numerical frequencies.

This optimization problem is solved using the *scipy.optimize.lsqn* function in Python. During each iteration, the parameters are updated by an amount $\Delta\theta$, which is the solution from the previous iteration:

$$\theta_{i+1} = \theta_i + \Delta\theta_i \tag{7}$$

The iteration process continues until the error between the FE model and the measurement results is reduced to an acceptable level, or when the values of θ_{i+1} and θ_i converge and are sufficiently close to each other. The workings of this algorithm have been previously presented by [15], where they also provide a code implementation of this method [16].

In practice, the FE model and measurement results yield various natural frequencies and mode shapes. Selecting which natural frequencies and mode shapes from the FE model to compare with the measured data is a challenge that needs to be addressed. To tackle this, a Mode Matching Index (MMI) has been introduced to find the natural frequencies and mode shapes of the FE model that closely match those of the measurement results. This is done based on the natural frequency values and the similarity in mode shapes, as quantified by the Modal Assurance Criterion (MAC) value

$$MMI = (1-\gamma) MAC_{m,n} - \gamma \frac{|f_m - f_n|}{f_m} \tag{8}$$

where f_m and f_n are measured and numerical frequencies respectively. To weight between mode shapes and frequencies, coefficient γ is introduced and has the range between 0 and 1. The value of γ is chosen as 0.5 in this study. For the updating purpose, only FE modes that have MAC value above 0.6 compare to measure modes, are selected for updating process.

Updating Parameters

It is important that the number of natural frequencies used for updating needs to be larger than the number of parameters to ensure unique solutions to the optimization problem [15]. The number of parameters also depends on the availability of the measured modes. In this study, four parameters were chosen; therefore, at least five natural frequencies must be used for

Table 1 Used parameters for updating routine and their limits

Paremeter	Initial value	Allowable change between iterations	Global bounds
ρ_{steel}	7850 kg/m^3	$\pm 5\%$	no bounds
k_1	10000 kN/m	$\pm 20\%$	no bounds
k_2	10000 kN/m	$\pm 20\%$	no bounds
E_{steel}	210 GPa	$\pm 5\%$	no bounds

finite element model updating. The first parameter chosen is the material density, ρ_{steel}, which accounts for possible errors in estimating non-structural mass and modeling errors. This is followed by Young's Modulus, E_{steel}, that can be associated with uncertainties in structural stiffness due to corrosion and degradation. The stiffness of the lifting towers, k_1 and k_2, is also included, as the support characteristics of this type are unknown. The parameters and their ranges are summarized in Table 1. Based on the study conducted in [13], the initial values for the stiffness of lifting towers were set to be 10000 kN/m. Allowable change of 5% was applied for steel density and Young's modulus since these two parameters were not expected to change much. However, considering the potential variability in lifting tower stiffness, a more substantial allowable change of 20% was established.

Results

The FEMU process was conducted for six iterations to minimize the objective function $J(\Delta\theta_i)^*$, as detailed in Fig. 8. A significant reduction in this quantity occurred within the first three iterations, followed by a gradual convergence. Updated parameter values are presented in Table 2, while the FEMU process's effectiveness in matching natural frequencies and mode shapes between the measured state and FE model is summarized in Table 3.

As anticipated, the stiffnesses of the lifting towers underwent the most substantial changes. Given that all measured frequencies exceeded those of the initial FE model, indicating a stiffer-than-estimated actual ferry dock state, the FEMU process increased values of the stiffness of the lifting towers. This is also reflected by a slight increase in Young's modulus. Conversely, a minor decrease in steel density might be attributed to modeling errors at joints and an inaccurate estimation of the side balconies' weight.

Figure 7 presents sensitivity index values (calculated using Eq. (4)) for the four considered parameters. The sensitivity indices of the lifting tower stiffnesses, G_{k1} and G_{k2}, reveal their primary influence on the natural frequencies of the first bending and first torsional modes. Their impact on other modes is less pronounced.

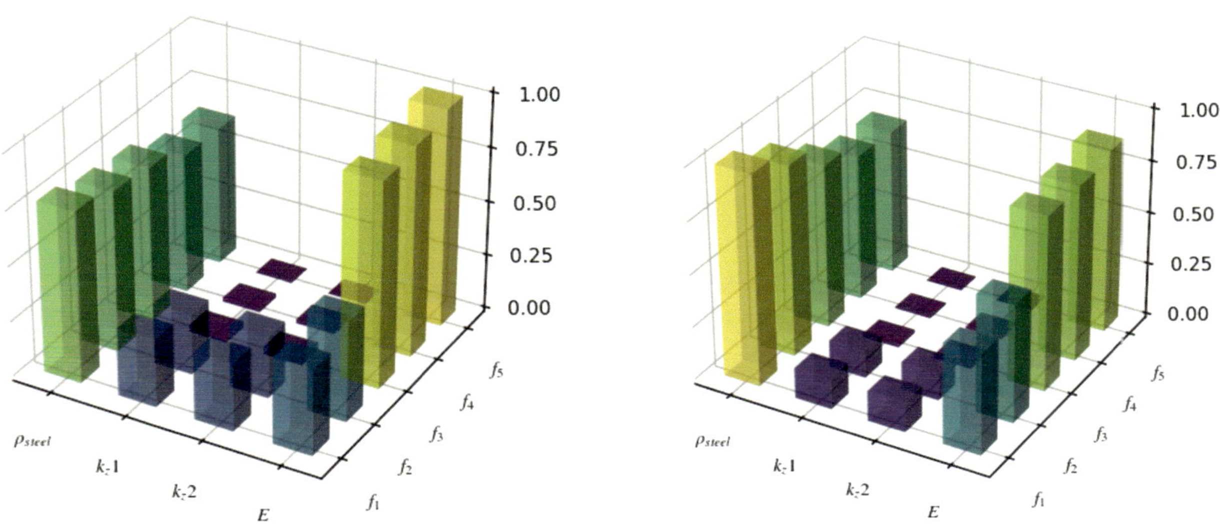

(a) Scaled sensitivity matrix of first iteration

(b) Scaled sensitivity matrix of last iteration

Fig. 7 Scaled sensitivity matrix of FEMU process

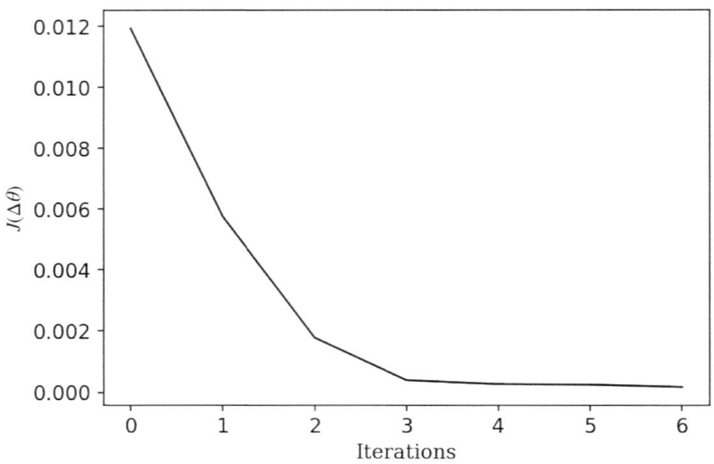

Fig. 8 Objective function $J(\Delta\theta_i)^*$ through iterations

Table 2 Parameter values before and after finite element updating

Paremeter	Initial value	Updated value	Change
ρ_{steel}	7850 kg/m^3	7039 kg/m^3	-811 kg/m^3
k_1	10000 kN/m	20736 kN/m	10736 kN/m
k_2	10000 kN/m	20736 kN/m	10736 kN/m
E_{steel}	210 GPa	218.9 GPa	8.9 GPa

Table 3 Natural frequencies and MAC values before and after updating

Mode	Frequency, f[Hz]							MAC value		
	Measured	Initial	Error[%]	Weighted errors[%]	Updated	Error[%]	Weighted errors[%]	Initial	Updated	Change
1	3.15	2.48	-21.27	-11.92	3.18	0.95	0.53	0.957	0.981	0.024
2	4.42	3.42	-22.62	-6.44	4.26	-3.62	-1.03	0.953	0.977	0.024
3	8.83	7.95	-9.97	-0.71	8.63	-2.27	-0.16	0.649	0.664	0.015
4	10.19	10.1	-0.88	-0.05	10.84	6.38	0.34	0.960	0.958	-0.002
5	13.52	14.39	6.43	0.20	15.2	12.43	0.38	0.699	0.703	0.004
Absolute average			**10.2**			**4.3**		**0.70**	**0.71**	

The updating process yielded a commendable reduction in average frequency errors from 10.2% to 4.3%. Notably, the most significant improvements were observed for the first two modes, aligning with the amplified weighting assigned to these modes. A slight increase in the MAC value suggests a closer approximation of the FE model's mode shapes to those extracted from measurements.

Sensitivity Analysis of Lifting Towers

One of the motivations for performing studies at Magerholm as a case study stems from the collapse of its ferry dock during Ingunn storm, one of the most powerful storms to impact Norway in 30 years [17], on 31st January 2024. Following the storm, the entire deck of the structure detached from the lifting towers and sank into the water, necessitating a salvage operation and reattachment to the towers. Although the exact cause of the collapse remains uncertain, the authors suspect that similar damages can be caused by failure of the lifting towers. Consequently, the authors conducted a sensitivity analysis on the updated model of lifting tower stiffness to assess its impact on the dynamic behavior of the linkspan.

The results are presented in Figs. 9 and 10. Figure 9 captures the sensitivity of frequencies when changing the stiffness of one tower and keep the other one constant at $k = 20736kN/m$ which is the stiffness of the towers after updating. On the other hand Fig. 10 capture that when changing the stiffness of both towers at the same time.

As expected, there is a clear correlation between tower stiffness and modal behavior. Most modes are sensitive to stiffness variations, except for mode 6, which remains relatively unaffected. The first bending mode (mode 1) is particularly sensitive to stiffness changes, while modes 3 and 6 show minimal sensitivity. Interestingly, the first torsional mode (mode 2) exhibits

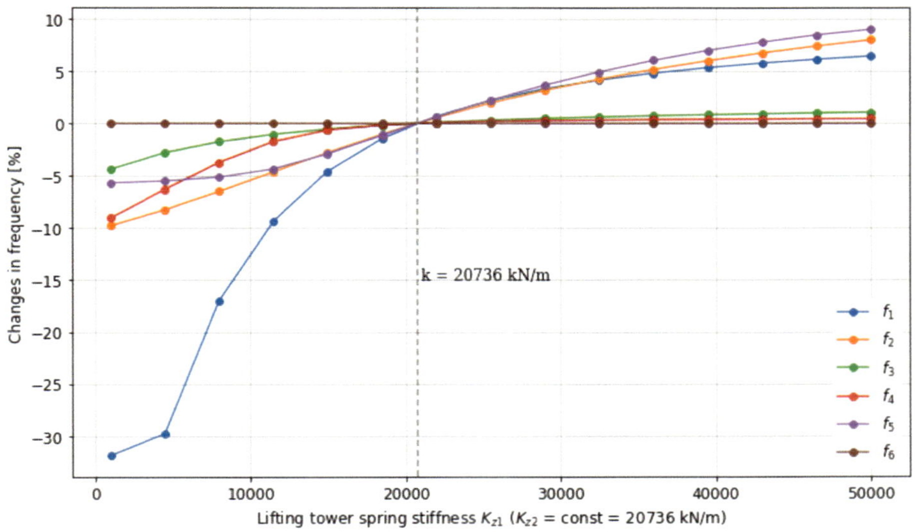

Fig. 9 Percentage changes in natural frequencies of 6 modes corresponded to different lifting tower stiffness values - Altering stiffness in a single tower. $k = 20736 kN/m$ is the stiffness of the towers after updating process

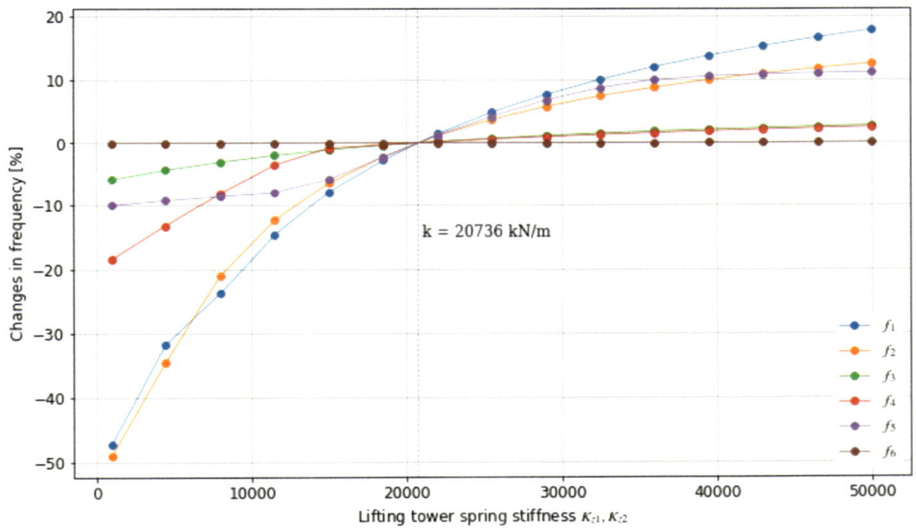

Fig. 10 Percentage changes changes in natural frequencies of 6 modes corresponded to different lifting tower stiffness values - Altering stiffness in both towers. $k = 20736 kN/m$ is the stiffness of the towers after updating process

significantly increased sensitivity when both tower stiffnesses are adjusted. Other modes experience a gradual frequency increase with rising stiffness.

Conclusion

This study provides a better understanding of the modal behavior of linkspans and examines the possibility of detecting lifting tower damage modeled by reduction in its stiffness using modal information. The key points can be summarized as follows:

- When employing wireless accelerometers, walking excitation serves as an effective input for the SSI algorithm in determining the modal characteristics of linkspans.

- There are challenges in selecting modes for FEMU application due to multiple modes with similar mode shapes and closely spaced natural frequencies. This is caused by the variable stiffness of the jacks used in lifting towers, which can fluctuate slightly during operation, resulting in nearly identical modes.
- Sensitivity-based FEMU has proven highly effective in constructing a FE model that replicates the actual condition of the linkspan. The error between the FE model and field measurement results was reduced to less than 5% within just six updating iterations.
- The sensitivity analysis shows a strong correlation between lifting tower stiffness and the docking bridge natural frequencies, especially when the stiffness of lifting towers is below 20,000 kN/m.
- While most modes are sensitive to stiffness variations, the first bending and first torsional modes are particularly susceptible to changes in lifting tower stiffness. This suggests that damage to the lifting towers would likely be reflected in changes to the natural frequencies of these two modes. After the updating process, the stiffness of lifting towers is estimated to be approximately 20,000 kN/m.

Acknowledgments The study was conducted with support from the Research Council of Norway through the Norwegian Regional Research Fund in Møre og Romsdal county (SHMBru project 331578). The authors gratefully acknowledge Møre og Romsdal fylke for financing the research and for helping during the planning and execution of instrumentation and measurements.

References

1. U. S. Department of Homeland Security Science and Technology. "Aging Infrastructure: Issues, Research, and Technology" (2010).
2. Kim, K.H., Nam, M.S., Hwang, H.H., and Ann, K.Y. "Prediction of remaining life for bridge decks considering deterioration factors and propose of prioritization process for bridge deck maintenance". *Sustain*, 12:1–25 (2020).
3. Noortwijk, J.M.V. and Klatter, H.E. "The use of lifetime distributions in bridge maintenance and replacement modelling". *Computers & Structures*, 82:1091–1099 (2004).
4. Jeong, Y., Kim, W.S., Lee, I., and Lee, J. "Bridge service life estimation considering inspection reliability". *KSCE Journal of Civil Engineering*, 21:1882–1893 (2017).
5. Agdas, D., Rice, J.A., Martinez, J.R., and Lasa, I.R. "Comparison of visual inspection and structural-health monitoring as bridge condition assessment methods". *Performance of Constructed Facilities*, 30(3):1–10 (2016).
6. Moughty, J.J. and Casas, J.R. "A state of the art review of modal-based damage detection in bridges: Development, challenges, and solutions". *Applied Sciences*, 7 (2017).
7. Srikanth, I. and Arockiasamy, M. "Deterioration models for prediction of remaining use-ful life of timber and concrete bridges: A review". *Traffic and Transportation Engineering*, 7:152–173 (2020).
8. Vegvesen, S. *Hånbok – Ferjestatistikk*. V620 (2018).
9. Siedziako, B. and Nord, T.S. *Experimental vibration analysis on the Rykkjem ferry dock during ferry berthing*. Presented on IMAC-XLI (In press) (2023).
10. Vegvesen, S. "Ferjestatistikk" (2024). Last accessed 20 August 2024.
11. Dassault Systemes Simulia Corp. "Abaqus/CAE 6.14 – Documentation" (2014).
12. Statens Vegvesen 2022 Brutus. "Management system for bridges, ferry quays and other load- bearing structures in Norway" (2022).
13. Siedziako, B., Nord, T.S., and Fenerci, A. "Finite element model updating of a ferry dock bridge". *Journal of Physics: Conference Series*, 2647:182001 (2024).
14. Mottershead, J.E., Link, M., and Friswell, M.I. "The sensitivity method in finite element model updating: A tutorial". *Mechanical Systems and Signal Processing*, 25:2275–2296 (2011).
15. Bjørn T. Svendsen, G.T.F., Øyvind W. Petersen and Rønnquist, A. "Improved finite element model updating of a full-scale steel bridge using sensitivity analysis". *Structure and Infrastructure Engineering*, 19(3):315–331 (2023).
16. Bjørn T. Svendsen, G.T.F., Øyvind W. Petersen and Rønnquist, A. "Fe model updating in python" (2020).
17. "New wind record in norway with storm ingunn". https://www.meteoiq.com/2024/02/02/new-wind-record-in-norway-with-storm-ingunn/Posted on 2.02.2024 by Dennis Schulze.

Chapter 6
A Robust Data-Driven Algorithm for Early Damage Detection in Structural Health Monitoring

Luigi Severa, Silvia Milana, Nicola Roveri, Eleonora Maria Tronci, Antonio Culla, and Antonio Carcaterra

Abstract In the field of Structural Health Monitoring (SHM), the ability to detect and identify damage at its early stage is necessary to maintain the safety and integrity of structures. Early damage detection not only prevents catastrophic failures but also reduces maintenance costs by enabling timely interventions. Presented here is a data-driven algorithm for SHM that extracts Damage Sensitive Features (DSFs) with high sensitivity to structural damage. The proposed method leverages a model-free approach, making it highly adaptable and suitable for real-world applications where models may not be available or feasible. Central to this approach is the use of blind source separation techniques, which isolate and amplify damage indicators from the complex structural response signals. This isolation is crucial for enhancing the sensitivity and specificity of damage detection, ensuring that even minor structural anomalies are accurately identified. By integrating artificial intelligence techniques, such as machine learning algorithms, the proposed method improves the identification accuracy of damage and significantly mitigates the effects of environmental and operational variabilities on DSFs. The efficacy of the algorithm is validated through comprehensive testing on a cylinder structure subjected to various damage scenarios and loading conditions. These scenarios are designed to be representative of real-world environmental and operational influences, ensuring the practical relevance of the results, which demonstrate a significant improvement in the robustness and accuracy of SHM practices, highlighting the algorithm's potential as an effective approach for the continuous monitoring and maintenance of critical infrastructures. Furthermore, the findings suggest that the proposed method could be generalized to other types of structures, making it a versatile tool in the field of SHM.

Keywords Structural Health Monitoring · Damage Detection · Damage Sensitive Features · Principal Component Analysis · Independent Component Analysis

Introduction

Ensuring the safety and durability of structures is an important concern in engineering applications, and Structural Health Monitoring (SHM) provides a valuable means of addressing this challenge. By detecting structural anomalies at an early stage, SHM helps prevent failures and optimizes maintenance processes, thereby reducing associated costs and disruptions [1, 2].

This is relevant in several sectors, like the mechanical and aerospace industries, civil infrastructures, and pipelines. Indeed, in industrial and civil applications, pipelines are critical components since they carry fluids and gases through plants. Therefore, any malfunction in these components can result in significant environmental impacts and economic losses [3, 4].

Vibration-based SHM methods are particularly effective in this context, as they monitor the dynamic behavior using sensors that collect vibration data. These data are then used to extract specific indicators, known as Damage Sensitive Features (DSFs), which serve as a baseline to assess structural integrity. Any deviation from the baseline DSFs of a healthy structure can identify potential damage [4, 5, 6]. As far as concerns the extraction of DSFs, it traditionally involves modal

Luigi Severa · Silvia Milana · Nicola Roveri · Antonio Culla · Antonio Carcaterra
Department of Mechanical and Aerospace Engineering, Sapienza University of Rome, Via Eudossiana 18, 00184 Rome, Italy
e-mail: luigi.severa@uniroma1.it; silvia.milana@uniroma1.it; nicola.roveri@uniroma1.it; antonio.culla@uniroma1.it; antonio.carcaterra@uniroma1.it

Eleonora Maria Tronci
Department of Civil and Environmental Engineering, Northeastern University, Snell Engineering Center, 400, 110 Forsyth St, Boston, 02115, MA, USA
e-mail: e.tronci@northeastern.edu

Brian Damiano et al. (eds.), *Structural Health Monitoring & Machine Learning, Vol. 12*, Conference Proceedings of the Society for Experimental Mechanics Series, https://doi.org/10.13052/9788743801573-6

parameters like natural frequencies and damping ratios, which are directly linked to a structure's mechanical properties [7, 8]. However, extracting these parameters can be computationally expensive and highly sensitive to environmental conditions, making them less reliable in practical applications, also because they require a great deal of expertise from the user, who interprets the data and assesses the health of the structure [9, 10]. Signal processing techniques such as the Wavelet Transform [3] and Hilbert-Huang Transform [11] have been explored as alternatives, as they decompose signals to capture distinctive patterns or signatures that indicate damage [12]. Despite their potential, these methods face limitations in automated systems due to generalization problems. In this framework, blind source separation techniques [13], including Principal Component Analysis (PCA),Independent Component Analysis (ICA), and Second-Order Blind Identification, have gained attention in SHM because they require minimal user input and are useful to extract meaningful DSFs [14, 15]. However, all the techniques employed to extract DSFs are not without limitations because they have to face the effect of EOV within the structural response. In particular, the reliability of these DSFs is related to their ability to distinguish between structural changes caused by damage and those caused by Environmental EOV. Sensitivity to damage and robustness to EOV are critical for minimizing false alarms. A pre-processing stage of the data recorded by sensors is typically performed to address this. This activity is generally performed in a pre-processing stage, where various machine learning techniques have been employed to achieve this. Among them, PCA stands out as particularly effective, compared with auto-associative neural networks, factor analysis, Mahalanobis distance, and singular value decomposition [16]. PCA projects data into lower-dimensional subspaces, focusing on the components least affected by EOVs, thereby improving the reliability of the extracted DSFs [9, 17]. In particular, projecting data onto the Minor Components (MCs) subspace has proven effective in enhancing the robustness of DSFs. This paper proposes an SHM approach that leverages the combined strengths of PCA and ICA to extract non-modal-based DSFs. Unlike most traditional methods, this approach is data-driven, relying solely on measured structural response data, making it suitable for real-world monitoring applications. The proposed method offers sensitivity to low-magnitude damage and demonstrates resilience to variable loading conditions, thanks to the use of MCs projection. To validate this approach, we applied it to a Finite Element model of a pipe structure, where damage was simulated by reducing the cross-sectional area at various locations. The results validate the method's capability to detect damage at early stages while remaining robust to EOV.

Background

The proposed methodology is based on the cascading application of PCA and ICA. The theoretical foundations of these techniques are presented in the following paragraphs.

Principal Component Analysis

Principal Component Analysis (PCA) is a powerful multivariate statistical technique commonly used to identify and extract the most significant patterns hidden within a dataset [18]. By reducing the dimensionality of the problem, PCA minimizes information loss while preserving as much variance as possible. This makes it especially valuable in the analysis of large datasets, where eliminating redundancy is mandatory to focus on the most relevant signals and trends and so to ensure that the most critical insights are retained.

PCA achieves this by transforming a set of potentially correlated variables into a new set of uncorrelated variables, called Principal Components (PCs), which represent the directions of maximum variance in the data, capturing the essential information in a more compact form. This is performed through an orthogonal transformation since the PCs' orthogonality ensures that each component captures unique information [18].

Given a data-acquisition matrix $\mathbf{Z} \in \mathbb{R}^{N \times N_s}$, its rows are the N observations, while its columns ($\mathbf{z_n}$) are the N variables available. The implementation of the PCA encounters several stages, as following listed [19]:

1. Data Standardization. In the beginning, data ($\mathbf{z_n}$) are standardized in order to ensure that variables with different measurement scales do not disproportionately influence the analysis. Without standardization, variables with larger scales could dominate the variance and skew the results. Generally, this stage consists of two sub-stages, giving the Z-score normalization, as in Eq. (1), which are:

   (a) Centering: each variable is set to zero-mean, otherwise the first PC would capture the mean (μ_n) of the data instead of their variance.

   (b) Scaling: each variable is divided by its standard deviation (σ_n) in order to ensure that all variables contribute equally to the process, which is not biased by different data magnitude.

$$\mathbf{x_n} = \frac{\mathbf{z_n} - \mu_n}{\sigma_n} \tag{1}$$

2. Covariance Matrix Computation. Starting from the standardized data collected in the $\mathbf{X}$ matrix, a covariance matrix is evaluated, as in $\mathbf{C} = \frac{\mathbf{X}^T\mathbf{X}}{N}$, to quantify the degree of correlation between the variables and how the co-vary with each other to identify the direction of maximum variance in the dataset.
3. Covariance Matrix Eigenproblem. This is the key step of the PCA algorithm, and it consists of an eigenvalue decomposition of the covariance matrix, as expressed in $\mathbf{Cv} = \lambda\mathbf{v}$. It is performed in order to find the eigenvectors ($\mathbf{v}$), or PCs, and their corresponding eigenvalues (λ). The eigenvectors represent the directions in which the data varies the most, and the corresponding eigenvalues indicate the amount of variance captured by each component. Each eigenvector corresponds to a PC, and the eigenvalues are ranked in descending order to prioritize the directions that capture the most variance. Since the eigenvalues are often referred to as active energies [12], representing the proportion of total variance explained by each component, PCs with larger eigenvalues capture more variance and are, therefore, more energetic and relevant to the data.
4. Dimensionality Reduction. Subsequently, which components to keep and to discard are selected. This selection process is guided by a threshold, typically based on the proportion of variance to retain or the mean of the eigenvalues, as in Eq. (2) [19].

$$\lambda_i > \frac{1}{N_s}\sum_{j=1}^{N_s}\lambda_j. \tag{2}$$

where λ_i is the eigenvalue of the $i-th$ component. Components with eigenvalues that exceed the mean eigenvalue are traditionally considered significant, while the others are the so-called Minor Components (MCs), which are the ones that exhibit less variability.
5. Projection onto Principal Components. Once the PCs are identified, the data can be projected into the new subspace, effectively reducing its dimensionality and making them more manageable for analysis or further processing.. The transformed data matrix $\mathbf{Y}$ is obtained as in $\mathbf{Y} = \mathbf{X}\ \mathbf{V_k}$, where $\mathbf{V_k}$ is the matrix of the previously selected k eigenvectors.

Thanks to this framework, PCA enhances the interpretability of the data, making it a suitable tool in data analysis for feature extraction, revealing relationships, and patterns that may not be immediately apparent in the original variable space. Additionally, PCA can improve the performance of ML algorithms by eliminating noise and redundant features.

Despite its strengths, PCA assumes that the components are linear combinations of the original variables. As a result, it may not capture complex nonlinear relationships present in the data. Additionally, while PCA is effective for variance-based feature selection, it does not explicitly consider the underlying distribution of the data, which may lead to the loss of important information, especially in cases with significant non-Gaussian characteristics.

Independent Component Analysis

Independent Component Analysis (ICA) is a computational technique that seeks to decompose multivariate data into statistically independent non-Gaussian components [13]. While similar to other dimensionality reduction techniques like PCA and factor analysis, ICA goes a step further by aiming to extract signals that are not only uncorrelated but also independent, meaning that the presence of one signal provides no information about the presence of the others. Thanks to this property, ICA is particularly useful in applications involving the analysis of mixed signals, such as in BSS, where the goal is to recover original source signals from observed mixtures without prior knowledge of the mixing process. One of the most classic examples is the cocktail party problem, in which multiple people are speaking simultaneously in a room, and ICA is used to isolate each individual voice from a set of mixed recordings captured by several microphones.

Assuming that the observed data are linear mixtures of statistically independent and non-Gaussian source signals, ICA aims to recover these unknown sources by finding components that are as far from Gaussian as possible, using measures like kurtosis (a measure of the "tailedness" of the distribution) or negentropy (a measure of how far a distribution is from Gaussianity).

To illustrate the underlying principles of ICA, consider the following mathematical formulation. Let $\mathbf{s} = \left(s_1, s_2, \ldots, s_{N_s}\right)^T$ represent the unknown source signals and $\mathbf{x} = \left(x_1, x_2, \ldots, x_{N_s}\right)^T$ represent the observed mixed signals. The mixing process can be expressed as in Eq. (3) [13], where $\mathbf{A}$ is the unknown mixing matrix.

$$\mathbf{x} = \mathbf{A}\mathbf{s} \tag{3}$$

Therefore, the challenge lies in estimating both $\mathbf{s}$ and $\mathbf{A}$ from the observable signals $\mathbf{x}$. This is achieved through various optimization techniques, commonly based on maximizing the non-Gaussianity of the estimated signals or minimizing the mutual information among them, like FastICA, kurtosis maximization ICA, Infomax and joint approximate diagonalization of eigenmatrices [13, 20, 21]. After the unmixing coefficients have been computed, the original Independent Components (ICs) are reconstructed from the mixed signals, using the relation $\mathbf{s} = \mathbf{W}\mathbf{x}$, where $\mathbf{W}$ is the estimated unmixing matrix. ICA's ability to leverage higher-order statistics and maximize non-Gaussianity makes it especially effective in scenarios where independence, rather than variance, is the primary concern. However, despite its effectiveness, ICA comes with certain limitations due to the unknown nature of both $\mathbf{s}$ and $\mathbf{A}$. One primary challenge is that the variances of the ICs remain indeterminable. This is because any scalar multiplier present in one of the source signals s_i can be compensated by adjusting the corresponding column $\mathbf{a_i}$ in the mixing matrix. To address this issue, a common approach is to assume unit variance for the sources. Additionally, a sign ambiguity exists: multiplying an IC by -1 does not violate the model, but this ambiguity is often inconsequential in most applications [20]. Another challenge is that the sequence of the ICs cannot be uniquely determined. The order of terms in the summation in the mixing equation allows for any IC to be designated as the primary one. A permutation matrix $\mathbf{P}$ can be introduced into the model, in this way $\mathbf{x} = \mathbf{A}\mathbf{P}^{-1}\mathbf{P}\mathbf{s}$, where the components of $\mathbf{P}\mathbf{s}$ are the original independent variables s_i but rearranged. Consequently, the matrix $\mathbf{A}\mathbf{P}^{-1}$ becomes an unknown mixing matrix that ICA algorithms must resolve [20]. This is one of the more important distinctions between ICA and PCA.

Overview and Description of the Technique

The proposed methodology, outlined in Fig. 1, involves several phases designed to enhance the detection of early-stage damage while remaining robust against variations of loading and operative conditions [22]. The first phase involves the application of PCA, with the data standardization outlined in Eq. (1), to the raw data collected by sensors. This step aims to reduce the dimensionality of the data and to isolate the most significant components that capture the underlying structural behavior [10]. As a result, the selected components are the Minor Components (MCs) [9].

Following PCA, ICA is applied to separate further the mixed signals recorded by the sensors, isolating the Independent Components (ICs). This step distinguishes the effects of structural damage from confounding factors such as noise or external environmental influences. Once the ICs are extracted, the next step is transforming these signals from the time domain to the frequency domain using the Fourier Transform (FT). Indeed, the frequency domain offers several advantages over the time domain when detecting damages, above all at their early stage: it simplifies the complexity of the raw vibratory data, making it easier to identify patterns associated with structural anomalies. Additionally, analyzing the frequency characteristics of the ICs helps reduce the impact of noise and other temporal variations, thereby improving the accuracy of the damage detection process.

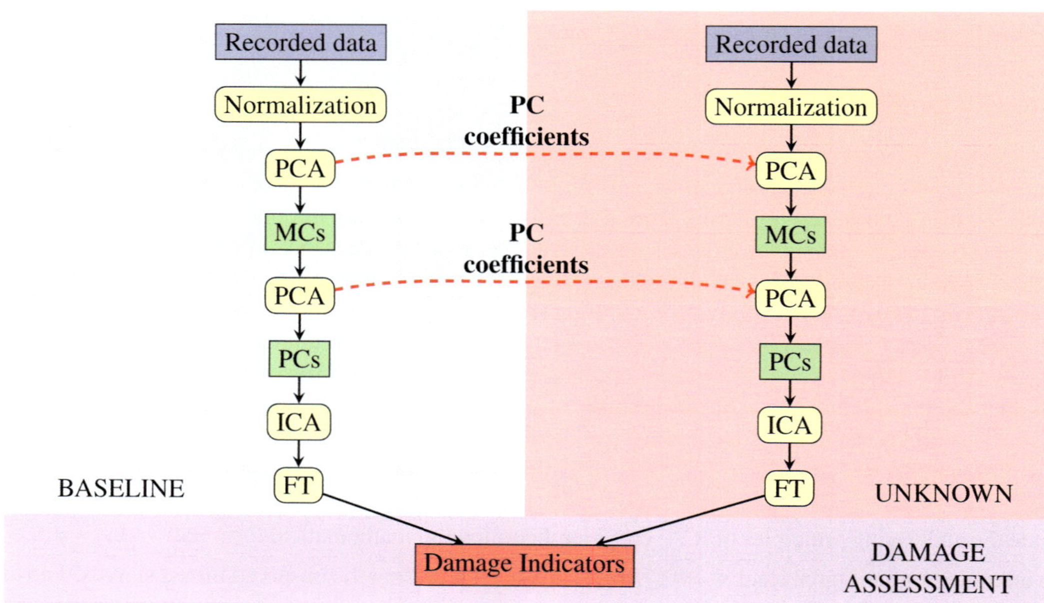

Fig. 1 Block diagram resuming the algorithm workflow [22]

In the final phase, the method compares the frequency spectra of ICs obtained from measurements taken at different time intervals, corresponding to the baseline and the actual states of the structure. The differential area (A), as in Eq. (4), is employed to quantify the overall difference between the spectra $x(f)$ and $y(f)$ of two signals, where the frequency vector f spans the bandwidth $[f_{min}, f_{max}]$. For this metric, larger values indicate more significant alterations in the structural response, thus warning for potential damage [22].

$$A(x, y) = \int_{f_{min}}^{f_{max}} |y(f) - x(f)| \, df \tag{4}$$

Analysis

This section is dedicated to the description of the structure to which the proposed methodology is applied, as well as the presentation of the results obtained.

Case Study: A Randomly Excited Cylindrical Pipe

The structure under investigation is a steel pipe, numerically modeled using the finite element software ANSYS, as detailed in [3]. The cylindrical structure has a length of $5m$, with a circular cross-section of $0.2m$ in radius and a uniform thickness of $0.01m$, and it is clamped at both ends to simulate fixed boundary conditions.

This study focuses on only one damage type, involving a 10% reduction in the section's thickness at six different locations along the cylinder's length, as detailed in Table 1. The type of damage was chosen to simulate a condition that affects the dynamic behavior of the pipe. Indeed, a reduction in thickness will impact the flexural stiffness of the cylinder, which in turn affects its frequency response.

Nine measurement points were selected on the test bed's external surface. These points, illustrated in Fig. 2, are evenly spaced along the cylindrical axis to cover the entire pipe, while their angular positions are evenly spaced along half of the cylinder's section to capture possible asymmetries in its behavior. These sensors collect the displacement time histories at the nodes where they are installed.

To evaluate the dynamic behavior of the pipe under a randomly distributed load ($p(x, t)$, a modal analysis is performed on ANSYS, identifying the first N_M natural mode shapes (ϕ_n). Then, using the modal superposition techniques, as in Eq. (5), the displacement at any point (x_0), where sensors are positioned, has been computed. In this approach, the displacement is evaluated as a combination of the single modal contributions, and the amplitude of each mode is governed by the modal coordinates (q_n), which can be calculated by solving the system of differential equations in Eq. (6) [11], where the natural

Table 1 Damage location along the longitudinal axis of the pipe for each scenario

	Scenario 1	Scenario 2	Scenario 3	Scenario 4	Scenario 5	Scenario 6
Description	Undamaged	Damaged	Damaged	Damaged	Damaged	Damaged
Damage intensity	-	10%	10%	10%	10%	10%
Damage location	-	$1.5m$	$2.0m$	$2.5m$	$3.0m$	$3.5m$

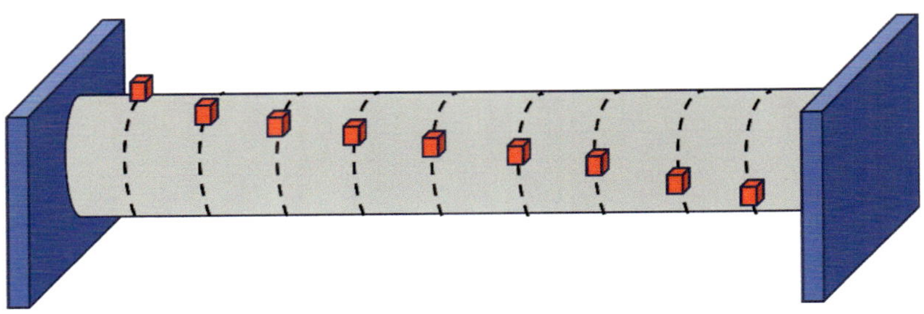

Fig. 2 Case study: the cylindrical pipe with sensors mounted on it (red cubes)

frequencies of each mode (f_n), ranging from $93.96Hz$ to $234.20Hz$ are given by the finite element model; while the the damping ratios (ζ_n) were then introduced in the system's response computation.

To better simulate the variability and uncertainty present in real-world conditions, random numerical noise is introduced into the computed displacements. This noise is proportional to 5% of the standard deviation of the displacement signal.

$$w(x_0, t) = \sum_{n=1}^{N_M} \phi_n(x_0)\, q_n(t) \tag{5}$$

$$\ddot{q}_n(t) + 2\zeta_n\omega_n\dot{q}_n(t) + \omega_n^2 q_n(t) = \int_0^L \phi_n(x)p(x,t)\, dx \tag{6}$$

Results and Discussion

The goal of this analysis is to evaluate how well the proposed method performs in assessing structural damage. For clarity and conciseness, the damage considered in all the figures is scenario 2 in Table 1, except for the illustration of the final result. The general behavior of the signal recorded by sensors is illustrated in Fig. 3a, where the damage influence in the pipe's response is barely noticeable. To gain deeper insights, its corresponding frequency spectrum is provided in Fig. 3b, where damage effects are typically more evident.

However, only a slight shift in modal peaks can be observed in this case. The analysis begins by applying PCA to data recorded by the N_s sensors. In this step, the most significant MCs are identified based on the formulation in Eq. (2). PCA is then reapplied on them to reduce the problem's dimensionality further, selecting the PCs from the application of Eq. (2). Subsequently, ICA is performed on the selected components, using the FastICA and the kICA algorithm [20], to extract the ICs. Figure 4 shows the spectra of the most damage-sensitive PC and IC, which are identified by the greater differential area. Notably, damaged IC's spectrum shows a pronounced increase in amplitude within the frequency band close to the first mode when the structure is damaged, demonstrating the algorithm's ability to highlight structural changes. In contrast, as sensors, PCA alone fails to reveal substantial differences between damaged and undamaged states, underlining the added value of ICA in improving the detection of structural anomalies (as illustrated in Fig.4b).

The next step involves the evaluation of the differential area, as in Eq. (4), which serves as a damage indicator. This is done for all damage scenarios in Table 1, within a damage detection framework [22], Specifically, for the evaluation of the differential area for each damage scenario j in Table 1, the ICs' spectra of the jth are compared against the first undamaged scenario (scenario 1). The results, depicted in Fig. 5, clearly demonstrate that the combination of PCA and ICA is more effective in detecting damage than PCA alone. Indeed, these findings highlight the presence of structural anomalies, confirming the occurrence of damage. Therefore, the method proves effective even in identifying damage at an early stage, where the damage intensity is as low as 10%.

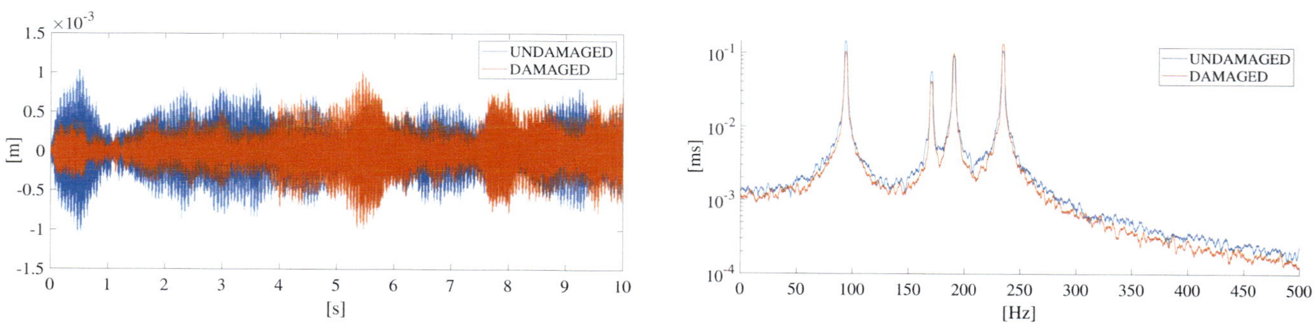

(a) Time histories of the displacement

(b) FT of the normalized displacement

Fig. 3 Signals recorded (and their FT) in the undamaged (blue) and damaged (orange) cases by the sensor placed at the midpoint of the cylinder axis on its surface

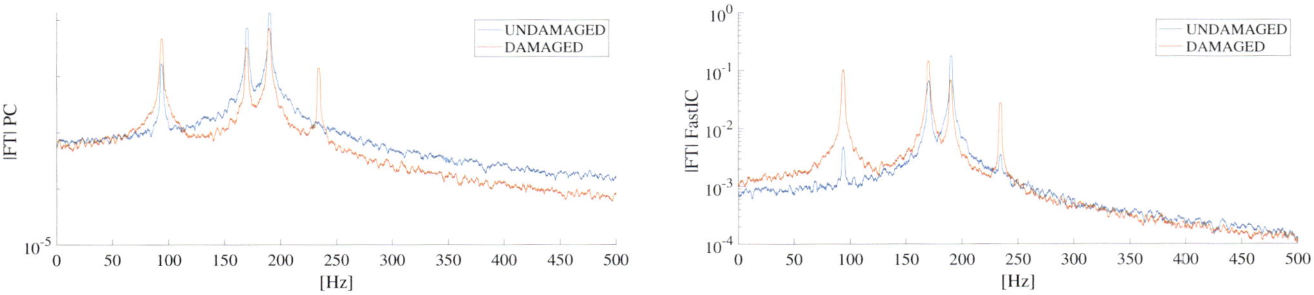

(a) PC (b) FastIC

Fig. 4 Best PC's FT and best FastIC's FT in the undamaged (blue) and damaged (orange) cases

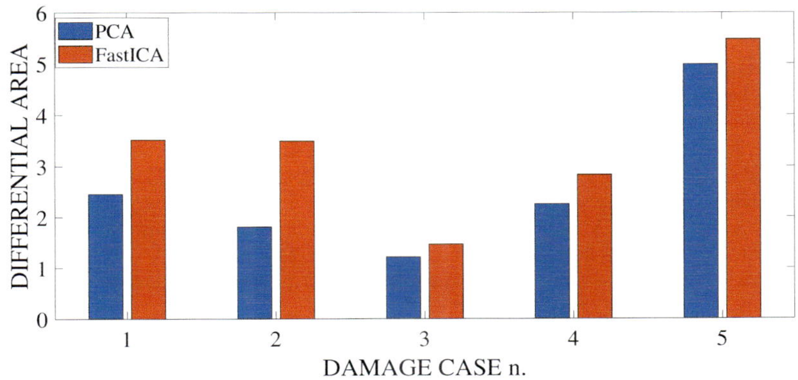

Fig. 5 Differential area for both PCs and ICs evaluated for damage detection for all the scenarios in Table 1

Conclusion

This research explores the ability of the proposed methodology, which integrates PCA and ICA, to detect early-stage damage. This is performed using the differential area as a key damage indicator. Applied to a FEM model of a pipe with simulated damage, the algorithm demonstrates superior performance when compared to PCA alone. Even under conditions where the structure is subjected to a randomly distributed load, the algorithm efficiently filters the noise by analyzing the Minor Components identified through PCA. The encouraging results suggest that this approach could be applied to various structural scenarios.

Future work will expand this analysis, considering multiple damage scenarios and locations to test the method further. Additionally, several environmental factors, such as temperature and humidity variations, will be included to evaluate how sensitive the damage indicator is under different conditions and the ability of PCA to filter out them.

Acknowledgments This research was supported by co-funding of the European Union - The National Recovery and Resilience Plan (NRRP) – Mission 4 Component 2 Investment 1.4 - NextGeneration EU Project - Project "MOST-Sustainable Mobility Center" - CUP B83C22002900007. This manuscript reflects only the authors' views and opinions, neither the European Union nor the European Commission can be considered responsible for them.

References

1. Abe, M. "Structural monitoring of civil structures using vibration measurement current practice and future". *Artificial intelligence in structural engineering: Information technology for design, collaboration, maintenance, and monitoring*, pages 1–18 (2005).
2. Abdo, M. "Structural health monitoring, history, applications and future". *A review book. Open Science* (2014).
3. Milana, S., Roveri, N., Carcaterra, A., and Culla, A. "Continuous wavelet transform for structural health monitoring of a pipe". *Proceedings of ISMA 2018 - International Conference on Noise and Vibration Engineering and USD 2018 - International Conference on Uncertainty in Structural Dynamics*, page 3925 – 3933 (2018).

4. Farrar, C. and Worden, K. "An introduction to structural health monitoring". *Philosophical Transactions of the Royal Society A: Mathematical, Physical and Engineering Sciences*, 365(1851):303–315 (2007).
5. Roveri, N., Pepe, G., Mezzani, F., Carcaterra, A., Culla, A., and Milana, S. "Optyre—real time estimation of rolling resistance for intelligent tyres". *Sensors (Switzerland)*, 19(23) (2019). Cited by: 8; All Open Access, Gold Open Access.
6. Stagi, L., Sclafani, L., Tronci, E.M., Betti, R., Milana, S., Culla, A., Roveri, N., and Carcaterra, A. "Enhancing the damage detection and classification of unknown classes with a hybrid supervised–unsupervised approach". *Infrastructures*, 9(3) (2024).
7. Farrar, C. and Jauregui, D. "Comparative study of damage identification algorithms applied to a bridge: I. experiment". *Smart materials and structures*, 7(5):704 (1998).
8. Tronci, E., De Angelis, M., Betti, R., and Altomare, V. "Multi-stage semi-automated methodology for modal parameters estimation adopting parametric system identification algorithms". *Mechanical Systems and Signal Processing*, 165:108317 (2022).
9. Morgantini, M., Betti, R., and Balsamo, L. "Structural damage assessment through features in quefrency domain". *Mechanical Systems and Signal Processing*, 147:107017 (2021).
10. Malekloo, A., Ozer, E., AlHamaydeh, M., and Girolami, M. "Machine learning and structural health monitoring overview with emerging technology and high-dimensional data source highlights". *Structural Health Monitoring*, 21(4):1906–1955 (2022).
11. Roveri, N. and Carcaterra, A. "Unsupervised identification of damage and load characteristics in time-varying systems". *Continuum Mechanics and Thermodynamics*, 27(4-5):531 – 550 (2015).
12. Roveri, N., Milana, S., Culla, A., and Carcaterra, A. "Damage diagnostic technique combining machine learning approach with a sensor swarm". *INTER-NOISE 2019 MADRID - 48th International Congress and Exhibition on Noise Control Engineering* (2019).
13. Stone, J. *Independent Component Analysis: A tutorial Introduction*. The MIT Press Cambridge (2004).
14. Hernández-González, I.A., García-Macías, E., Costante, G., and Ubertini, F. "Ai-driven blind source separation for fast operational modal analysis of structures". *Mechanical Systems and Signal Processing*, 211:111267 (2024).
15. Milana, S., Roveri, N., Culla, A., and Carcaterra, A. "Model-free experimental damage identification by symbolic data analysis". *Proceedings of ISMA 2022 - International Conference on Noise and Vibration Engineering and USD 2022 - International Conference on Uncertainty in Structural Dynamics*, page 3781 – 3791 (2022).
16. Figueiredo, E., Park, G., Farrar, C., Worden, K., and Figueiras, J. "Machine learning algorithms for damage detection under operational and environmental variability". *Structural Health Monitoring*, 10(6):559–572 (2011).
17. Deraemaeker, A. and Worden, K. "A comparison of linear approaches to filter out environmental effects in structural health monitoring". *Mechanical systems and signal processing*, 105:1–15 (2018).
18. Greenacre, M., Groenen, P.J.F., Hastie, T., D'Enza, A.I., Markos, A., and Tuzhilina, E. "Principal component analysis". *Nature Reviews Methods Primers*, 2(1) (2022).
19. Abdi, H. and Williams, L. "Principal component analysis". *Wiley interdisciplinary reviews: computational statistics*, 2(4):433–459 (2010).
20. Hyvärinen, A. and Oja, E. "Independent component analysis: algorithms and applications". *Neural networks*, 13(4-5):411–430 (2000).
21. Hyvarinen, A. "Fast and robust fixed-point algorithms for independent component analysis". *IEEE transactions on Neural Networks*, 10(3):626–634 (1999).
22. Severa, L., Roveri, N., Milana, S., Tronci, E.M., Culla, A., Betti, R., and Carcaterra, A. "An integrated pca-ica approach for early-stage damage detection". *Lecture Notes in Civil Engineering*, 515 LNCE:216 – 227 (2024).

Chapter 7
Real-Time Structural Health Assessment of a Tension Rod Assembly Using Machine Learning

Ahmad Rababah, Osama Abdeljaber, Aniston Cumbie, Lauren Harpenau, and Onur Avci

Abstract This paper introduces a vibration-based damage detection method for monitoring the condition of structural members at a local level. The technique employs a piezoelectric patch as an actuator to excite the monitored member and another patch as a sensor to measure the resulting vibration response. The measured signal is processed by a one-dimensional convolutional neural network (1D CNN), which classifies the input signal segment as either undamaged or damaged. By calculating the classification output over multiple signal segments, an index representing the estimated structural health is determined, quantifying the deviation from the undamaged member's response. In this study, the method was experimentally evaluated on a tension rod assembly, where damage was simulated by reducing the tension applied to the rod. This application aims to demonstrate the method's potential for real-world structures, such as suspension bridge cables and prestressed concrete elements. The results indicated that the health values obtained using the proposed method closely matched the actual damage severity applied to the assembly.

Keywords Real-time anomaly detection · Structural health assessment · Piezoelectric patch · Structural Health Monitoring (SHM) · Structural Damage Detection (SDD)

Introduction

Structural health refers to a structure's ability to maintain its initial "undamaged" condition. Structural Health Monitoring (SHM) and Structural Damage Detection (SDD) focus on identifying deviations from this baseline. One of the methods used in SHM is vibration-based damage detection (VBDD), which involves applying a controlled excitation force to a structure and capturing the resulting responses with sensors. The collected data is then processed by certain algorithms, which analyze, classify, and evaluate the structural health.

Ahmad Rababah
Graduate Student, Department of Civil and Environmental Engineering, Engineering Sciences Building, 1306 Evansdale Drive, West Virginia University, Morgantown, WV, 26506, USA
(Corresponding author)
e-mail: ayr00002@mix.wvu.edu

Osama Abdeljaber
Associate Senior Lecturer, Department of Building Technology, Linnaeus University, 351 95 Växjö, Sweden
e-mail: osama.abdeljaber@lnu.se

Aniston Cumbie
Graduate Student, Department of Civil and Environmental Engineering, University of Illinois Urbana-Champaign, Newmark Civil Engineering Laboratory, 205 N. Matthews Avenue, Urbana, IL, 61801
e-mail: aniston2@illinois.edu

Lauren Harpenau
Undergraduate Student, Department of Civil and Environmental Engineering, Iowa State University, 813 Bissell Road, Ames, IA, 50011
e-mail: llh1@iastate.edu

Onur Avci
Assistant Professor, Department of Civil and Environmental Engineering, Engineering Sciences Building, 1306 Evansdale Drive, West Virginia University, Morgantown, WV, 26506, USA
e-mail: onur.avci@mail.wvu.edu

Brian Damiano et al. (eds.), *Structural Health Monitoring & Machine Learning, Vol. 12*, Conference Proceedings of the Society for Experimental Mechanics Series, https://doi.org/10.13052/9788743801573-7

Piezoelectric patch transducers offer a unique solution for SHM of structural members due to their ability to convert mechanical energy to electrical and vice versa based on the piezoelectric material principle [1]. When mechanical stress or strain is applied to them, an electrical field response is produced. Conversely, they undergo mechanical energy when exposed to an electric field. This phenomenon allows for the use of such transducers for both actuating (i.e., applying artificial excitations on the monitored structural member) or sensing (i.e., measuring the response due to the applied excitation) [2].

Utilizing piezoelectric patch transducers in SHM has increased considerably in recent decades. These transducers have been deployed across various structural types to detect damage, including cracks, loose bolts in connections, corrosion, debonding, and fatigue, among other forms of degradation. Markovic et al. (2015) employed piezoelectric patches in active monitoring systems for reinforced concrete structures to detect damage, such as notch and hole located at the middle of the beam, using wave propagation methods [3]. Sun et al. (2015) proposed a method for identifying midspan debonding in reinforced concrete beams strengthened with fiber-reinforced polymer (FRP) strips using piezoelectric patches attached to the FRP strips, enabling high-frequency structural excitations [4]. Fan et al. (2016) Investigated damage detection in a laboratory-constructed truss. They utilized piezoelectric patches to detect damage simulated by removing specific bolts. This method enabled the observation of the impact on the impedance-measured signals [5]. Pavelko et al. (2014) examined the full-scale tail beam of a Mi-8 helicopter to evaluate the condition of its bolt joints. By comparing the frequency domain impedance responses of undamaged and damaged structures, they successfully detected damage. One of the connecting frames of the tail beam was equipped with piezoelectric patches attached to the surface near the bolts. The study focused on investigating bolt loosening using Electrical Impedance Monitoring (EMI) technology [6]. Meyers et al. (2013) employed the VBDD method on an aluminum plate to identify simulated damage, which was introduced by progressively drilling deeper holes through the center of the plate. The plate was excited using a PZT actuator, and wave propagation was monitored by a piezoelectric transducer positioned on the opposite side. The detected wave patterns were then compared to a predefined baseline to assess the extent of the damage [7].

The integration of machine learning (ML) and artificial intelligence (AI) has significantly improved SHM and SDD. These technologies have revolutionized structural monitoring practices by providing powerful tools for the analysis of large datasets collected from pre-installed sensors, enabling continuous, automated, real-time monitoring and early detection of potential damages before they escalate into critical failures. AI algorithms enhance SHM systems by extracting relevant features from datasets and classifying structural conditions based on these features [8].

Several researchers have demonstrated the effectiveness of ML in creating highly reliable and accurate SDD systems. Khan et al. (2020) introduced a method that utilizes a one-dimensional convolutional neural network (1D CNN) to detect cracks by analyzing EMI signatures from piezoelectric patches. The study involved testing fiber-reinforced concrete specimens under compression loading, and the method achieved a mean accuracy of 95.24% in damage detection [9]. Xu et al. (2019) employed the EMI method alongside Back Propagation Neural Networks (BPNNs) to identify bolt looseness in bolted spherical joints (BSJs). Different torque levels were applied to the sleeve to represent varying degrees of joint looseness. As the torque increased, the looseness of the joint also increased proportionally. The root-mean-square deviation (RMSD) of the conductance signatures from the piezoelectric patches served as the primary metric for monitoring and evaluating the extent of joint looseness [10]. Teng et al. (2019) developed a parametric vibration-based model using a CNN to identify damage features in steel frame structures. They employed the finite element method (FEM) to analyze free vibrations and calculate the first-order modal strain energy (MSE) for various damage scenarios, which were used as training data for the CNN. Data were collected using ten accelerometers to capture vibrations from a hammer impact. The damage was simulated by a 50% reduction in the rod's cross-sectional area [11].

This paper introduces a novel approach for detecting damage in structural components by utilizing piezoelectric patches for both sensing and actuation. The sensor patch captures signals that are then analyzed using a one-dimensional convolutional neural network (1D CNN). The 1D CNN's output is used to compute an index that quantifies the severity of the damage. Unlike previous methods, such as the one by Khan et al. (2020), which were only validated numerically on finite element models, this approach has been experimentally validated using a tension rod assembly with varying tension levels. The aim of this work is to demonstrate the method's ability to detect tension loss in suspension bridge cables and prestressed concrete elements.

Methodology

The proposed method relies on a 1D CNN trained to classify the response measured by the sensor patch into two classes: healthy or damaged. The following subsections describe the architecture of the 1D CNN, the test structure used to train and evaluate the model, the training procedure, and the process of estimating damage severity based on the classification output of the 1D CNN.

CNN Architecture

Convolutional Neural Networks (CNNs) have been pivotal in image classification and segmentation tasks, particularly because of their ability to efficiently extract features from images. Unlike traditional computer vision and machine learning techniques, which depend on manually engineered low-level features, CNNs use their large number of parameters to automatically learn complex mid- to high-level image representations from pixel tensors [12]. 1D CNNs are a variant of CNNs specifically designed to deal with 1D data (i.e., signals) rather than images. This is achieved by using 1D convolution filters instead of 2D filters in conventional 2D CNNs. These models consist of three components: convolution layers, subsampling (or pooling) layers, and fully connected layers. Convolution layers extract features from small regions of the input data. Each convolution layer is followed by a subsampling (or pooling) layer that reduces the dimensionality of the feature maps and lowers the number of parameters while keeping essential information. Finally, the fully connected layers or multilayer perceptron (MLP) aggregate these extracted features to compute class scores, which represent the model's predictions, serving as the output for tasks such as classification or object recognition.

In this work, the implemented 1D CNN architecture consists of two convolution layers, each with 64 filters, a kernel size of 80, and rectified linear unit (ReLU) activation. After each convolution layer, a max pooling layer with a pool size of 2 is applied to downsample the input. The output is then flattened and processed by two fully connected dense layers with ten neurons each, also using ReLU activation. Finally, softmax activation is applied in the output layer to generate the binary classification results (damaged or undamaged), as illustrated in Figure 1.

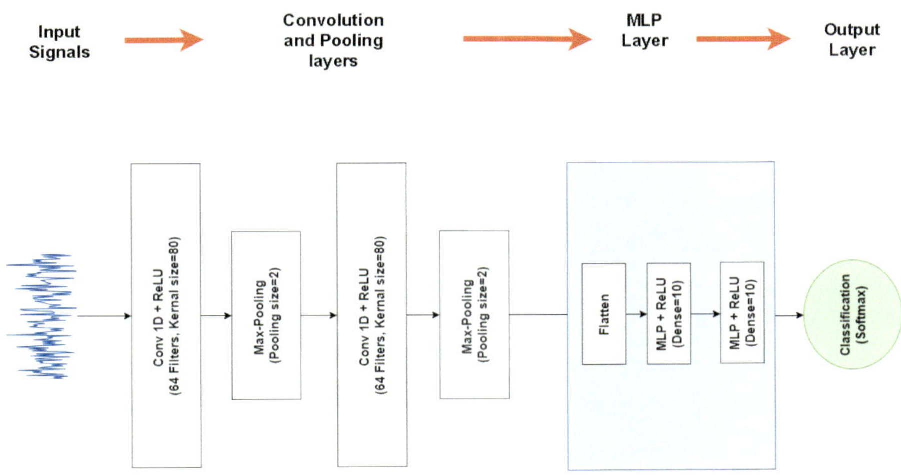

Fig. 1 Architecture of the 1D CNN.

Test Structure

A small-scale setup, illustrated in Figure 2, has been developed for training and testing the 1D CNN. This setup consists of a hollow steel section (540mm x 50.8mm x 38mm) with a tension rod extended through its center. Wing nuts were affixed on either side of the rod and can be adjusted to increase or decrease the tensile stress on the rod. Additionally, two PZTs (P-876.A15, 61 mm × 35 mm × 0.8 mm) were attached to the setup, serving as both actuator and sensor. These PZTs were mounted onto the steel section using wooden pieces and steel clamps. Attention was given to ensuring that the clamps were neither overly tightened, which could affect the PZTs' functioning, nor too loose, which could lose their stability and signal transmission. A data acquisition device (NI USB-6212) was used to drive the actuator patch and acquire the response from the sensor patch. A piezo amplifier (E-835.00) was used to amplify the low-voltage signal generated by the data acquisition device.

Training Procedure

The 1D CNN model was trained to distinguish between two conditions: healthy (undamaged) and damaged states. The training process involved the following steps:

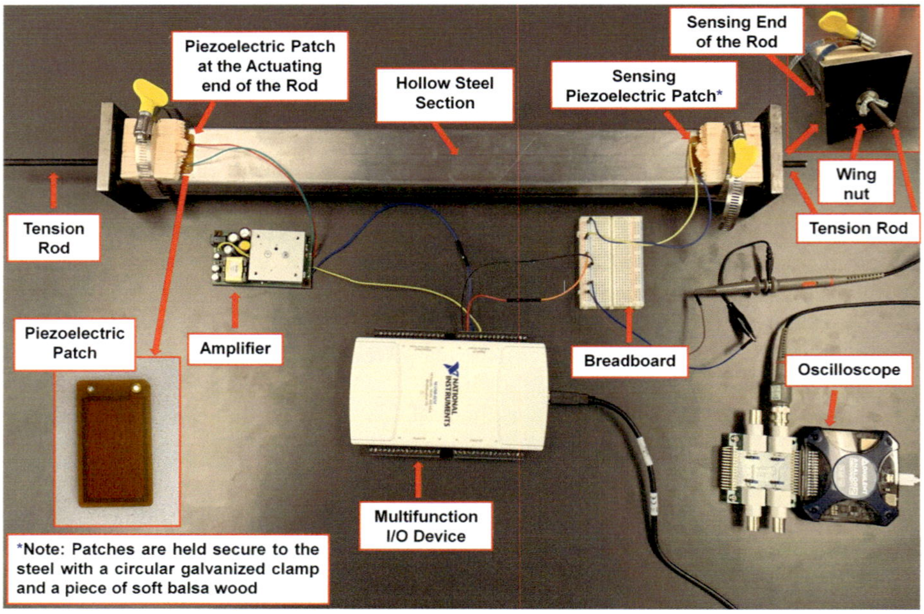

Fig. 2 Labeled diagram of the setup used in testing.

1. The wing nuts were fully tightened to represent the completely undamaged structural state. The actuator patch was then subjected to random white noise excitation, and the vibration response was recorded by the sensor patch for 60 seconds at a sampling frequency of 250 kHz.
2. The same procedure was repeated with the wing nuts completely loosened to simulate a fully damaged state.
3. The 60-second signals from both healthy and damaged states were divided into 256-sample segments, resulting in 58,594 segments for each condition.
4. Each segment was normalized between 0 and 1.
5. The segments were labeled, randomly shuffled, and split into 95% for training and 5% for validation.
6. The training was conducted using TensorFlow 2.10 [13], with Adam optimizer, a learning rate of 0.001, and a batch size of 64. The loss function used was binary cross-entropy between the model's predictions and the true labels. The classification error was evaluated on the validation set at the end of each epoch. The training was terminated when the error did not decrease for 8 consecutive epochs.

Structural Health Estimation

The training procedure described in Section 2.3 resulted in a binary 1D CNN that classifies an input 256-sample segment into two classes: completely healthy or completely damaged. However, it is possible to use the 1D CNN to quantify damage severities between these two extremes by calculating a damage severity index representing the estimated structural health (H%) according to the following steps:

1. Excite the structure with a white noise excitation for a short period of time (e.g., 2 seconds) at the same sampling frequency (250 kHz) and measure the response by the sensor patch.
2. Divide the measured signal into n segments, each having 256 samples.
3. Process each segment using 1D CNN to obtain its binary class (undamaged or damaged).
4. H% is calculated according to the following expression:

$$H(\%) = \frac{Number\ of\ segments\ classified\ as\ undamaged}{n} \times 100 \quad (1)$$

The methodology is depicted in Figure 3 below.

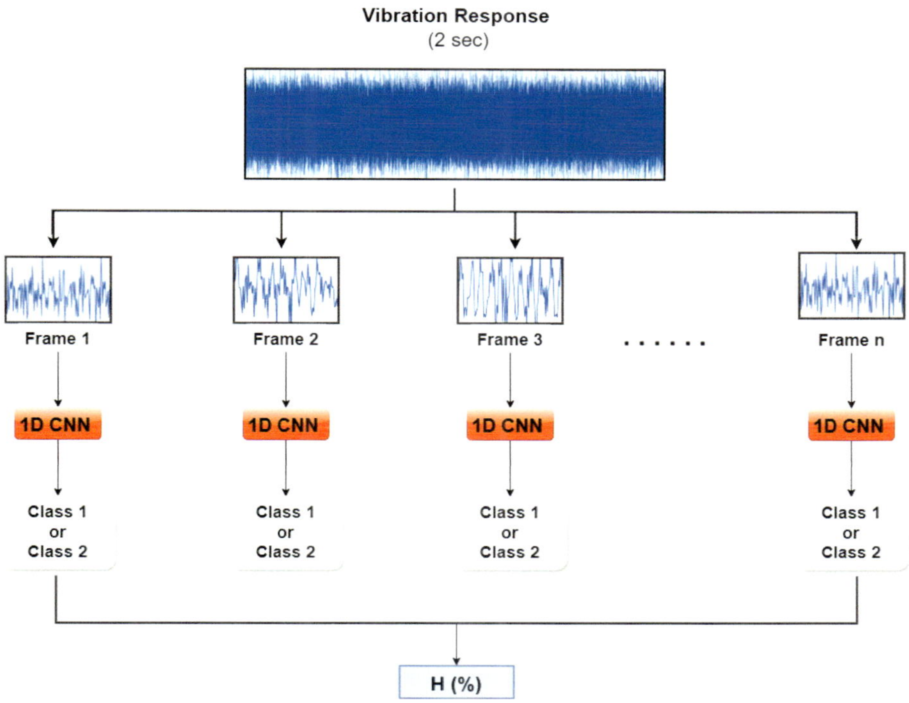

Fig. 3 Methodology for calculating the structural health (H%) using a 1D CNN classification model.

Results and discussions

After training the network as detailed in Section 2.2, it was employed to monitor changes in the health percentage (H%) resulting from variations in rod tension. During testing, the beam was continuously excited using white noise, and H% was recalculated every 2 seconds as outlined in Section 2.3. The wing nut was adjusted by tightening and loosening it to different extents to simulate various damage levels. Figure 4 illustrates the H% calculated during multiple cycles of tightening and loosening. Initially, the wing nut was fully tightened, and the estimated health was nearly 100%, indicating a completely healthy structure. As the wing nut was gradually loosened, the H% dropped below 40%, indicating an increased likelihood of structural damage. Repeating this process multiple times caused the H% levels to fluctuate between high and low values, depending on the current tension level. This demonstrates the model's accuracy and capability to reflect the real-time condition of the setup.

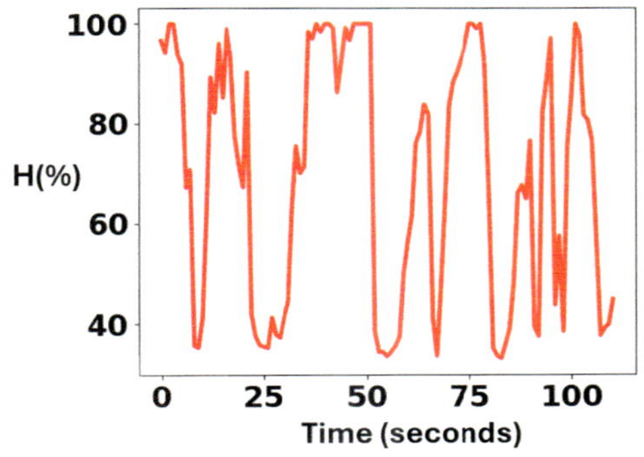

Fig. 4 Real-time structural health percentage, H(%), calculated using the 1D CNN.

During the testing process, several challenges were identified that impacted monitoring accuracy. One critical issue was the method of attaching the piezoelectric patches using steel clamps and wooden pieces, which notably affected the system's performance and outcomes. As shown in Figure 5a, if the clamps were tightened excessively, both the actuators and the sensor could not function optimally for excitation and data collection, leading to an underestimation of the damage. Conversely, if the clamps were too loose, the patches failed to maintain proper contact with the surface, resulting in inaccurate measurements and unreliable results. In this scenario, the excitation from the actuator would not be fully transferred to the setup, causing issues with measuring the initial healthy condition. As illustrated in Figure 5b, the fully healthy state does not accurately represent the connector health as 100%.

Additionally, disturbances from external sources, such as vibrations from movement and contact with the setup or vibrations from the desk, adversely affected the health estimation. While these disturbances were managed in a controlled laboratory environment, scaling the model for application in various conditions requires addressing this issue.

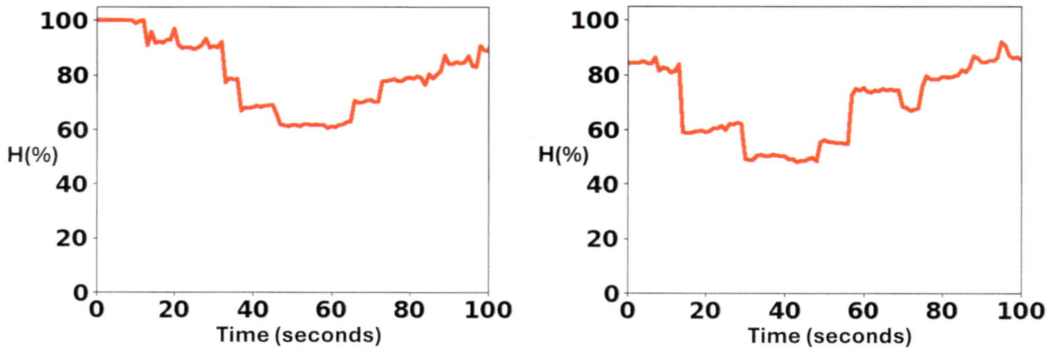

Fig. 5 Impact of clamp tightness on structural health accuracy: (a) Over-tightened clamps, (b) Under-tightened clamps.

Conclusions

This study proposed a vibration-based damage detection technique for monitoring the health of a tension rod assembly. The method utilized piezoelectric patch transducers for both sensing and actuating. A 1D CNN was trained to estimate the current tension level applied to the rod. The experimental verification showed that the proposed method successfully calculated a damage index H% that reflects the actual structural health of the monitored member. In future studies, the method can be extended and applied to detect damage in the strands of the prestressed concrete beams.

References

1. Qing, X., Li, W., Wang, Y. and Sun, H., Piezoelectric transducer-based structural health monitoring for aircraft applications. Sensors, 2019, pp. 19(3), p.545.
2. Lin, B. and Giurgiutiu, V., Modeling and testing of PZT and PVDF piezoelectric wafer active sensors. Smart Materials and Structures, 2006, pp. 15(4), p.1085.
3. Markovic, N., Nestorovic, T., & Stojic, D., Numerical modeling of damage detection in concrete beams using piezoelectric patches. Mechanics Research Communications, 2015, pp. 64, 15–22.
4. Sun, R., Sevillano, E. and Perera, R., Debonding detection of FRP strengthened concrete beams by using impedance measurements and an ensemble PSO adaptive spectral model. Composite Structures, 2015, pp. 125, pp.374–387.
5. Fan, X., Li, J. and Hao, H., Piezoelectric impedance based damage detection in truss bridges based on time frequency ARMA model. Smart Struct. Syst, 2016, pp. 18(3), pp.501–523.
6. Pavelko, I., Pavelko, V., Kuznetsov, S. and Ozolinsh, I., Bolt-joint structural health monitoring by the method of electromechanical impedance. Aircraft Engineering and Aerospace Technology: An International Journal, 2014, pp. 86(3), pp.207–214.
7. Meyers, F.N., Loh, K.J., Dodds, J.S. and Baltazar, A., Active sensing and damage detection using piezoelectric zinc oxide-based nanocomposites. Nanotechnology, 2013, pp. 24(18), p.185501.
8. Gomez-Cabrera, A. and Escamilla-Ambrosio P.J., Review of machine-learning techniques applied to structural health monitoring systems for building and bridge structures. Applied Sciences, 2022, pp. 12(21), p.10754.
9. Khan, A., Shin, J.K., Lim, W.C., Kim, N.Y. and Kim, H.S., A deep learning framework for vibration-based assessment of delamination in smart composite laminates. Sensors, 2020, pp. 20(8), p.2335.

10. Xu, J., Dong, J., Li, H., Zhang, C. and Ho, S.C., Looseness monitoring of bolted spherical joint connection using electro-mechanical impedance technique and BP neural networks. Sensors, 2019, pp. 19(8), p.1906.
11. Teng, S., Chen, G., Liu, G., Lv, J. and Cui, F., Modal strain energy-based structural damage detection using convolutional neural networks. Applied Sciences, 2019, pp. 9(16), p.3376.
12. Gao, Y., and Mosalam, K.M. Deep transfer learning for image-based structural damage recognition. Computer-Aided Civil and Infrastructure Engineering, 2018, pp. 33(9), pp.748–768.
13. Mattmann, Chris. Machine learning with tensorflow. Second Edition. s.l. : Simon and Schuster, 2020.

Chapter 8
Multi-Bridge Indirect Structural Health Monitoring: Leveraging Big Data and Drive-By Crowdsensing Techniques

Jiangyu Zeng, Qipei Mei, and Mustafa Gül

Abstract This paper presents a novel structural health monitoring (SHM) methodology that analyzes in-vehicle data from vehicle-bridge interaction (VBI) signals across multiple bridges to detect damage in individual structures. Unlike traditional SHM methods that monitor each bridge independently, the proposed approach compares the dynamic responses across a network of bridges using vehicle-collected data. By analyzing changes in correlation coefficients between these bridges, our method improves the accuracy of damage detection while reducing the likelihood of missed detections. Numerical simulations demonstrate the effectiveness of the method for both single-span and multi-span bridges. This scalable approach offers a significant advancement in SHM systems, particularly suited for smart cities where large-scale, cost-effective monitoring is essential.

Keywords Structural Health Monitoring (SHM) · Bridge Network Monitoring · Multi-Bridge Damage Detection · Drive-By Monitoring · Smart Cities · Scalable Infrastructure Monitoring

Introduction

Structural health monitoring (SHM) is essential for maintaining bridge safety and serviceability, particularly as aging infrastructure necessitates proactive interventions to prevent failures [1]. Traditional SHM methods, which rely on fixed sensors installed on bridges, face limitations such as high costs, logistical challenges, and scalability issues, especially in large bridge networks [2–4]. Recent advancements, such as drive-by monitoring techniques, utilize vehicle data to infer bridge health, eliminating the need for permanent sensors and offering more flexible, cost-effective solutions for infrastructure monitoring [5–10]. These methods, however, often focus on individual bridges, limiting their effectiveness when applied to networks of bridges within smart cities [11].

The key innovation of this paper is the use of in-vehicle data from multiple bridges to determine the structural health of a single bridge. By comparing the correlation between dynamic responses across a network of bridges, this signal-level SHM approach leverages the collective information from other bridges to improve damage detection accuracy. This simultaneous monitoring of multiple bridges offers a significant improvement over traditional methods that evaluate each bridge independently. This concept is inspired by the work of Catbas *et al.* [12], Malekzadeh *et al.* [13], and Riasat Azim and Gül [14], who demonstrated a similar approach by tracking correlation coefficients and vibration data to monitor structural health in various types of bridges. The method, validated through numerical simulations, shows strong potential for large-scale SHM in urban environments, making it particularly well-suited for smart city applications.

Jiangyu Zeng
PhD Student, Department of Civil & Environmental Engineering, University of Alberta, Canada
e-mail: jiangyu1@ualberta.ca

Qipei Mei
Assistant Professor, Department of Civil & Environmental Engineering, University of Alberta, Canada
e-mail: qipei.mei@ualberta.ca

Mustafa Gül
Professor, Department of Civil & Environmental Engineering, University of Alberta, Canada
Corresponding author
e-mail: mustafa.gul@ualberta.ca

Brian Damiano et al. (eds.), *Structural Health Monitoring & Machine Learning, Vol. 12*, Conference Proceedings of the Society for Experimental Mechanics Series, https://doi.org/10.13052/9788743801573-8

Numerical Simulations

This study employs numerical simulations to collect vehicle vertical acceleration signals as vehicles traverse bridges under various conditions. The data collection focuses on both the baseline and damaged states of bridges, with the dynamic interaction between vehicles and bridges simulated using an iterative decoupled Vehicle-Bridge Interaction (VBI) model.

In the baseline case, vertical vibration signals were recorded as twelve distinct vehicles, modeled using a one-axle moving spring-mass system, traversed the bridges. These vehicles varied in mass, spring constant, and speed, with combinations of three masses, two spring constants, and two speeds to represent different vehicle types. Each vehicle made 20 passes over each bridge, generating a total of 240 signals per bridge. The bridges used in these simulations shared identical properties except for their lengths. Bridges Bridge-1-SS through Bridge-10-SS were single-span bridges, while bridges Bridge-11-TS through Bridge-20-TS were two-span bridges with an additional support located at mid-span.

A validation case, identical to the baseline, was included to ensure consistency and reliability in the monitoring process. The validation state served as a baseline comparison against future damaged scenarios, ensuring that the monitoring system can differentiate between normal and damaged conditions accurately.

To simulate structural damage, a reduction in stiffness was introduced. Specifically, a 30% stiffness reduction was applied to the mid-span region of the bridges, affecting 1/4 of the total bridge length. This damage was designed to reflect realistic structural deterioration and assess the method's ability to detect such changes. As in the baseline and validation cases, each vehicle crossed the damaged bridges 20 times, generating 240 signals for each damaged bridge. The study focuses on two representative bridges: Bridge-4-SS (Single-Span) and Bridge-17-TS (Two-Span), chosen to assess the method's performance across different structural types. .

During all simulations, the vertical acceleration signals of the vehicles were collected. To mimic real-world conditions, 10% artificial noise was added to these signals. To enhance the clarity of the signals, a Gaussian low-pass filter was applied to suppress high-frequency noise while preserving the key signal components related to the bridge's structural response.

Analysis

This section presents the analysis of the structural health monitoring process using the signal-level approach, focusing on direct comparisons of the vehicle acceleration signals collected from multiple bridges. The goal of this method is to identify structural damage by analyzing changes in the correlation coefficients between the signals from different bridges over time.

Signal-Level comparison and correlation coefficient calculation

The analysis begins with preprocessing the vehicle acceleration signals. The original time-domain signals collected from vehicles crossing the bridges are transformed into the frequency domain and resampled to focus on the 0-20 Hz range[6]. This frequency range is chosen because it encompasses the typical fundamental frequencies of bridges. In our study, the highest first-mode frequency among all the bridges is 5.7 Hz, and the highest second-mode frequency is 8.5 Hz. Both of these frequencies occur on the shortest two-span bridge, ensuring that no critical information is lost by focusing on the 0-20 Hz range.

Following the preprocessing, the Correlation Coefficient (CC) Matrix is constructed. For a system of m bridges, indexed by $i = 1, 2, \ldots, m$, the Correlation Coefficient Matrix $CC[i, j]$ is computed to quantify the correlation between the vehicle acceleration signals of Bridge i and Bridge j.

$$CC[i,j] = \frac{1}{P \times Q} \sum_{p=1}^{P} \sum_{q=1}^{Q} R(S_p^i, S_q^j) \tag{1}$$

In this equation, S_p^i represents the resampled frequency-domain signal from the p-th run on Bridge i, and S_q^j denotes the resampled frequency-domain signal from the q-th run on Bridge j. The terms P and Q refer to the total numbers of vehicle runs on Bridges i and j, respectively. The function $R(S_p^i, S_q^j$ denotes the Pearson correlation coefficient between the signals S_p^i and S_q^j.

The vehicles entering each bridge are entirely random, meaning that no specific sequence or order of vehicles is assumed across the bridges. This randomness is important to consider in the correlation analysis, as it reflects realistic traffic conditions and ensures that the method can handle different vehicle combinations over time.

This average pooling technique provides a robust summary of the correlations between the structural responses of the bridges. The focus of our method is not on the absolute correlation values, but rather on how these correlations change when structural damage occurs. These changes help detect potential structural discrepancies.

System-wide cross-comparison and separation factor calculation

Following the construction of the Correlation Coefficient Matrix, the next step is to assess the changes in correlation coefficients between the baseline, validation, and unknown states of the bridges. This is achieved through the calculation of Percentage Difference Matrices (PDMs) between the correlation coefficients in these states. For every pair of bridges i and j, the Percentage Difference $\Delta CC[i,j]$ is calculated as follows:

$$\Delta CC_{\text{state}}[i,j] = \frac{CC_{\text{state}}[i,j] - CC_{\text{baseline}}[i,j]}{CC_{\text{baseline}}[i,j]} \times 100\%, \quad \text{where } i \neq j \tag{2}$$

Here, "state" refers to either the validation or unknown state, depending on the context. For the diagonal elements ($i = j$), which represent the correlation between a bridge and itself, the percentage difference is defined as:

$$\Delta CC_{\text{state}}[i,i] = 0 \tag{3}$$

These diagonal elements are zero since the correlation between the same bridge in different states does not change. The PDMs constructed using these percentage differences enable visualization of the changes in correlation values between the baseline and the unknown or validation states, helping to identify potential damage in any of the bridges.

Relative damage index and threshold calculation

To quantify the extent of structural damage, the Relative Damage Index (RDI) is computed for each bridge, which measures the change in its correlation coefficients relative to the rest of the system. The RDI is derived from the Separation Factor (SF), which quantifies how distinctly a bridge's response deviates from others in the system. The SF for each bridge i is calculated as:

$$SF_i = \frac{\sum_{k=1}^{m} \Delta CC[i,k] + \sum_{k=1,k\neq i}^{m} \Delta CC[k,i]}{\sum_{h=1}^{m} \sum_{k=1}^{m} \Delta CC[h,k]} \tag{4}$$

Next, the RDI for the unknown state is computed as:

$$RDI_i = \frac{e^{SF_{i,\text{unknown}}} - 1}{e^{SF_{i,\text{baseline}}} - 1} \tag{5}$$

The Threshold Relative Damage Index (TRDI) is calculated similarly but based on the validation state, replacing the unknown state in the equation above. The TRDI sets a threshold for identifying damage and accounts for environmental and operational variations.

Finally, the RDI is compared against the TRDI. If the RDI exceeds the TRDI, the bridge is considered damaged; otherwise, it remains classified as undamaged. This method provides a robust and scalable approach to detecting damage across a network of bridges by analyzing changes in correlation values over time.

Results and Discussions

This section presents the outcomes of the signal-level comparison approach applied to two damaged bridge cases: Bridge-4-SS (single-span) and Bridge-17-TS (two-span). We demonstrate the method's effectiveness in identifying structural damage by comparing the PDMs and RDI for both cases.

Percentage difference matrices

The PDMs illustrate the changes in correlation coefficients between pairs of bridges, revealing how the structural responses deviate from the baseline state. Figures 1 and 2 display the PDMs for Bridge-4-SS and Bridge-17-TS under damaged conditions, each having experienced a 30% stiffness reduction at mid-span.

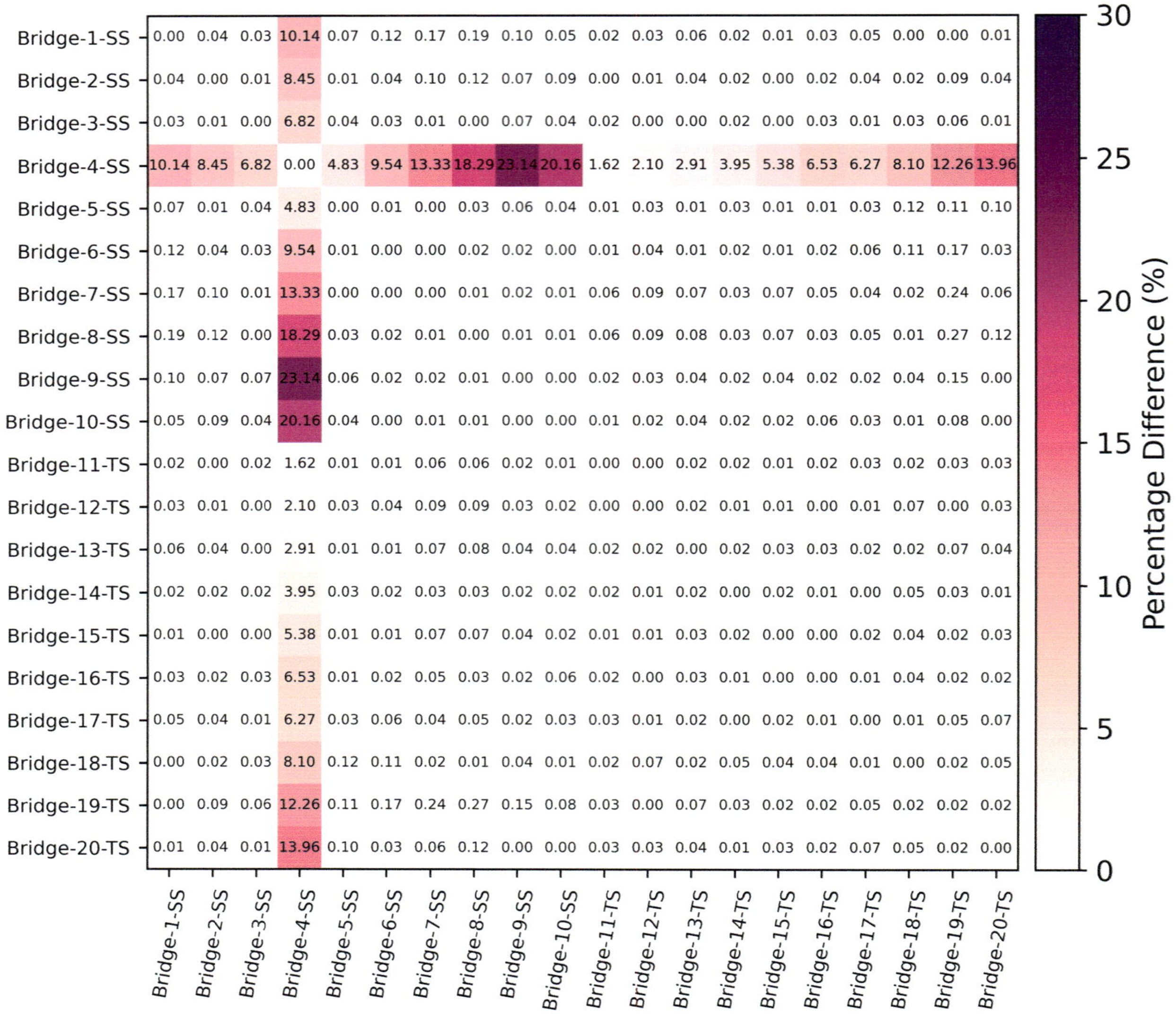

Fig. 1 Percentage Difference Matrix for the damaged state: Bridge-4-SS.

In the case of Bridge-4-SS (Figure 1), the PDM exhibits pronounced differences, with values reaching as high as 23.14%. This indicates significant structural changes, particularly when comparing Bridge-4-SS with other bridges in the system. These elevated values reflect the localized damage and the limited ability of the single-span structure to redistribute the effects of the damage, making the changes more concentrated around the affected bridge. The high percentage difference clearly signals that the single-span structure is vulnerable to localized damage, and the signal-level comparison method is effective in detecting these changes.

Conversely, the PDM for Bridge-17-TS (Figure 2) shows much lower percentage differences, even though the same level of damage (30% stiffness reduction) was applied. The largest percentage differences remain below 4%, indicating a more subdued response to the damage. The lower PDM values suggest that the multi-span structure, with its more complex geometry and additional support at mid-span, is able to distribute the effects of the damage across multiple spans, thereby reducing the severity of localized structural responses[15, 16]. This highlights a key difference between single-span and multi-span bridges, where the structural complexity in the latter allows for better redistribution of stresses, leading to less pronounced changes in correlation coefficients.

While these visual insights from the PDMs provide an initial understanding of the changes in structural behavior, they are limited in detecting more subtle deviations that may occur across the bridge network. To address this, the RDI offers a more comprehensive, quantitative measure for assessing structural health.

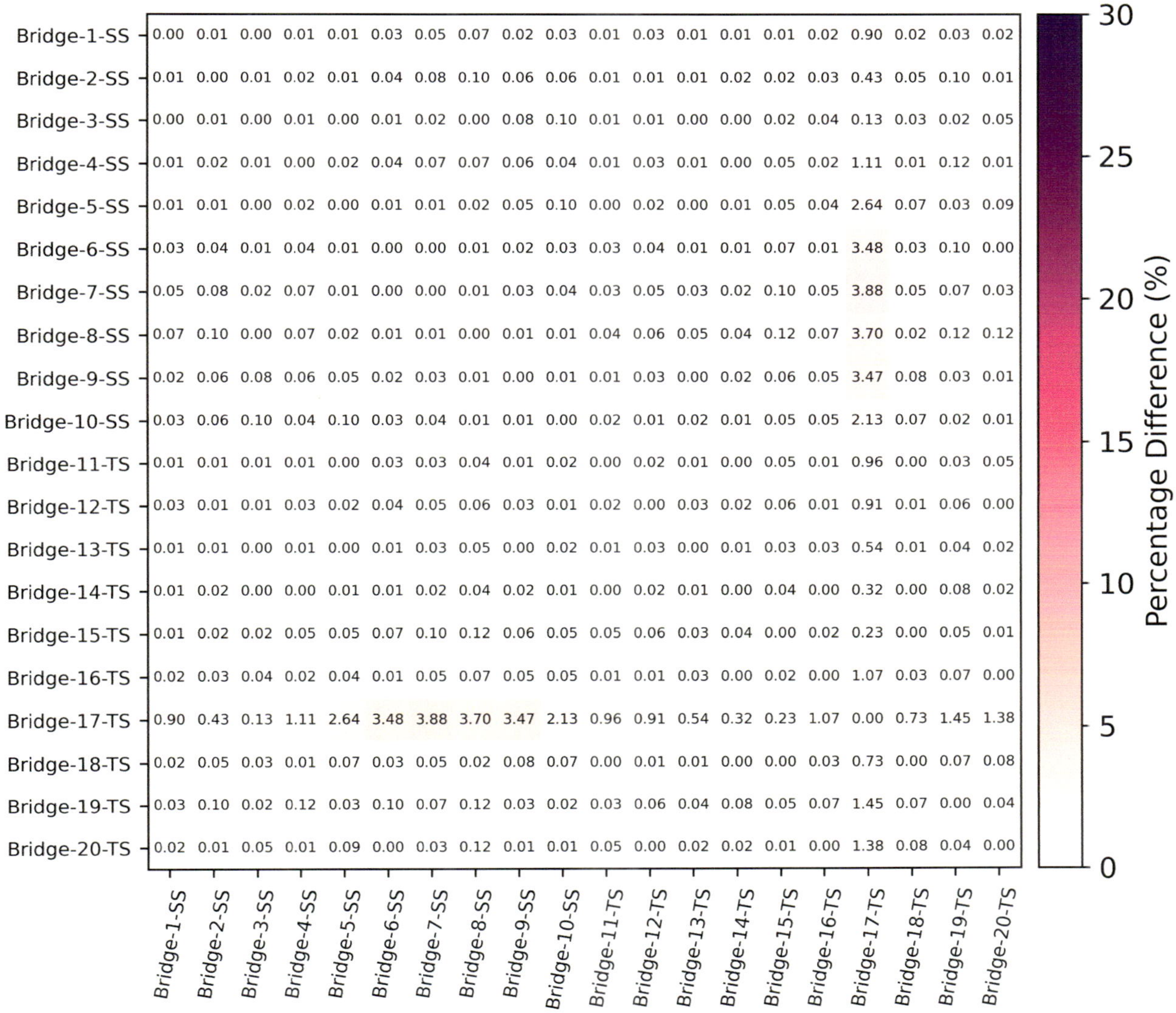

Fig. 2 Percentage Difference Matrix for the damaged state: Bridge-17-TS.

RDI and TRDI results

The RDI is particularly effective as it considers not just individual bridges, but the system-level comparison—i.e., the changes in correlation coefficients between a specific bridge and all other bridges in the network. By taking a system-wide approach, the RDI increases sensitivity to subtle changes in a bridge's behavior, which might be missed when analyzing the bridge individually. This is particularly important in cases like Bridge-17-TS, where stress redistribution across multiple spans might lead to less pronounced changes in the PDM.

Additionally, normalization in the RDI calculation helps reduce the impact of external factors like environmental conditions and traffic variations, isolating the changes caused by structural damage. The RDI is computed as shown in Equation 5. This normalization ensures robustness and emphasizes damage-related structural changes. Moreover, the exponential function amplifies even minor deviations, which further enhances the ability to detect damage even when the PDM differences are small, such as in the case of Bridge-17-TS.

Figures 3 and 4 display the RDI distributions for Bridge-4-SS and Bridge-17-TS under damaged conditions, calculated using five repeated experiments for each bridge.

For Bridge-4-SS (Figure 3), which represents a single-span bridge, the RDI values for the damaged bridge significantly exceed the threshold value, confirming the presence of structural damage. Specifically, Bridge-4-SS exhibits RDI values of approximately 16, well above the threshold. However, Bridge-9-SS's RDI values are slightly higher than its threshold, falling within 20% of the threshold, as indicated by the triangle markers. This suggests a possible false positive or minor sensitivity in the model for Bridge-9-SS. Nevertheless, all other bridges remain well below their respective thresholds, reinforcing the localized nature of the damage in Bridge-4-SS.

Similarly, for Bridge-17-TS (Figure 4), representing a two-span bridge, the RDI results indicate structural damage. The RDI values for Bridge-17-TS exceed the threshold, with values around 14 to 16. However, unlike the single-span bridge, the magnitude of the difference is slightly lower, reflecting the distribution of damage across the multiple spans. Despite this, the method effectively identifies the presence of damage in a more complex structural configuration, while other bridges maintain RDI values below their thresholds.

These observations demonstrate the effectiveness of the signal-level approach in detecting structural anomalies across both single-span and multi-span bridges, with the RDI values serving as a robust indicator of damage. The method's ability to consistently identify damage in various bridge types underlines its applicability in diverse structural health monitoring scenarios.

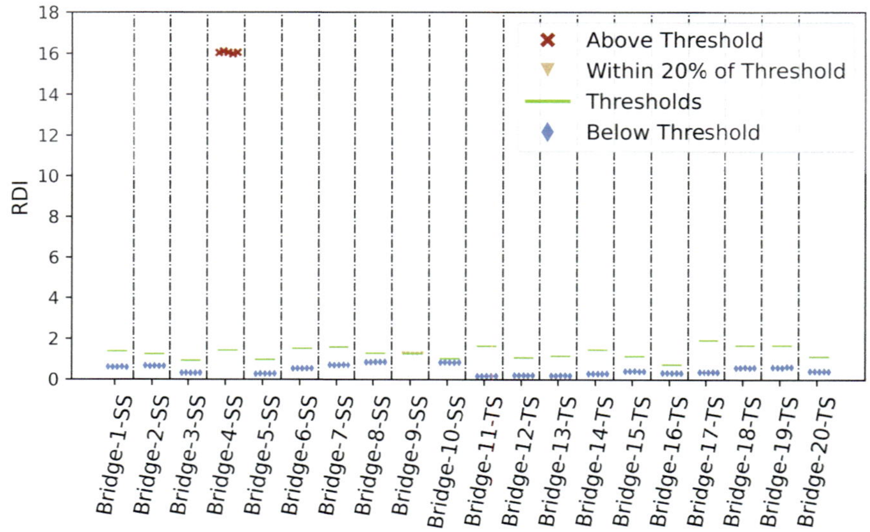

Fig. 3 Distribution of RDI and TRDI values for the damaged state: Bridge-4-SS.

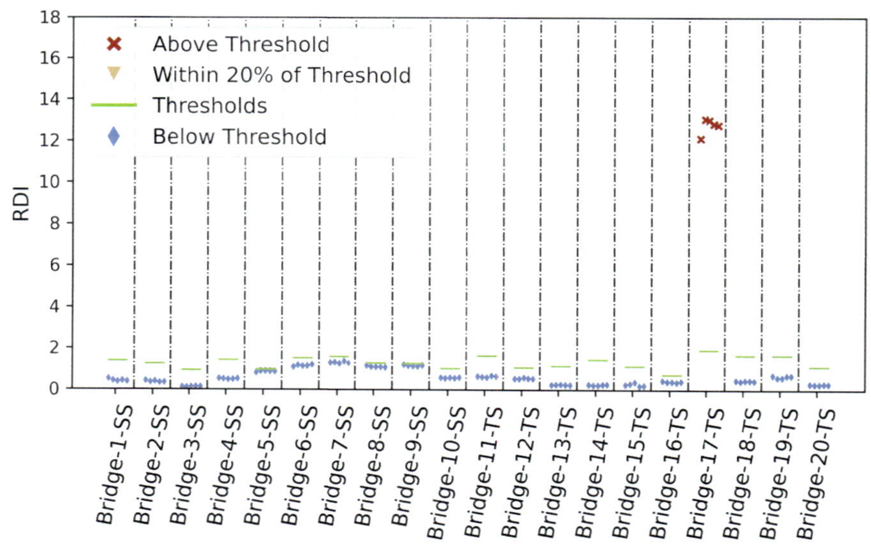

Fig. 4 Distribution of RDI and TRDI values for the damaged state: Bridge-17-TS.

Conclusion

This paper introduces an innovative signal-level approach for SHM that leverages information from multiple bridges to enhance damage detection accuracy. By utilizing correlation changes between dynamic responses across a network of bridges, this methodology departs from traditional SHM methods, which focus on monitoring individual structures in isolation. The ability to infer damage in a single bridge by analyzing data from the entire bridge network offers a more comprehensive understanding of structural health and reduces the likelihood of missed detections. Simulations for both single-span and multi-span bridges confirm the robustness of the proposed method. This approach is particularly well-suited for smart city applications, providing a scalable, cost-effective solution for monitoring large infrastructure networks.

References

1. Wang, G. and Ke, J. "Literature Review on the Structural Health Monitoring (SHM) of Sustainable Civil Infrastructure: An Analysis of Influencing Factors in the Implementation". *Buildings*, 14(2):402 (2024)
2. Ntotsios, E., Papadimitriou, C., Panetsos, P., Karaiskos, G., Perros, K., and Perdikaris, P.C. "Bridge health monitoring system based on vibration measurements". *Bull Earthquake Eng*, 7(2):469–483 (2009)
3. Catbas, F.N., Gokce, H.B., and Gul, M. "Nonparametric analysis of structural health monitoring data for identification and localization of changes: Concept, lab, and real-life studies". *Structural Health Monitoring*, 11(5):613–626 (2012)
4. Gul, M. and Catbas, F.N. "Structural health monitoring and damage assessment using a novel time series analysis methodology with sensor clustering". *Journal of Sound and Vibration*, 330(6):1196–1210 (2011)
5. Yang, Y.B., Lin, C., and Yau, J. "Extracting bridge frequencies from the dynamic response of a passing vehicle". *Journal of Sound and Vibration*, 272(3-5):471–493 (2004)
6. Shirzad-Ghaleroudkhani, N. and Gül, M. "Inverse Filtering for Frequency Identification of Bridges Using Smartphones in Passing Vehicles: Fundamental Developments and Laboratory Verifications". *Sensors*, 20(4):1190 (2020)
7. Matarazzo, T.J., Santi, P., Pakzad, S.N., Carter, K., Ratti, C., Moaveni, B., Osgood, C., and Jacob, N. "Crowdsensing Framework for Monitoring Bridge Vibrations Using Moving Smartphones". *Proc. IEEE*, 106(4):577–593 (2018)
8. Matarazzo, T.J., Kondor, D., Milardo, S., Eshkevari, S.S., Santi, P., Pakzad, S.N., Buehler, M.J., and Ratti, C. "Crowdsourcing Bridge Vital Signs with Smartphone Vehicle Trips" (2022) arXiv:2010.07026 [cs].
9. Liu, J., Chen, S., Bergés, M., Bielak, J., Garrett, J.H., Kovačević, J., and Noh, H.Y. "Diagnosis algorithms for indirect structural health monitoring of a bridge model via dimensionality reduction". *Mechanical Systems and Signal Processing*, 136:106454 (2020)
10. Aalto University, Li, Z., Aalto University, Lan, Y., Aalto University, and Lin, W. "Crowdsensing-based automatic bridge health condition assessment using drive-by measurements and deep learning". *eJNDT*, 29(7) (2024)
11. Mei, Q., Gül, M., and Shirzad-Ghaleroudkhani, N. "Towards smart cities: crowdsensing-based monitoring of transportation infrastructure using in-traffic vehicles". *J Civil Struct Health Monit*, 10(4):653–665 (2020)
12. Catbas, F.N., Gokce, H.B., and Gul, M. "Nonparametric analysis of structural health monitoring data for identification and localization of changes: Concept, lab, and real-life studies". *Structural Health Monitoring*, 11(5):613–626 (2012)
13. Malekzadeh, M., Gul, M., and Catbas, F. "Application of multivariate statistically based algorithms for civil structures anomaly detection". In Catbas, F., Pakzad, S., Racic, V., Pavic, A., and Reynolds, P., editors, *Topics in Dynamics of Civil Structures, Volume 4*, Conference Proceedings of the Society for Experimental Mechanics Series. Springer, New York, NY (2013)
14. Riasat Azim, M. and Gül, M. "Damage Detection of Steel-Truss Railway Bridges Using Operational Vibration Data". *J. Struct. Eng.*, 146(3):04020008 (2020)
15. Zhang, Y., Xie, Q., Li, G., and Liu, Y. "Multi-Damage Identification of Multi-Span Bridges Based on Influence Lines". *Coatings*, 11(8):905 (2021)
16. Brinissat, M., Ray, R.P., and Kuti, R. "Multi-Span Box Girder Bridge Sensitivity Analysis in Response to Damage Scenarios". *Buildings*, 14(3):667 (2024)

Chapter 9
A Comparative Study of Feature Selection Methods for Wind Turbine Gearbox Bearing Fault Prognosis

Feras Abla, Mohammad Hesam Soleimani-Babakamali, Sahabeddin Rifai, Ahmad Rababah, Shawn Sheng, Ertugrul Taciroglu, Serkan Kiranyaz, and Onur Avci

Abstract This paper focuses on comparing two main approaches for selecting input and target features for training a normal behavior model (NMB) using wind turbines' SCADA data. The NMB models aid in predicting gearbox failure in wind turbine structures. In the first approach, the target feature is excluded from the input features, and in the second approach, the NBM models are trained using lagged measurements of the target feature. Historical SCADA data from a wind farm are used in this study. The SCADA data are preprocessed and used to train four sequential artificial neural network long short-term memory (LSTM) models to predict the normal behavior of the target feature. The analysis of the errors between the predicted and measured output feature indicates that the first approach is more promising in failure prognosis, and the gearbox oil temperature is found to be the optimal target feature to foreshadow deterioration in components.

Keywords SCADA data · Wind Turbine · Prognosis

Introduction

The continuous monitoring of wind turbine (WT) components is critical for the early detection of potential failures. Operation and maintenance (O&M) of wind farms can account for a significant portion of their lifetime expenses, with some offshore projects reporting costs as high as 30% of the total expenditure [1]. To reduce these costs, condition-based maintenance

Feras Abla · Sahabeddin Rifai · Ahmad Rababah
Graduate Student, Department of Civil and Environmental Engineering, Engineering Sciences Building, 1306 Evansdale Drive, West Virginia University, Morgantown, WV 26506
Corresponding author: fa00060@mix.wvu.edu
e-mail: sr00090@mix.wvu.edu; ayr00002@mix.wvu.edu

Mohammad Hesam Soleimani-Babakamali
Postdoctoral Research Associate, Department of Civil and Environmental Engineering, 5731K Boelter Hall, University of California, Los Angeles | UCLA, Los Angeles, CA 90095
e-mail: soleimanisam92@g.ucla.edu

Shawn Sheng
Senior Researcher Engineer, National Renewable Energy Laboratory (NREL), Golden, Colorado, 80401
e-mail: shawn.sheng@nrel.gov

Ertugrul Taciroglu
Department Chair, Department of Civil and Environmental Engineering, 5731K Boelter Hall, University of California, Los Angeles, UCLA, Los Angeles, CA 90095
e-mail: etacir@ucla.edu

Serkan Kiranyaz
Professor, Department of Electrical Engineering, Qatar University, Doha 2713, Qatar
e-mail: mkiranyaz@qu.edu.qa

Onur Avci,
Assistant Professor, Department of Civil and Environmental Engineering, Engineering Sciences Building, 1306 Evansdale Drive, West Virginia University, Morgantown, WV 26506
e-mail: onur.avci@mail.wvu.edu

Brian Damiano et al. (eds.), *Structural Health Monitoring & Machine Learning, Vol. 12*, Conference Proceedings of the Society for Experimental Mechanics Series, https://doi.org/10.13052/9788743801573-9

systems are essential. These systems often require additional devices to measure and record the system behavior via various indicators, such as vibration response. In contrast, using Supervisory Control and Data Acquisition (SCADA) systems for WT condition monitoring is more cost-effective, as the manufacturer already integrates them into WTs.

Gearbox failures in WTs are particularly costly and result in the longest downtimes [2], making their prognosis highly critical. Previous research has focused on using SCADA data for WT fault prognosis. For instance, using high-frequency SCADA data, a neural network model combined with a one-class support vector machine classifier was employed by [3] to detect early gearbox faults. Their framework successfully predicted anomalies weeks in advance as it detected 80.9% of anomalies one week before failure. Another study investigated WT gearbox bearing failure prognosis using SCADA data alongside modeled data [4]. The authors trained and tested four algorithms and concluded that the LSTM model outperformed others in detecting faulty data during the month preceding failure. Previous research has also shown that failures of other turbine components, such as the main bearing, can be detected several months before a catastrophic breakdown [5].

When using neural networks to analyze SCADA data, one of the main challenges is selecting the most relevant features to ensure accurate predictions of the target feature. Additionally, it is crucial to identify the target feature that best reflects the deterioration of the component of interest when its behavior deviates from the norm. This study uses only SCADA data to compare two modeling strategies for predicting WT gearbox bearing failure. In one approach, the target feature is excluded from the input features, while in the other, the target feature is included as an input. The study also investigates which target feature is the most reliable indicator of impending WT gearbox bearing failure.

Methodology

The framework in this study consists of three main stages: 1) data preprocessing, 2) training and validating the normal behavior models (NBMs), and 3) testing the models on unseen data to compare the capacity of different approaches in performing gearbox bearing fault prognosis.

Data preprocessing

The data used in this study was collected by a research partner from a wind farm in the southern USA from December 1, 2008, to October 31, 2018. Table 1 details the available SCADA data per channel and unit. Only one WT was analyzed from the dataset. The selected WT experienced a high-speed shaft gearbox bearing failure. The gearbox was replaced on January 13, 2011, which is considered as the failure date in this study.

Table 1 SCADA channels for the available data.

SCADA channel	Units
Power	kW
Rotor speed	rpm
Wind speed	m/s
Wind direction (10 sec)	-
Wind direction (1 sec)	-
Gearbox oil temperature	°C
Gearbox bearing temperature	°C
Ambient temperature	°C
Nacelle temperature	°C

Since the impact of installing new components in the WT is not within the scope of this research, data collected after the gearbox replacement is omitted. Additionally, data recorded during low or extremely high wind speeds and during maintenance periods were excluded. Only data collected under normal running conditions were retained. Despite the discontinuity in the data, and given that the potential imputation methods may impact the comparison, no data imputation was performed.

The dataset was split into training, validation, and test sets, as shown in Figure 1. To ensure the model is trained only on healthy data, the last 9 months before the failure date (which may contain faulty data) were reserved for testing, while the remaining data was used for model training. Finally, the data was normalized to a [0, 1] range since the features have varying scales.

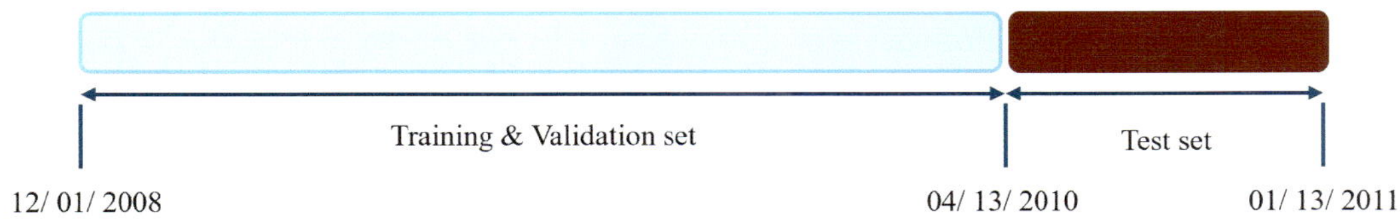

Fig. 1 Training, validation, and test data split for the studied WT.

Normal Behavior Model Development

Recurrent neural networks are designed for temporal data [6], preserving the running flow of information for their decision-making process. Long Short-Term Memory (LSTM), a type of recurrent neural network, is thus chosen to build four neural network architecture models to accommodate various features to be chosen as input and target features. The input and target features for each model are shown in Table 2. Gearbox oil and bearing temperatures, which are relevant to the component of interest, are selected as target features. Two models with different input features are built to predict each target feature. Models 1 and 2 predict future instances of the gearbox oil temperature from past measurements of the input features—*i.e.,* to predict the gearbox oil temperature at time t, observations of the input features at times $(t-1), (t-2)\ldots, (t-n)$ where $n=144$, which is equivalent to the number of recorded measurements per day are fed to the model. Similarly, Models 3 and 4 are built to predict the gearbox-bearing temperature.

Table 2 Input and target features for each model.

Model 1		Model 2		Model 3		Model 4	
Input Features	**Target Feature**	**Input Feature**	**Target Feature**	**Input Features**	**Target Feature**	**Input Feature**	**Target Feature**
Power				Power			
Rotor Speed				Rotor Speed			
Wind Speed				Wind Speed			
Gearbox Bearing Temperature	Gearbox Oil Temperature	Gearbox Oil Temperature	Gearbox Oil Temperature	Gearbox Oil Temperature	Gearbox Bearing Temperature	Gearbox Bearing Temperature	Gearbox Bearing Temperature
Ambient Temperature				Ambient Temperature			
Nacelle Temperature				Nacelle Temperature			

Testing the NBMs and Gearbox Bearing Fault Prognosis

In the final stage, the trained models were tested on unseen data to evaluate their ability to predict gearbox bearing faults. The test data was used to assess the models' performance in identifying early signs of gearbox deterioration. The models' accuracy in forecasting abnormal behavior and potential failures was evaluated by comparing the predicted values to the actual SCADA measurements during the test period. The effectiveness of each model was determined based on how well it detected deviations from normal operating conditions leading up to the gearbox failure.

Results and Discussion

After training the four NBM models, they were used to predict the target features. Figures 2(a) and 2(b) show the predicted and measured target features over a specific period from the test set. The predictions closely align with the measured normal signals, demonstrating that the models learned the normal data patterns with a high degree of accuracy.

Table 3 presents the root mean squared errors (RMSEs) for comparing the predicted and actual target features during the last three months before the reported failure. All models show an increasing trend in the RMSE as the failure date

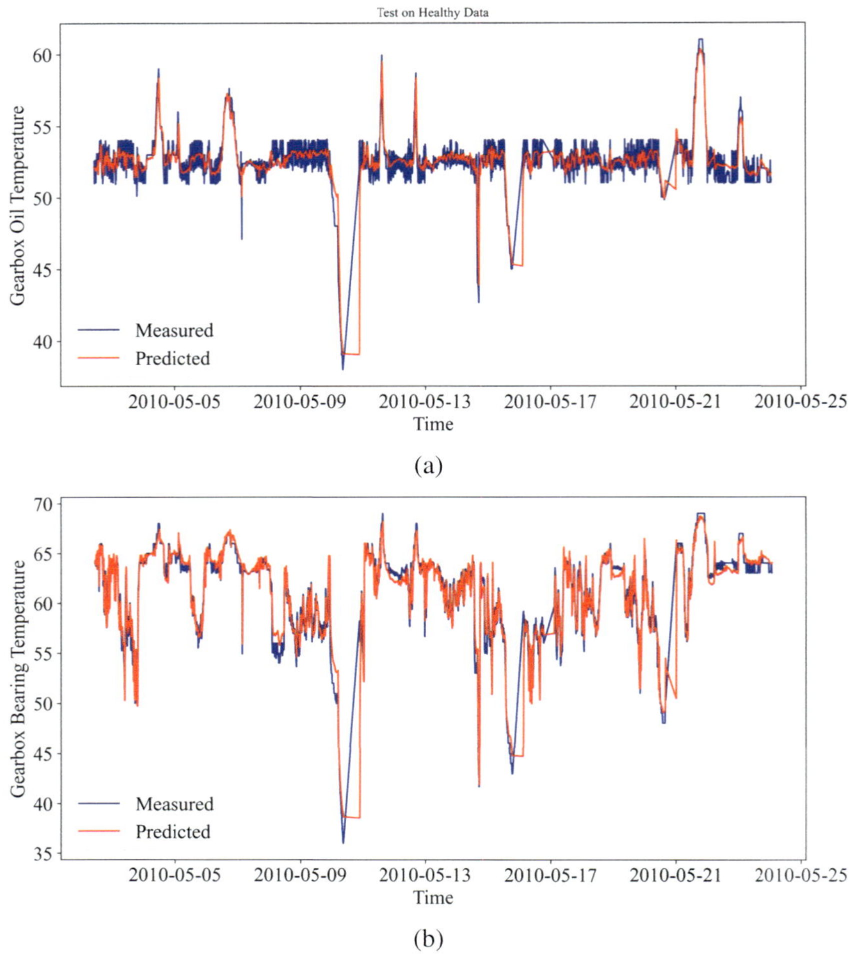

Fig. 2 Target feature prediction: (a) measured and predicted Gearbox Oil Temperature for a specific period in the test set, b): measured and predicted Gearbox Bearing Temperature for a specific period in the test set.

approaches, suggesting that the rising error is likely due to the progressive deterioration of the component before the actual failure occurs. For Model 1, which predicts gearbox oil temperature, the RMSE increased by 13% from the third-to- last month before failure to the second-to-last month, and 70% from the second-to-last month to the final month. Similarly, for Model 2, which also predicts gearbox oil temperature, the RMSE rose by 15% from the third-to-last month before failure to the second-to-last month, and 37% from the second-to-last month to the final month. For Models 3 and 4, which predict gearbox bearing temperature, the RMSE increased by 2.5% (Model 3) and 15% (Model 4) from the third-to-last month to the second-to-last month before failure. From the second-to-last month to the final month, the RMSE increased by 46% for Model 3 and 25% for Model 4. These results indicate that Models 1 and 3, which predict their target features using six input features, are more indicative of impending failure compared to Models 2 and 4, which use past measurements of the target feature as input. Furthermore, the changes in error between the predicted and actual gearbox oil temperature provide more reliable predictions of future failures than those between the predicted and actual gearbox bearing temperature.

Table 3 RMSE for the four models for the last month before gearbox bearing failure.

	Model 1	Model 2	Model 3	Model 4
Period of testing	RMSE			
Third last month before failure	0.0195	0.0159	0.0197	0.0164
Second last month before failure	0.0222	0.0183	0.0202	0.0189
Last month before failure	0.0378	0.0251	0.0295	0.0237

Conclusions

This paper investigated two alternative approaches for training NBMs for WT gearbox bearing fault prognosis and explored the optimal feature for detecting deterioration in the component of interest. The analysis of four different NBM models demonstrated that training the model using features that exclude the target feature is more effective for fault prognosis than the approach that utilizes past measurements of the target feature. Additionally, the results revealed that gearbox oil temperature is a more reliable indicator of gearbox bearing deterioration than gearbox bearing temperature.

Future work will employ generative models, such as Generative Adversarial Networks (GANs), for WT gearbox prognosis. Moreover, the potential of analyzing the frequency domain instead of the time domain will also be investigated.

References

1. Crabtree, C. J., Zappalá, D., & Hogg, S. I. (2015). Wind energy: UK experiences and offshore operational challenges. Proceedings of the Institution of Mechanical Engineers, Part A: Journal of Power and Energy, 229(7), 727–746.
2. Reder, M. D., Gonzalez, E., & Melero, J. J. (2016, September). Wind turbine failures-tackling current problems in failure data analysis. In Journal of Physics: Conference Series (Vol. 753, No. 7, p. 072027). IOP Publishing.
3. Verma, A., Zappalá, D., Sheng, S., & Watson, S. J. (2022, May). Wind turbine gearbox fault prognosis using high-frequency SCADA data. In Journal of Physics: Conference Series (Vol. 2265, No. 3, p. 032067). IOP Publishing.
4. Desai, A., Guo, Y., Sheng, S., Phillips, C., & Williams, L. (2020, November). Prognosis of wind turbine gearbox bearing failures using SCADA and modeled data. In Annual Conference of the PHM Society (Vol. 12, No. 1, pp. 10–10).
5. Bermúdez, K., Ortiz-Holguin, E., Tutivén, C., Vidal, Y., & Benalcázar-Parra, C. (2022, May). Wind turbine main bearing failure prediction using a hybrid neural network. In Journal of Physics: Conference Series (Vol. 2265, No. 3, p. 032090). IOP Publishing.
6. Malhotra, P., Vig, L., Shroff, G., & Agarwal, P. (2015, April). Long short term memory networks for anomaly detection in time series. In Esann (Vol. 2015, p. 89).

Chapter 10
Damage Identification on Gear Drivetrains Using Neural Networks Trained by High-Fidelity Multibody Simulation Data

J. Koutsoupakis, D. Giagopoulos, G. Karyofyllas, P. Seventekidis, and S. Natsiavas

Abstract In this work, structural health monitoring of an experimental gear drivetrain is examined by means of machine learning algorithms trained though high-fidelity data, generated by optimal Multibody Dynamics models. The model's accuracy is enhanced through detailed modeling of the contact mechanics in gear meshing, via the development of a novel contact force model dedicated to gears, which accounts for the effects emanating from the time varying mesh stiffness, transmission error and backlash between them. This detailed contact force formulation takes into account the geometry of the gears, allowing for modeling potential asperities in them, such as surface roughness, spalls or missing teeth, which may lead to errors during motion transmission and produce greater damages in a mechanical system. Data is then generated through repetitive simulations of the optimal numerical model, simulating the system's operation in its healthy state as well as in the presence of faults. The produced data is then used to train an ensemble of neural networks for the task of structural health monitoring on the gear drivetrain through analysis of its response in the frequency domain. The trained algorithms are then employed in damage detection and characterization on the physical drivetrain, proving that they can generalize their health state predictions on unknown, real-world data successfully, and validating the proposed structural health monitoring framework of utilizing training data from the numerical domain.

Keywords Time Varying Mesh Stiffness · Backlash · Transmission Error · Nonlinear Dynamics · Machine Learning

Introduction

As awareness regarding the benefits of proper maintenance of machinery increases, the need for timely detection of defects in transmission systems, particularly those used in critical applications such as industrial machinery or vehicles has led to the development of a series of Condition Monitoring (CM) methods. Vibration-based methods in particular have been extensively applied to gear transmission systems due the large amount of information contained in the system's vibration response and the accessibility of data even during operation of a system [1][2][3]. While, traditionally, damage detection would be based on signal analysis tools and fault indices, such as the Root Mean Square (RMS) or kurtosis of a measured signal, as well as the analysis of a system's response from a professional, the rapid increase in Machine Learning (ML) algorithms and tools has provided additional options in the task of CM [4][5][6]. While powerful, as ML methods such Artificial Neural Networks (ANNs) are global approximators, use of such tools requires vast amounts of data, particularly for labeled classification tasks, such as damage detection and characterization, that is, accurately predicting the health state of a mechanical system requires that the ML algorithm has been trained on similar, labeled data. This data, however, is usually scarce or even inexistent, due to the prohibiting cost of extensively instrumenting machinery or, in the case of collecting damaged state data, deliberately causing defects to a machine's components. To mitigate this shortcoming, multiple data augmentation methods can be found in literature [7][8], as a means of producing more samples based on a small number of physical measurements. These data augmentation methods, however, require measurements of every defect of interest, thus not being practical in cases where no data from nominally identical structures and cases is available.

To this end, numerical simulations have been explored as a means of synthetic data generation, where using methods such as Finite Element Modeling (FEM) [9] or Multibody Dynamics (MBD) analysis [10], one can generate a virtually infinite amount of data from models corresponding the different health states of a system. Using this simulation data, algorithms

J. Koutsoupakis · D. Giagopoulos · G. Karyofyllas · P. Seventekidis · S. Natsiavas
Aristotle University of Thessaloniki, Department of Mechanical Engineering, Thessaloniki, GR, 54124
Corresponding author: dgiagopoulos@auth.gr
e-mail: jkoutsoup@meng.auth.gr; gdkaryof@meng.auth.gr; seventep@meng.auth.gr; natsiava@auth.gr

Brian Damiano et al. (eds.), *Structural Health Monitoring & Machine Learning, Vol. 12*, Conference Proceedings of the Society for Experimental Mechanics Series, https://doi.org/10.13052/9788743801573-10

such as ANNs can be trained in the numerical domain and employed in making predictions in the physical domain, so long as the simulated data hold similar characteristics as those contained in the physical measurements. This similarity between the numerical and physical data is achieved by optimizing the models using a small number of healthy state measurements as well as powerful optimization techniques [11], aiming to minimize an objective function between simulated and real system responses. While this framework has previously been tested, it has become obvious that its capacity is limited by the capacity of the numerical models, that is, especially in cases where machinery is concerned, the MBD models must be able to simulate the various mechanisms of the system with as much accuracy as possible. Gear transmission systems in particular comprise complex mechanisms, where phenomena such as gear meshing dominate the system's response and are usually the key features in a measured signal. Additionally, wear-related faults in gear transmission systems most commonly appear in components such as bearings (inner/outer race defects, etc.), and gears, where cracks or spalls can appear in gear teeth. To accurately model such phenomena, mechanisms such as the Time Varying Mesh Stiffness (TVMS), dynamic error and backlash between gear teeth must be taken into account in the model, aiming to increase the accuracy and fidelity of the results. In this work, a detailed gear meshing force formulation is developed, aiming to achieve high-fidelity simulations where the time varying effects of gear meshing are accurately presented in the numerical model of an experimental gear drivetrain system. The enhanced model, after being properly optimized, is employed in data generation for different health states of the drivetrain, producing the data necessary to train an ensemble of Deep Neural Networks (DNNs) for classifying the physical system's health state.

The rest of this work is structured as follows: First, the theoretical formulation used in this work is described in the Background section. Afterwards the experimental set-up and corresponding MBD models are shown in the Analysis section, where the results of the numerical simulations and damage classification are also presented, aiming to validate the proposed method experimentally. Finally, the findings of this work are discussed in the Conclusions section and further developments are briefly discussed.

Background

The stiffness of a tooth in a meshed gear pair can be broken down to five components based on the potential energy method as [12]:

$$K_h = \frac{\pi E L}{4(1-\nu^2)} \tag{1}$$

$$\frac{1}{K_b} = \int_{-\varphi 1}^{\varphi 2} \frac{3[1 + (\varphi_2 - \varphi)\, sin\varphi cos\varphi_1 - cos\varphi cos\varphi_1]^2\, (\varphi_2 - \varphi)\, cos\varphi}{2EL[(\varphi_2 - \varphi)\, cos\varphi + sin\varphi)]^3} d\varphi \tag{2}$$

$$\frac{1}{K_s} = \int_{-\varphi 1}^{\varphi 2} \frac{1.2\,(1+v)\,(\varphi_2 - \varphi)\, cos\varphi \cos^2\varphi 1}{2EL\,[(\varphi_2 - \varphi)\, cos\varphi + sin\varphi)]} d\varphi \tag{3}$$

$$\frac{1}{K_a} = \int_{-\varphi 1}^{\varphi 2} \frac{(\varphi_2 - \varphi)\, cos\varphi sin^2\varphi 1}{2EL\,[(\varphi_2 - \varphi)\, cos\varphi + sin\varphi)]} d\varphi \tag{4}$$

$$\frac{1}{K_f} = \frac{\cos^2\varphi 1}{EL}[L^*\left(\frac{u_f}{S_f}\right)^2 + M^*\left(\frac{u_f}{S_f}\right) + P^*(1 + Q^*\tan^2\varphi 2)] \tag{5}$$

where K_h, K_b, K_s, K_a and K_f denote the Hertzian, bending, shear, axial and fillet foundation stiffness. The terms E, L and ν are the tooth material modulus of elasticity, the width of the gear tooth and Poisson's ratio respectively and φ_1 and φ_2 are explained schematically in Figure 1. Last, the rest of the terms of Equation (5) are derived from [13].

Note that the Line of Action (LoA) is estimated as the tangent between the two gear base circles. As such, depending on the number of gear teeth, the potential energy method may lead to an over or underestimation of the meshing stiffness. To take this error into account, the meshing stiffness estimation must be split to two cases, based on the minimum number of teeth in a gear, which can be estimated as:

$$z_{min} = 2h_a/\sin^2 a \tag{1}$$

where $h_a$is the addendum of the gear and a is the nominal pressure angle of the gear. The distinction between the two cases can also be achieved by estimating the root and base radii of the gear as:

$$R_B = \frac{mzcosa}{2} \tag{2}$$

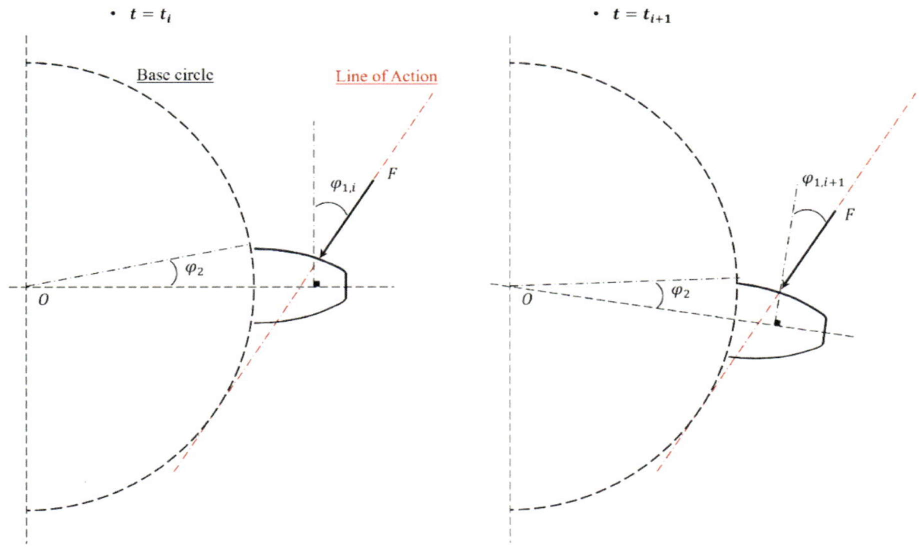

Fig. 1 Cross-section of a gear tooth profile.

$$R_R = \frac{mz}{2} - (h_a + c_n)\, m \tag{3}$$

where m is the normal module, and c_n is the tip clearance coefficient. Depending on the actual teeth in a gear, the stiffness components can be estimated as:

Case 1: $z < z_{min}$

$$\frac{1}{K'_b} = \frac{1}{K_b} + \int_{\varphi 2}^{\varphi 3} \frac{3[1 + (\varphi_2 - \varphi)\, sin\varphi cos\varphi_1 - cos\varphi cos\varphi_1]^2\, (\varphi_2 - \varphi)\, cos\varphi}{2EL[(\varphi_2 - \varphi)\, cos\varphi + sin\varphi)]^3} d\varphi \tag{4}$$

$$\frac{1}{K'_s} = \frac{1}{K_s} + \int_{\varphi 2}^{\varphi 3} \frac{1.2\,(1 + v)\, (\varphi_2 - \varphi)\, cos\varphi cos^2\varphi 1}{2EL\,[(\varphi_2 - \varphi)\, cos\varphi + sin\varphi)]} d\varphi \tag{5}$$

$$\frac{1}{K'_a} = \frac{1}{K_a} + \int_{\varphi 2}^{\varphi 3} \frac{(\varphi_2 - \varphi)\, cos\varphi sin^2\varphi 1}{2EL\,[(\varphi_2 - \varphi)\, cos\varphi + sin\varphi)]} d\varphi \tag{6}$$

Case 2: $z \geq z_{min}$

$$\frac{1}{K'_b} = \frac{1}{K_b} - \int_{-\varphi 3}^{\varphi 2} \frac{3[1 + (\varphi_2 - \varphi)\, sin\varphi cos\varphi_1 - cos\varphi cos\varphi_1]^2\, (\varphi_2 - \varphi)\, cos\varphi}{2EL[(\varphi_2 - \varphi)\, cos\varphi + sin\varphi)]^3} d\varphi \tag{7}$$

$$\frac{1}{K'_s} = \frac{1}{K_s} - \int_{-\varphi 3}^{\varphi 2} \frac{1.2\,(1 + v)\, (\varphi_2 - \varphi)\, cos\varphi cos^2\varphi 1}{2EL\,[(\varphi_2 - \varphi)\, cos\varphi + sin\varphi)]} d\varphi \tag{8}$$

$$\frac{1}{K'_a} = \frac{1}{K_a} - \int_{-\varphi 3}^{\varphi 2} \frac{(\varphi_2 - \varphi)\, cos\varphi sin^2\varphi 1}{2EL\,[(\varphi_2 - \varphi)\, cos\varphi + sin\varphi)]} d\varphi \tag{9}$$

This error in the estimated stiffness is better explained in Figure 2, where the relation between angles φ_2, φ_3 as well as between the base and root circles is shown.

For a single tooth pair contact, the stiffness can be estimated based on Equations (1) - (9) as:

$$K_{STP} = \frac{1}{\frac{1}{K'_{h,i}} + \frac{1}{K'_{b,i}} + \frac{1}{K'_{s,i}} + \frac{1}{K'_{a,i}} + \frac{1}{K_{f,i}}} \qquad with\ i = 1, 2 \tag{10}$$

Similarly, for the case where more than one gear tooth pair is in contact, the meshing stiffness can be estimated as:

$$K_{MTP} = \frac{1}{\frac{1}{K'_{h,i,j}} + \frac{1}{K'_{b,i,j}} + \frac{1}{K'_{s,i,j}} + \frac{1}{K'_{a,i,j}} + \frac{1}{K_{f,i,j}}} \qquad with\ i = 1, 2\ \&\ j = 1, 2, \ldots N \tag{11}$$

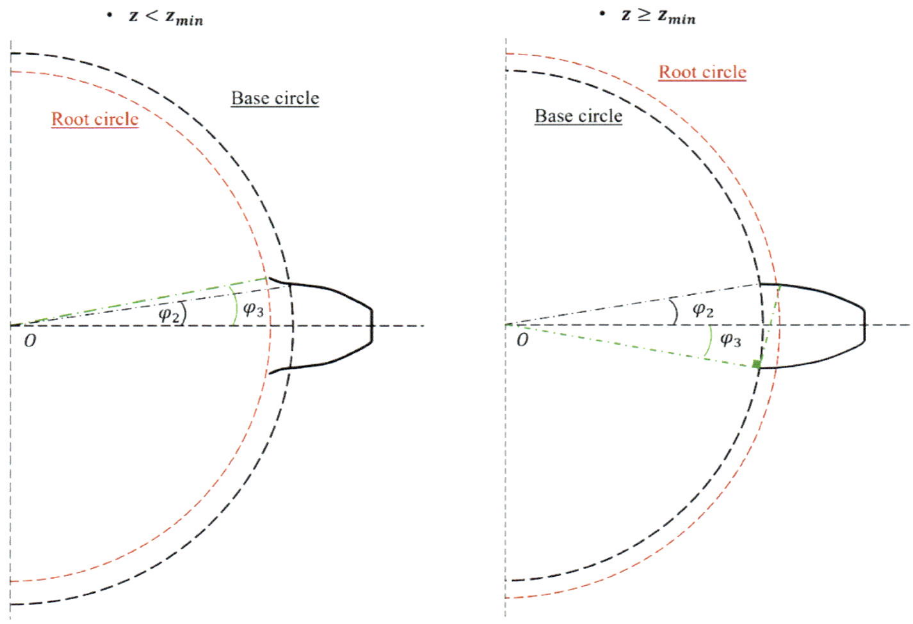

Fig. 2 Cross-section of a gear tooth profile.

Here, the subscript i denotes the pinion (1) and driven (2) gear and j denotes the tooth pair up to N meshed tooth pairs.

In literature, there is a multitude of models which can be used to estimate the normal force between to contacting bodies, such as two gears in mesh. The general expression of the contact normal force is given as:

$$F_N = K\delta^n + \chi\delta^n\dot{\delta} \tag{12}$$

where K denotes stiffness, δ and $\dot{\delta}$ are the indentation depth between the contacting bodies and the respective indentation velocity, n is the nonlinear exponent and χ is the hysteresis damping coefficient which, based on the formulation used, is given in Table 1. In the equations shown in the table, c_r is the coefficient of restitution.

The formulation described in Equations (1) - (11) describes the TVMS for spur gears, where the contact angle is constant for the whole width of a gear tooth. In helical gears, however, due to the helix angle of the gear teeth, the contact angle changes along the width of the gear teeth. To account for this, the slicing method is used to split the gear tooth into subsections and the stiffness is estimated for each slice individually [12]. Then, the total stiffness of a tooth pair can be estimated as the sum of the individual slice stiffnesses as:

$$K_{tot} = \sum_{i=1}^{M} K_i \tag{13}$$

where K_i denotes the stiffness of each slice.

Table 1 Hysteresis damping factor χ with respect to the contact force model.

Gharib & Hurmuzlu	Herbert & McWhannel	Flores et al.	Lee & Wang
$\frac{1}{c_r}\frac{K}{\dot{\delta}^{(-)}}$	$\frac{6(1-c_r)}{(2c_r-1)^2+3}\frac{K}{\dot{\delta}^{(-)}}$	$\frac{8(1-c_r)}{5c_r}\frac{K}{\dot{\delta}^{(-)}}$	$\frac{3(1-c_r)}{4}\frac{K}{\dot{\delta}^{(-)}}$
Hunt & Crossley	**Lankarani & Nikravesh**	**Zhiuing & Qishao**	**Gonthier et al.**
$\frac{3(1-c_r)}{2}\frac{K}{\dot{\delta}^{(-)}}$	$\frac{3(1-c_r^2)}{4}\frac{K}{\dot{\delta}^{(-)}}$	$\frac{3(1-c_r^2)e^{2(1-c_r)}}{4}\frac{K}{\dot{\delta}^{(-)}}$	$\frac{1-c_r^2}{c_r}\frac{K}{\dot{\delta}^{(-)}}$

Aiming to improve the accuracy of the MBD model developed on this work, the Covariance Matrix Adaptation Evolution Strategy (CMAES) was employed. The CMAES algorithm is a powerful population-based method, which is well suited for optimization of non-linear problems, such as the one tackled in this work [9][10][11]. The objective function used in this work is formulated as:

$$J\left(\underline{\theta}\right)=\sum_{i=1}^{M}\sqrt{\sum_{j=1}^{N}\left(\hat{y}_{ij}\left(\underline{\theta}\right)-y_{ij}\right)^{2}} \tag{14}$$

where $\hat{y}_{ij}\left(\underline{\theta}\right)$ and y_{ij} denote the frequency responses of the numerical and experimental acceleration data respectively, $\underline{\theta}$ denotes the vector containing the contact force related parameters. The subscripts i, j correspond to the measurement location and data point respectively.

In this work, health state classification is achieved in an automated manner by utilizing an ensemble of Deep Learning (DL) classifiers, namely Convolutional Neural Networks (CNNs), trained on data generated from the optimal MBD models of the system in its healthy and damaged states. The trained network ensemble is capable of making predictions on the health state of the physical drivetrain due to the fact that the numerical data is provided through high-fidelity, optimal MBD models, as well as due to the powerful feature extraction capabilities of the convolutional layers. This method of health state classification is presented in the flowchart of Figure 3.

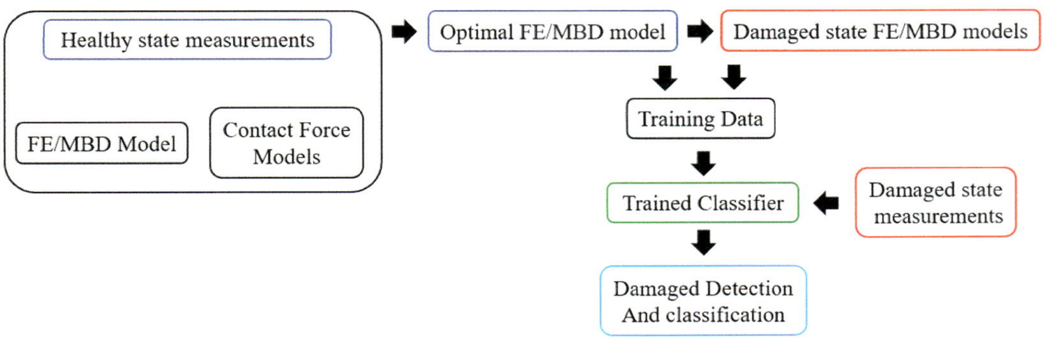

Fig. 3 Numerical data-based ANN training and health state classification method.

Analysis

The experimental system examined in this work is the single stage helical gear transmission system which is shown in Figure 4. The shafts are mounted on the gearbox via deep groove ball bearings while the gears are fixed on the shafts using a screw-wedge mechanism. The gearbox cap is made out of plexiglass, allowing for viewing the gears during operation. Two electric motors are used in the system, comprising the drive and load motors at the inlet and outlet of the setup respectively. The characteristics of the gears used in the experimental setup are explained in detail in Table 2. Experiments were conducted for three inlet velocity values, namely 450, 775 and 1100 RPM, with the load at the outlet shaft kept constant at 10 Nm. Two triaxial accelerometers, denoted as A1 & A2, were placed on the gearbox, above the inlet and outlet shafts respectively, and measurements were extracted with a sampling frequency of 5120 Hz.

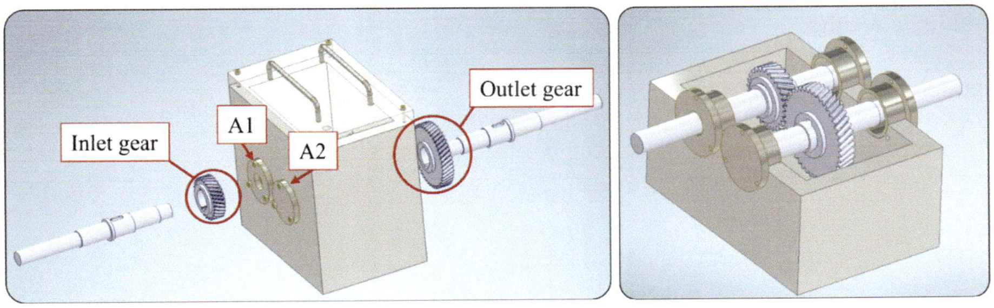

Fig. 4 Single stage helical gear transmission system.

Table 2 Gear geometry related parameters.

Gear	Inlet	Outlet
Module *[mm]*	2.25	2.25
Number of teeth [−]	29	44
Pitch Diameter [mm]	72.7	110.3
Pressure angle [deg]	20	20
Helix angle [deg]	26	26
Helix hand [-]	R	L

The corresponding MBD model of the single stage gearbox is shown in Figure 5.

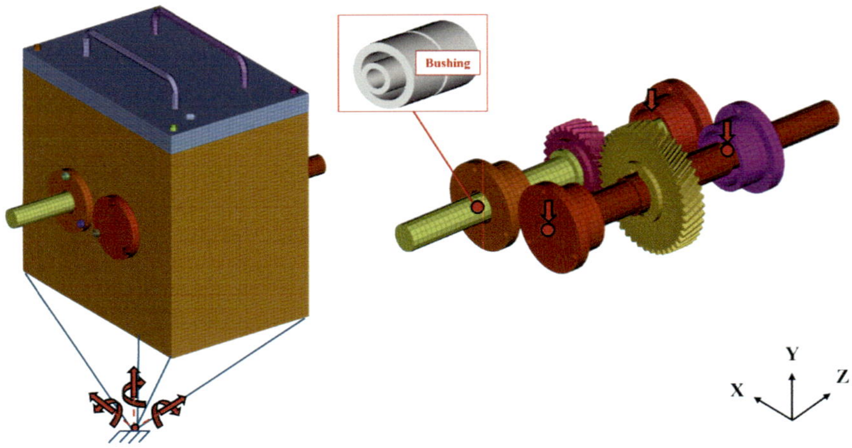

Fig. 5 Single stage helical gear transmission system – MBD model.

A spring-damper force is used to simulate the stiffness at the bolted joints at the base of the gearbox, while the shafts are connected to the gearbox through bushing forces, used as a simplified means of modeling bearings. While this does not allow for modeling the precise bearing dynamics, it was sufficient for the present work, where gear-related phenomena are of interest. Last, the gears are considered fixed to the shafts and a contacting force is acting between them. A constant velocity profile is used as an input to the model while a torque acts on the outlet shaft, simulation the load at the end of the gearbox.

Following the optimization process described in the theoretical background section, the model was optimized based on the healthy state acceleration measurements of the gearbox. The parameters used in the optimization process were the elastic modulus of the gears, assumed equal for both gears, the contact force model (Table 1), the coefficient of restitution and the nonlinear exponent. The final contact stiffness value was estimated based on the Hertzian stiffness formula Equation (1). The updated values for these parameters are shown in Table 3. It should be noted that the parameters of the bushings used in the shafts as well as the spring-damper component that was used to connect the gearbox to the ground could have also been included in the optimization but were omitted for the sake of speeding up the process. This is due to the fact that population-based methods, such as the CMAES algorithm used in this work, require a large number of instances/population for each iteration, which increases as the number of model parameters increases. For these components, nominal values were derived from literature, based on properties used in similar applications, and were then fine-tuned manually, ensuring the final model yielded realistic results.

Table 3 Optimal model and parameters.

Contact force model	$E\,[\frac{N}{mm^2}]$	$c_r[-]$	$n\,[-]$
Lankarani & Nikravesh	2.08e5	0.95	2.13

Figure 6 shows a comparison between the experimental and optimal MBD frequency responses of the single stage drivetrain, measured at the Y axis of accelerometer A. As shown, while both systems display peaks at the orders corresponding to the Gear Mesh Frequency (GMF) and its harmonics, there are some visible differences in the magnitude of the vibrations. Considering that the model was optimized based on the healthy response of the system, this difference in the two responses can be attributed to the limitations imposed due to the modeling of the contact mechanism in the numerical model. That is, while the MBD takes into account phenomena such as the varying backlash between gear teeth as well as the geometry of the tooth, the contact normal force model does not account for the TVMS between gear teeth.

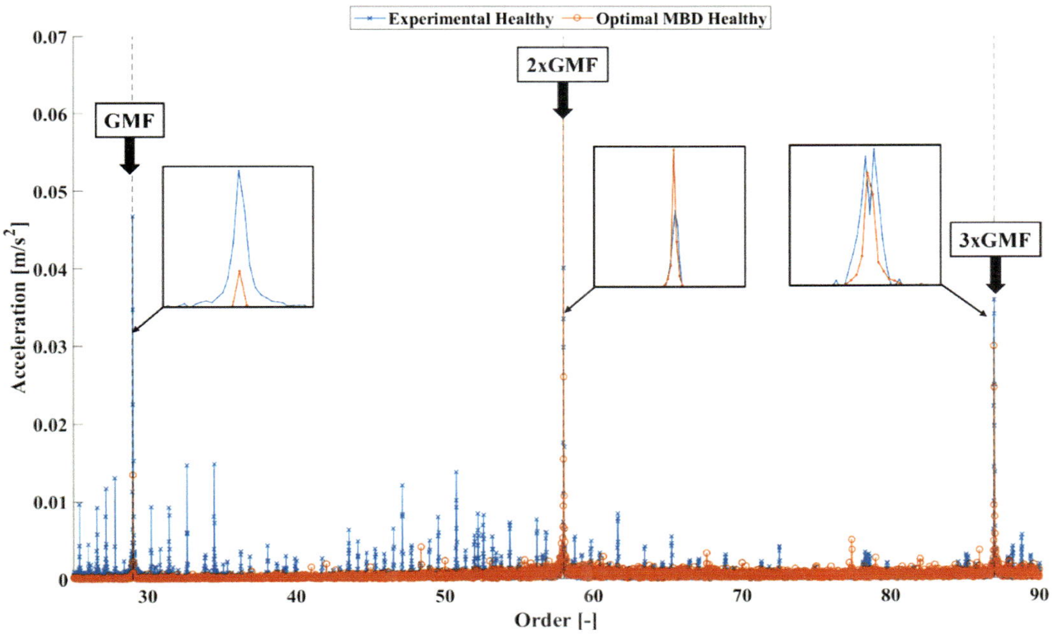

Fig. 6 Frequency response comparison between the experimental and optimal MBD system in its healthy state at 775 RPM.

Aiming to include the effects of TVMS in the MBD model, an augmented contact normal force model was constructed based on the formulation of Equations (1) - (12). By combining this detailed stiffness formulation with the MBD model, the contact forces between gear teeth can be estimated with increased accuracy, as the effects of the varying stiffness due to the changes in the contact angle are taken into account in addition to the force being estimated for infinitely small slices of the gear teeth, due to the contact detection algorithm that is built-in in the MBD model. The operations used in this augmented contact normal force model are described in Algorithm 1, and the stiffness profile resulting from the TVMS formulation is shown in 7.

Algorithm 1. Gear contact normal force algorithm.

- At time t_j, simulation step j:

Step 1. Detect contact between gear teeth at points $\boldsymbol{loc_i}$, $i = 1:N$
For $\boldsymbol{loc}$ in $\boldsymbol{loc_i}$:

Step 2. Calculate the angle φ between the LoA and the normal to tooth surface at $\boldsymbol{loc}$

Step 3. Calculate the mesh stiffness $\mathbf{K}$ at $\boldsymbol{loc}$ using Equation (10)

Step 4. Calculate the normal force $\mathbf{F}_{N,i}$ at $\boldsymbol{loc}$ using Equation (12)

Step 5. *Return* $\mathbf{F}_N = \sum_{i=1}^{N} \mathbf{F}_{N,i}$

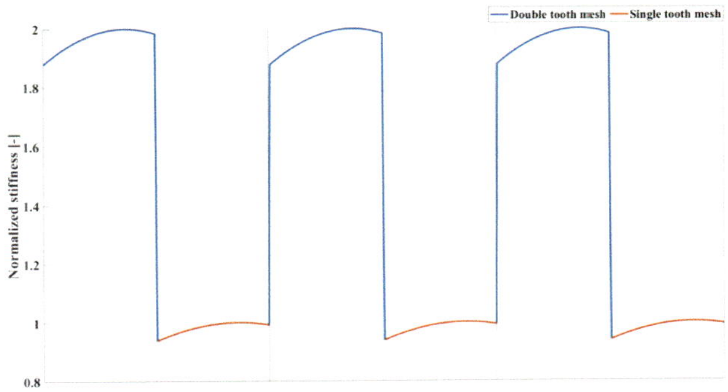

Fig. 7 Time Varying Mesh Stiffness profile.

The effects of the TVMS model are shown in Figure 8 where comparison between the measured and simulated responses is shown for the Y axis of Accelerometer A1.

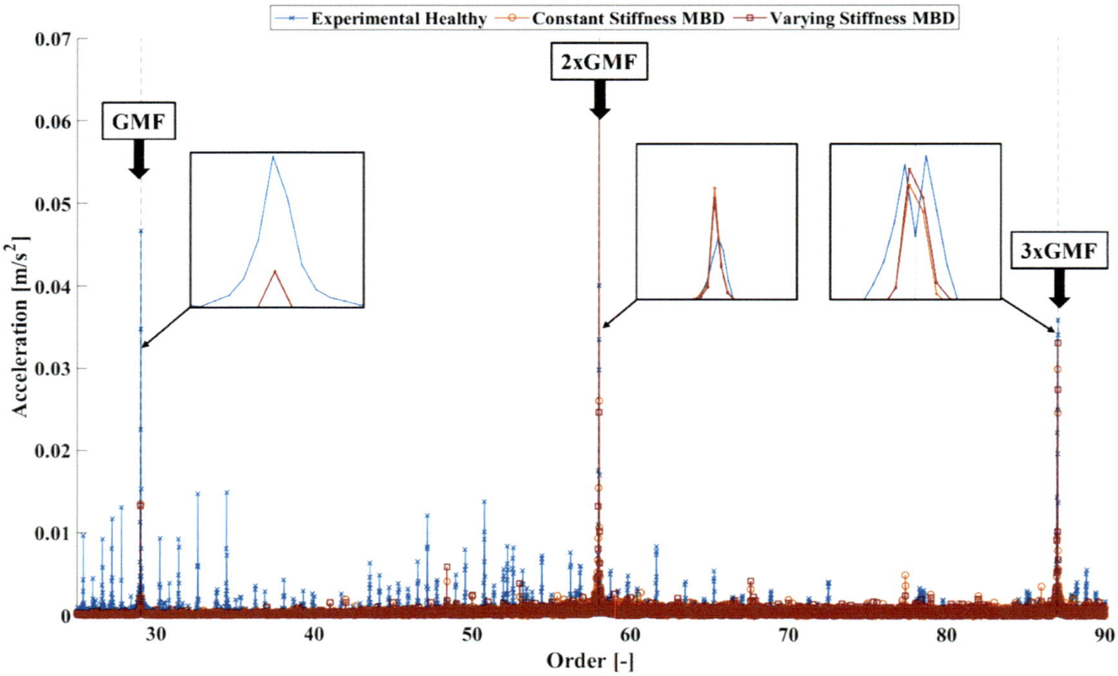

Fig. 8 Comparison between the experimental and the constant and varying stiffness MBD models of the system in its healthy state at 775 RPM.

In this work, two defects were examined to validate the modeling and CM framework. The first case, which for the rest of this text is denoted as Damage 1 (D1), is that of a missing tooth on the inlet gear. The second case, henceforth denoted as Damage 2 (D2) is that of a surface defect on one of the gear teeth. The respective fault cases are shown in Figure 9.

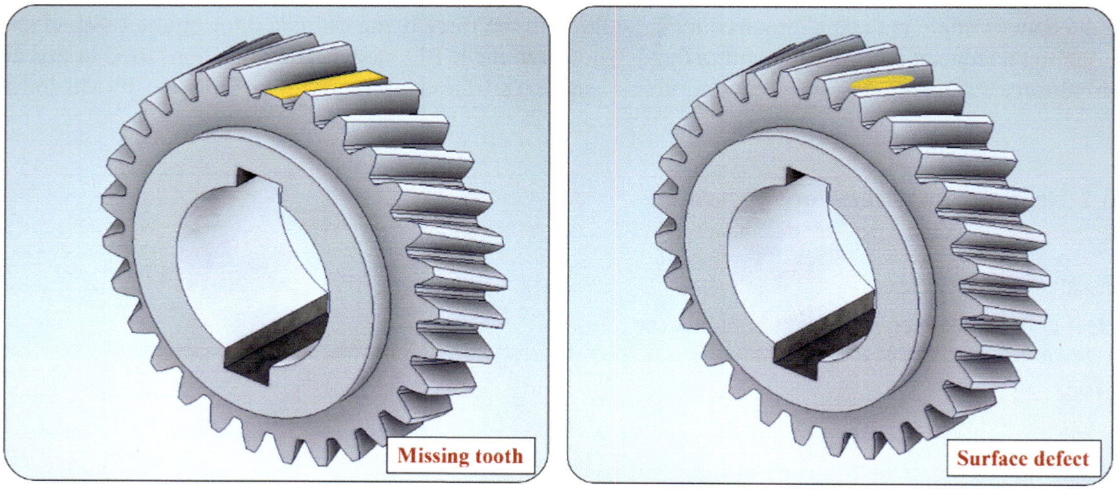

Fig. 9 Experimental drivetrain defective gear cases.

The results from analysis of the system through the MBD simulations of the two damaged gear cases are shown in Figure 10. As indicated by the figure, the damages result in changes in the magnitudes of the GMF and its harmonics, a change in the features of the signal that the DL classifier is expected to be able to identify with great accuracy.

While the results from the optimal MBD simulations in the healthy state of the system indicate a high fidelity between the simulated and measured system responses, validating the proposed numerically trained – experimentally validated CM

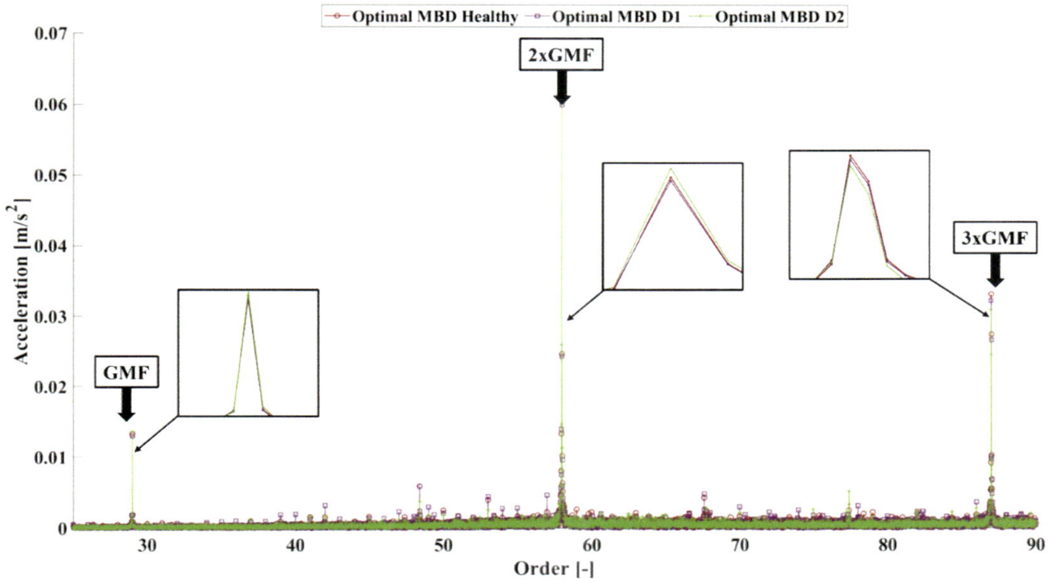

Fig. 10 Comparison between the optimal MBD frequency responses of the three health states at 775 RPM.

framework requires that the DL algorithms are proven capable of generalizing their predictions on unseen, physical measurements. To this end, an ensemble of 10 CNNs is created for the task of multiclass classification. The CNNs, whose architecture is shown in Figure 11, were trained for 25 epochs, on 2000 samples for each health state of the system, generated from the optimal MBD models. The loss function used in the training process was the categorical cross entropy and the optimizer selected was Adam, with a learning rate of 0.002.

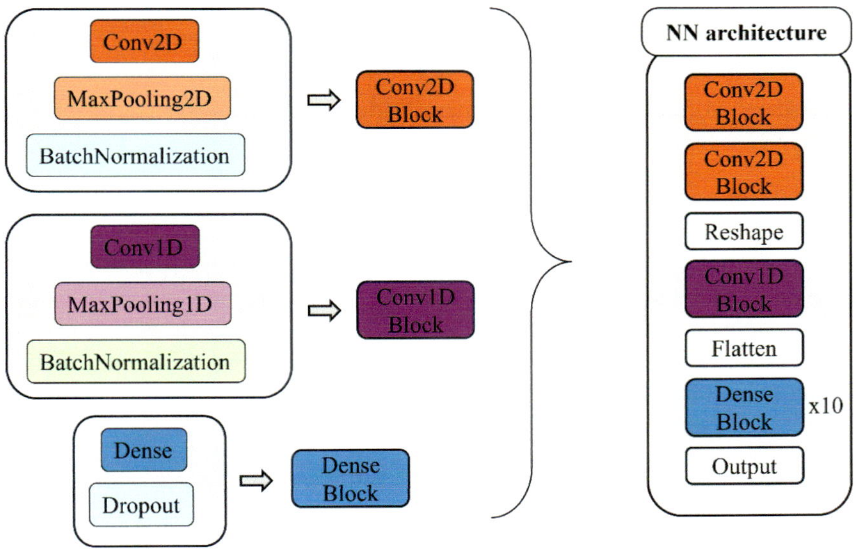

Fig. 11 DL classifier architecture – CNN ensemble.

The CNN ensemble was tested against a total of 300 experimental samples, corresponding to 100 samples for each of the health states. The health state classification results, which are shown in Figure 12, indicate a high level of accuracy and robustness in the predictions of the CNN ensemble. The networks are proven capable of making accurate predictions for each of the three different operating velocity values. Here, it should be noted that the networks are always capable of identifying the D1 case, that is, the missing tooth one, due to the fact that its much more extensive a defect compared to the surface defect. Similarly, most misclassification errors are observed between the healthy and D2 states, where the surface fault is not as extensive and, as such, affects the system's response much more subtly.

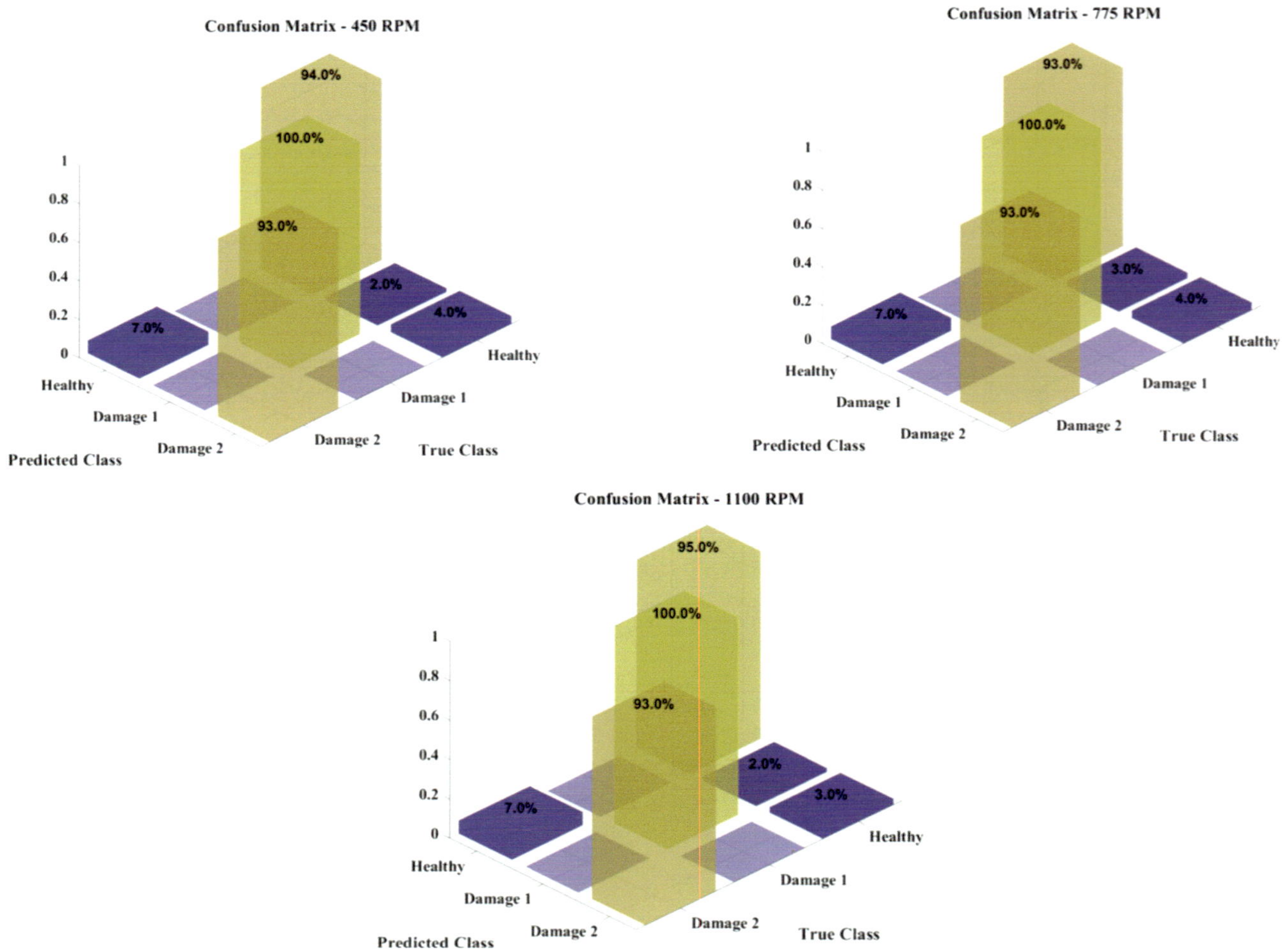

Fig. 12 Health states classification results for the experimental single stage gear drivetrain.

Conclusion

In this work, an augmented optimal MBD model of a single stage gear drivetrain is developed in order to create high-fidelity data for training an ensemble of DL classifiers for CM on the corresponding physical system. This augmented model incorporates an advanced contact normal force module, dedicated to gear meshing, where the effects of the TVMS are taken into account during simulation. This formulation, which is proven to yield improved results compared to the constant stiffness modeling of the contact forces between gears, results in highly accurate numerical data, whose features indicate increased similarity with the physical system's measured response. The developed CNN ensemble which is trained on numerical data alone is proven capable of making accurate predictions of the system's health state, while its robustness is also validated through its application on three different operating velocity conditions. The results derived from this work indicate that modeling mechanisms such as contacts, which are dominant in gear-related applications, with greater detail can significantly improve the simulation accuracy, aiding in the development and improvement of simulation-based DL methods.

Acknowledgments This project is carried out within the framework of the National Recovery and Resilience Plan Greece 2.0, funded by the European Union – NextGenerationEU (Implementation body: HFRI). Project Code: 16381.

References

1. Yuanning Mao, Jun Tong, Zhan Yie Chin, Pietro Borghesani, Zhongxiao Peng, Transmission-error- and vibration-based condition monitoring of gear wear with contaminated lubricant, Wear, Volume 523, 2023, 204760, https://doi.org/10.1016/j.wear.2023.204760.

2. Ke Feng, J.C. Ji, Qing Ni, Michael Beer, A review of vibration-based gear wear monitoring and prediction techniques, Mechanical Systems and Signal Processing, Volume 182, 2023, 109605, https://doi.org/10.1016/j.ymssp.2022.109605.
3. Miljković, Dubravko. (2015). Brief Review of Vibration Based Machine Condition Monitoring. CrSNDT Journal. 5. 14–23.
4. Zhuang Ye, Jianbo Yu, Deep morphological convolutional network for feature learning of vibration signals and itsapplications to gearbox fault diagnosis, Mechanical Systems and Signal Processing, Volume 161, 2021, 107984.
5. R.-B. Sun, Z.-B Yang, L.-D. Yang, B.-J Qiao, X.-F. Chen, K. Gryllias, Planetary gearbox spectral modeling based on the hybrid method of dynamics and LSTM, Mechanical Systems and Signal Processing, Volume 138, 2020,106611.
6. Moslem Azamfar, Jaskaran Singh, Inaki Bravo-Imaz, Jay Lee, Multisensor data fusion for gearbox fault diagnosis using 2-D convolutional neural network and motor current signature analysis, Mechanical Systems and Signal Processing, Volume 144, 2020, 106861.
7. A. L. Marra, R. Juliani and C. Garcia, "Data Augmentation for Vibration Signals using System Identification Techniques," 2021 5th International Conference on System Reliability and Safety (ICSRS), Palermo, Italy, 2021, pp. 281–285, doi:10.1109/ICSRS53853.2021.9660628
8. Timo Koenig, Luca Cadau, Fabian Wagner, Markus Kley, A generative adversarial network-based data augmentation approach with transient vibration data, Procedia Computer Science, Volume 225, 2023, Pages 1340–1349, ISSN 1877–0509, https://doi.org/10.1016/j.procs.2023.10.122.
9. P. Seventekidis, D. Giagopoulos, A. Arailopoulos, O. Markogiannaki, Structural Health Monitoring using deep learning with optimal finite element model generated data, Mechanical Systems and Signal Processing, Volume 145, 2020.
10. Koutsoupakis, J., Seventekidis, P., Giagopoulos, D. (2022). Machine Learning-Based Condition Monitoring with Multibody Dynamics Models for Gear Transmission Faults. Data Science in Engineering, Volume 9 (pp. 51–59). Springer International Publishing.
11. D. Giagopoulos, A. Arailopoulos, Computational framework for model updating of large scale linear and nonlinear finite element models using state of the art evolution strategy. Computers & Structures, 2017. 192: p. 210–232
12. Hongbo Yang, Wenku Shi, Zhiyong Chen, Niancheng Guo, An improved analytical method for mesh stiffness calculation of helical gear pair considering time-varying backlash, Mechanical Systems and Signal Processing, Volume 170, 2022, 108882, https://doi.org/10.1016/j.ymssp.2022.108882.
13. P. Sainsot, P. Velex, O. Duverger, Contribution of gear body to tooth deflections-A new bidimensional analytical formula, J. Mech. Des. 126 (2004) 748–752.

Chapter 11
Advanced Condition Monitoring framework for CFRP Gear Drivetrains Using Machine Learning and Multibody Dynamics Simulations

G. Karyofyllas, J. Koutsoupakis, and P. Giagopoulos

Abstract The advancements in key industry sectors such as automotive, wind turbines, oil, and gas have led to the increased use of Carbon-Fiber Reinforced Polymer (CFRP) materials in constructing shafts and gears with metal connectors for transmission drivetrain applications. Monitoring the health of these drivetrain components can prevent failures and enable effective maintenance schedules, ensuring high availability, reliability, and maintainability. Real-time condition monitoring (CM) via vibration measurements allows for fault detection and predictive maintenance. The accuracy and robustness of a CM application depend significantly on the availability of data for various health states, which typically necessitates comprehensive experimental measurements. In this work, an innovative condition monitoring (CM) framework for detecting and localizing damage in a lab-scale gear drivetrain system is presented. The framework leverages Machine Learning (ML) models that are trained on data produced through numerical simulations based on an Optimal Multibody Dynamics (MBD) model of the physical system. The experimental drivetrain is a single-stage system using CFRP shafts and gears, necessitating a high-fidelity MBD model to accurately represent the nonlinear material properties and layup of the CFRP shaft, as well as the 3D-printed gear set. The system, comprising shafts and gears, is mounted in four support bearings included in the MBD model. The model's precision is improved by thoroughly modeling the contact mechanics involved in gear meshing. This includes the development of an innovative contact force model that considers the influences of variable mesh stiffness, transmission error, and backlash. The objective is to perform damage identification across different health states using simulated responses for supervised health state classification, rather than relying solely on experimental data. Damage scenarios considered include cracks and delamination in the composite shaft and surface roughness, spalls, or missing teeth in the gear pair. The robustness and accuracy of the ML models are validated by accurately classifying faults in the physical system, demonstrating the proposed damage detection method's generalization capabilities and potential.

Keywords Carbon-Fiber Reinforced Polymer (CFRP) · Condition Monitoring (CM) · Multibody Dynamics (MBD) · Machine Learning (ML) · Gear Drivetrain · Damage Detection · Contact Mechanics

Introduction

In recent years, the increasing adoption of advanced materials like Carbon-Fiber Reinforced Polymer (CFRP) in key industry sectors, including automotive, wind turbines, and oil and gas, has sparked a transformation in the design and manufacturing of critical drivetrain components such as shafts and gears. The superior mechanical properties of CFRP, including a high strength-to-weight ratio, fatigue resistance, and corrosion resistance, make it an ideal choice for applications requiring high-performance, lightweight components [1]. These materials are particularly suited for transmission drivetrain systems, where energy efficiency, durability, and reliability are paramount. However, as CFRP components are integrated more widely into complex mechanical systems, the need for effective monitoring and maintenance strategies becomes increasingly important to prevent unexpected failures and optimize operational performance [2].

A crucial aspect of ensuring the reliability and performance of drivetrain systems is the ability to monitor the health of components in real time. Condition monitoring (CM) plays a vital role in detecting early signs of wear, damage, or faults in

G. Karyofyllas · J. Koutsoupakis · P. Giagopoulos
Aristotle University of Thessaloniki, Department of Mechanical Engineering, Thessaloniki, GR, 54124
Corresponding author: dgiagopoulos@auth.gr
e-mail: gdkaryof@meng.auth.gr; jkoutsoup@meng.auth.gr

Brian Damiano et al. (eds.), *Structural Health Monitoring & Machine Learning, Vol. 12*, Conference Proceedings of the Society for Experimental Mechanics Series, https://doi.org/10.13052/9788743801573-11

drivetrain components, enabling predictive maintenance and reducing the risk of costly breakdowns [3]. Among the various CM techniques, vibration-based monitoring is a well-established method for identifying faults in rotating machinery [4]. By analyzing the vibrational response of components, it is possible to detect deviations from normal operating conditions that may indicate the presence of damage, such as cracks, surface roughness, or gear tooth wear [5]. This approach provides a non-invasive and efficient means of assessing the health of drivetrain systems [6].

Despite the advantages of vibration-based condition monitoring, one of the key challenges is the requirement for a comprehensive dataset that accurately represents various health states of the system. In traditional CM approaches, this dataset is typically generated through extensive experimental measurements, which can be time-consuming, costly, and sometimes impractical, especially when dealing with novel materials like CFRP [7]. Moreover, obtaining experimental data for different damage scenarios and fault types may be difficult due to the complexity and diversity of possible failure modes in drivetrain systems. Therefore, there is a need for innovative methods to complement or replace experimental data collection for the development of robust condition monitoring frameworks [8].

In this work, is proposed an innovative condition monitoring framework that addresses these challenges by leveraging numerical simulations to generate training data for machine learning (ML) models. The proposed framework focuses on the detection and localization of damage in a lab-scale gear drivetrain system that incorporates CFRP shafts and gears. Rather than relying solely on experimental data, a high-fidelity multibody dynamics (MBD) model of the drivetrain system to simulate is utilized the vibrational responses under various health states [9]. The MBD model incorporates the nonlinear material properties and layup of CFRP shafts, as well as the intricate contact mechanics involved in gear meshing, including variable mesh stiffness, transmission error, and backlash [10]. These factors are essential for accurately simulating the physical behavior of the drivetrain components, particularly under different damage conditions [11].

The use of CFRP in shafts and gears presents unique challenges for condition monitoring due to the material's anisotropic behavior and complex damage mechanisms, such as delamination and cracking [12]. Additionally, the gear pair, constructed using 3D-printed materials, introduces further complexity due to the possibility of defects such as surface roughness, spalling, or missing teeth [13]. To address these challenges, an innovative contact force model that captures the dynamic interactions between the gear teeth is developed, enabling accurate simulation of the vibrational response under healthy and damaged conditions. The simulated responses generated from the MBD model serve as the training data for the machine learning models, which are then used to classify the health state of the drivetrain system. Supervised learning algorithms are employed to differentiate between normal operation and various damage scenarios, including cracks and delamination in the composite shaft and gear defects such as surface roughness and missing teeth. By training the ML models on numerically simulated data, we can bypass the need for exhaustive experimental measurements while still achieving high levels of accuracy and robustness in fault detection and classification.

The key contributions of this research are twofold. First, is presented a comprehensive MBD model of a drivetrain system with CFRP components that accurately simulates the complex dynamics of the system under different health conditions. This model includes detailed representations of the material properties, contact mechanics, and gear meshing behavior, providing a realistic basis for generating training data [14]. Second, is demonstrated the effectiveness of machine learning techniques in classifying faults based on the simulated data, showcasing the potential for integrating numerical simulations and data-driven methods in condition monitoring frameworks [15]. The proposed approach not only reduces the reliance on experimental data but also improves the generalization capabilities of the CM system, making it applicable to a wide range of drivetrain applications [16].

The remainder of this paper is organized as follows: First, the **Background** section outlines the theoretical foundation, including the multibody dynamics (MBD) model and the associated theoretical equations. This section also covers the modeling of contact forces between the gears and bushings, as well as the data mining process used to train the machine learning (ML) model. Additionally, the basic formulation for identifying the drivetrain's condition through the ML model is presented. Next, the **Analysis** section provides a detailed description of the drivetrain system under investigation, focusing on the CFRP shafts and 3D-printed gears, as well as the development of the MBD model to simulate the system's dynamics. This section also discusses the model updating process, in which the MBD model is refined using experimental datasets from the drivetrain's healthy state. Simulated damage scenarios are introduced as part of this section. In this section, the results of the fault classification experiments are also presented, accompanied by an analysis of the model's accuracy and its ability to generalize across different conditions. Finally, the paper concludes with a **Conclusion** section, summarizing the findings and providing recommendations for future research directions in condition monitoring for CFRP-based drivetrain systems.

Background

Multibody Dynamics (MBD) is a framework used to describe the dynamic interactions between interconnected bodies in a system. These bodies are connected through kinematic constraints and are influenced by both internal and external forces. When a system consists of components with varying degrees of stiffness or flexibility, its equations of motion can be expressed generally as:

$$\begin{cases} M\underline{\ddot{q}} + C\underline{\dot{q}} + K\underline{q} = \underline{f}(t) + A^T\underline{\lambda} \\ \underline{\Phi}(q,t) = \underline{0} \end{cases} \tag{1}$$

In this formulation, M, C, and K represent the system's mass, damping, and stiffness matrices, respectively. The terms $\underline{\ddot{q}}$, $\underline{\dot{q}}$, and $\underline{q}$ denote the acceleration, velocity, and displacement vectors of the system's generalized coordinates. $\underline{f}$ refers to external forces acting on the system, while $A^T\underline{\lambda}$ accounts for the constraints imposed by Lagrange multipliers. The constraint equations $\underline{\Phi}(q,t) = \underline{0}$ ensure that the kinematic constraints defined by the system's ideal joints are satisfied, allowing an accurate depiction of the dynamics of both rigid and flexible components [17].

In the drivetrain MBD model, bushings are introduced to act as both supports and flexible connectors between components. Bushings allow relative motion between parts while providing resistance to specific degrees of freedom, adding flexibility compared to rigid connections. They are typically characterized by their stiffness and damping properties, and their force-displacement behavior is often modeled using a spring-damper system. The equation governing the forces exerted by a bushing is typically:

$$F = -k * \delta - c * \dot{\delta} \tag{2}$$

In this equation, F represents the force exerted by the bushing, k is the stiffness, c is the damping coefficient, δ is the deformation of the bushing, and $\dot{\delta}$ is the rate of deformation (velocity). This model effectively captures the compliance and damping behavior of the bushing, which plays a crucial role in the dynamics of the system by allowing controlled flexibility.

In the drivetrain MBD model, contact between the gear pair is defined to accurately capture the interaction forces during meshing. To simulate the energy dissipation within the system, a damping component is introduced alongside the stiffness component of the contact force. This damping is represented using a hysteresis damping factor, which accounts for energy loss due to material deformation and contact mechanics. The hysteresis factor χ is determined using one of several available models, with each model providing a distinct relationship between the hysteresis factor, coefficient of restitution (c_r), and the initial indentation velocity $(\dot{\delta})$ at the moment of contact [18]. The general form of the damping model is given by:

$$F_n = -k * \delta^n - \chi * \delta^n * \dot{\delta} \tag{3}$$

Table 1 provides a summary of different models used to estimate the hysteresis damping factor χ based on the contact force model.

Table 1 Hysteresis damping factor χ with respect to the contact force model.

Gharib & Hurmuzlu	Herbert & McWhannel	Flores et al.	Lee & Wang
$\frac{1}{c_r}\frac{K}{\dot{\delta}^{(-)}}$	$\frac{6(1-c_r)}{(2c_r-1)^2+3}\frac{K}{\dot{\delta}^{(-)}}$	$\frac{8(1-c_r)}{5c_r}\frac{K}{\dot{\delta}^{(-)}}$	$\frac{3(1-c_r)}{4}\frac{K}{\dot{\delta}^{(-)}}$
Hunt & Crossley	**Lankarani & Nikravesh**	**Zhiuing & Qishao**	**Gonthier et al.**
$\frac{3(1-c_r)}{2}\frac{K}{\dot{\delta}^{(-)}}$	$\frac{3(1-c_r^2)}{4}\frac{K}{\dot{\delta}^{(-)}}$	$\frac{3(1-c_r^2)e^{2(1-c_r)}}{4}\frac{K}{\dot{\delta}^{(-)}}$	$\frac{1-c_r^2}{c_r}\frac{K}{\dot{\delta}^{(-)}}$

The contact forces between the gears and the forces in the bushings of the drivetrain model are then optimized for best performance by tuning the model parameters using the Covariance Matrix Adaptation Evolution Strategy (CMA-ES). CMA-ES is particularly effective in handling complex optimization scenarios characterized by discontinuities, noise, local optima, and other challenges [19]. The goal is to optimize a set of model parameters θ by minimizing the error between the experimental dataset and the predicted model's response in the frequency domain, obtained through Fast Fourier Transformation (FFT) of the accelerations at the bearing positions.

The error between the experimental and numerical responses for the $i-th$ predicted model can be minimized using the following cost function:

$$J_i(\theta) = \frac{1}{N}\sum_{i=1}^{N}\frac{\sum_{j=1}^{m}(\hat{a}(\theta)_{ij} - a_{ij})^2}{\sum_{j=1}^{m}(a_{ij})^2} \tag{4}$$

In this equation, $\hat{a}(\theta)_{ij}$ represents the FFT of the acceleration response at the $j-th$ bearing location for the $i-th$ frequency in the numerical model, and a_{ij} is the FFT of the experimental acceleration data at the same bearing location.

The optimization starts with an initial set of parameters in the vector θ, which represent the parameters for the drivetrain's numerical model.

The CMA-ES algorithm iteratively updates the parameters by calculating the numerical model's response and minimizing the cost function $J(\theta)$, which is based on normalized least squares error. The process continues until the parameter values are refined, aligning the numerical and experimental frequency responses, and ensuring a more accurate representation of the drivetrain's dynamics.

Next, the optimal MBD model is utilized to generate labeled data for training the proposed supervised machine learning framework. This numerical model produces a comprehensive dataset that encompasses various health states in the rotor dynamics model under investigation, providing detailed information about both the health status and specific instances of damage occurring at discrete locations within the structure. To account for the inherent uncertainty in real-world systems, key hyperparameters θ are sampled from a Gaussian distribution. In practical experiments, uncertainty is always present, resulting in discrepancies between experimental responses and those predicted by the model. By sampling the model's hyperparameters, these issues are addressed, mitigating discrepancies observed between numerical and experimental data across different trials.

To facilitate the generation of N labeled datasets, an automated algorithm, as shown in Figure 1, has been developed. This algorithm leverages the numerical model's response to compute Fast Fourier Transforms (FFTs) from the acceleration data in the X and Y directions, which serve as the primary input for the machine learning framework. At the end of the process, the algorithm determines the model's health status and returns both the FFTs and the health label Y. This label, represented as a single integer, indicates the simulated health state, designating whether the corresponding MBD model instance is healthy or exhibiting specific damage forms. Essentially, Y acts as a categorical indicator linked to the configuration of the solved MBD model, distinguishing between healthy and compromised states. The simulated FFT response data is then organized into a complete labeled dataset, expressed as:

$$Train\_set = \{(FFT_1, Y_1), (FFT_2, Y_2) \cdots (FFT_n, Y_n)\}, \text{ with } FFT_n = [FFT_n^X, FFT_n^Y] \tag{5}$$

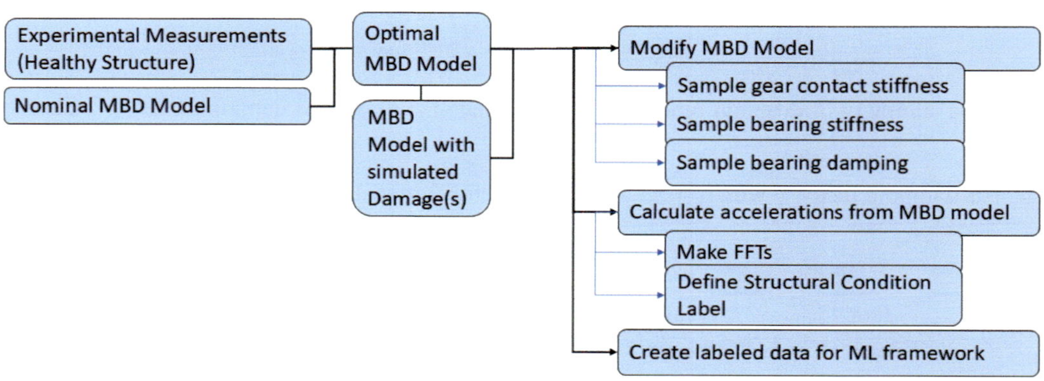

Fig. 1 Numerical data generation framework.

The simulated dataset for supervised damage detection and identification in the drivetrain system is processed using a Support Vector Machine (SVM) with a Radial Basis Function (RBF) kernel [20]. SVM is a robust classification algorithm that works by transforming the input data into a higher-dimensional space, allowing it to handle complex decision boundaries. The classification problem is expressed as:

$$y(x) = w^T \varphi(x) + b \tag{6}$$

where $\varphi(x)$ is the feature-space transformation function, and b is the bias term. The RBF kernel provides flexibility through hyperparameters and is defined as:

$$K(\boldsymbol{x}, \boldsymbol{y}) = e^{-\gamma \|\boldsymbol{x} - \boldsymbol{y}\|^2} \tag{7}$$

Where $K(\boldsymbol{x}, \boldsymbol{y})$ represents the kernel function applied to input vectors **x** and $\boldsymbol{y}$, and γ is a hyperparameter controlling the decision boundary's smoothness. The training dataset $T = \{x_i \in \mathbb{R}^n, \quad i = 1, \ldots, \ N\}$ and labels from two classes $y_i \in \{-1, 1\}$ are used to optimize the model.

During training, the SVM seeks to maximize the margin between classes by solving the optimization problem:

$$Maximize : W(a) = \sum_{i=1}^{N} a_i - \frac{1}{2} \sum_{i=1}^{N} \sum_{j=1}^{N} (a_i \cdot a_j \cdot y_i \cdot y_j \cdot K(x_i, x_j)) \tag{8}$$

subject to $0 \leq a_i \leq C$, where C is a regularization parameter, and $a_i$are the Lagrange multipliers. The decision function is then used for classification:

$$f(\boldsymbol{x}) = sign\left(\sum (a_i \cdot y_i \cdot K(\boldsymbol{x}, \boldsymbol{x}_i)) + b)\right) \tag{9}$$

Where, $f(x)$ is the predicted class label for input vector x and b is a constant value. This SVM-RBF model, trained using the scikit-learn Python library, can accurately classify new data and identify health states in real-time, making it suitable for condition monitoring in non-linear systems characterized by complex patterns.

The overall process of the proposed methodology is summarized in the flowchart presented in Figure 2. This flowchart outlines the key steps, starting from the development of a high-fidelity MBD model of the drivetrain system, including the CFRP shafts and 3D-printed gears. Numerical simulations are then performed using this model to generate data for various health states. The data is processed through FFT to capture the frequency domain responses at the bearing positions. Following this, a SVM model with RBF kernel is trained using the simulated dataset to classify different health states. The SVM-RBF is optimized by tuning its hyperparameters, such as the kernel parameter γ and regularization parameter C. Once trained, the model is capable of performing real-time condition monitoring by accurately detecting and identifying damage based on new input data.

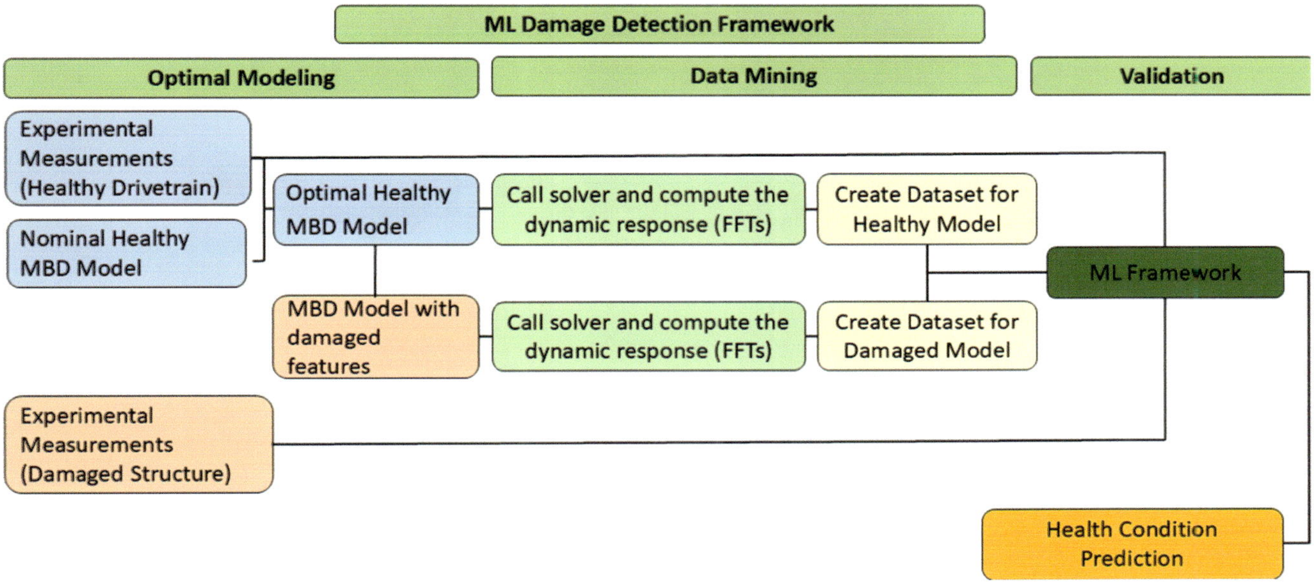

Fig. 2 Flowchart of the proposed framework.

Analysis

The experimental setup used to conduct dynamic testing of the drivetrain with Carbon Fiber Reinforced Polymer (CFRP) gears and shafts is illustrated in Figure 3. The system consists of two main components: the drive motor (1) and the load motor (2), both of which are three-phase electric motors. Additionally, it includes two shafts (3), four shaft mounting ball bearings (4), a pair of gears (5) and (6), and a mounting frame (7). To monitor the system's dynamic response, four tri-axial accelerometers are mounted on the bearings (4), allowing for measurement of acceleration in the radial direction. A torque meter is also placed on the input shaft, positioned directly after the electric drive motor, to capture the input torque of the drivetrain. The tests are conducted over a rotational speed range from 450 RPM to 1100 RPM, with increments of 250 RPM between each test. Data is recorded at a sampling rate of 5120 Hz to capture the detailed dynamic behavior of the system. The corresponding MBD model, which accurately represents the experimental drivetrain system, is illustrated in Figure 4. Table 2 summarizes the material properties of CFRP used in the MBD model for both the CFRP gears and shaft.

The optimal contact force model, along with its corresponding parameters as estimated through the optimal selection using the Covariance Matrix Adaptation Evolution Strategy (CMA-ES) algorithm, is presented in Table 3. In addition to this, the table summarizes the stiffness and damping values for the bushings used in the system.

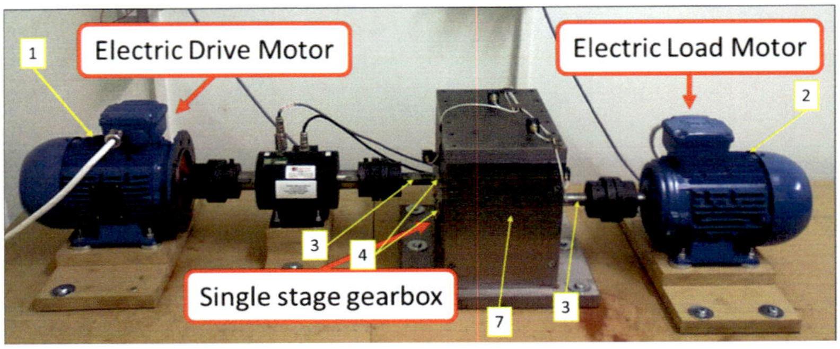

Fig. 3 Experimental drivetrain system and measuring equipment.

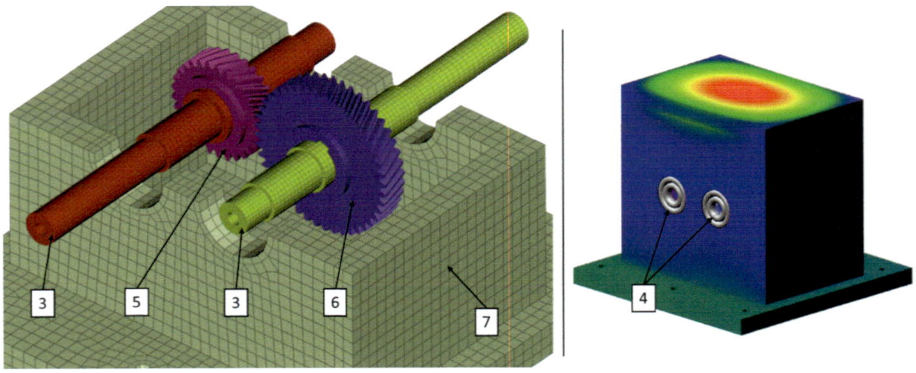

Fig. 4 Drivetrain system numerical model (MBD).

Table 2 CFRP material properties.

Property		
Modulus of Elasticity in X	E_1[GPa]	138.945
Modulus of Elasticity in Y	E_2[GPa]	6.6154
In-plane Shear Modulus & Transverse Shear Modulus 1-Z plane	$G_{12} = G_{1z}$ [GPa]	3.387
Transverse Shear Modulus 2-Z plane	G_{2z} [GPa]	2.2864
Density	ρ[kg/m³]	1560

Table 3 Optimal force model and parameters.

Contact force model	$K\,[\frac{N}{mm^2}]$	$c_r[-]$	$n\,[-]$
Flores et al.	3.25e5	0.96	1.2
Bushing force model	$K\,[\frac{N}{mm^2}]$	$C\,[\frac{N*s}{mm}]$	
$F = -K*\delta - C*\dot{\delta}$	1.825e5	12.3	

To accurately replicate the damage scenarios and develop a machine learning (ML)-based model capable of identifying the health state of the drivetrain, two new MBD models were created, each representing specific damage conditions. These models, combined with the existing healthy state model, enable a comprehensive analysis of the system's behavior across different health conditions. In this study, three distinct health states of the drivetrain were analyzed. The first is the baseline "healthy" state, where no faults or damage are present. The second state represents a surface fault, characterized by wear or degradation on the pinion gear teeth surface. This condition was simulated by reducing the contact stiffness of the gears by 15%, mirroring the reduction in stiffness typically observed in real-world surface damage scenarios. The third state represents a more severe fault, a missing tooth on the pinion gear, which drastically alters the dynamic behavior of the drivetrain due to the abrupt change in contact mechanics. Figure 5 illustrates the gear models used for each of these health states. By incorporating these different damage conditions into the MBD framework, the study provides a robust dataset for training the ML-based damage detection system, which is designed to classify the health states based on the system's dynamic responses under varying operational conditions.

Fig. 5 Gear geometry for different health states.

Figure 6 presents the acceleration responses in the frequency domain for the optimal MBD models at rotational speed of 450RPM. The responses are shown for the first nine harmonics of the Gear Mesh Frequency (GMF) of the gear pair, providing insight into the system's dynamic behavior at various speeds. Figure 7 compares the simulated responses of the drivetrain system in both its healthy and damaged states. This comparison highlights the differences in dynamic behavior and helps in identifying damage by observing the variations between the healthy and faulty conditions.

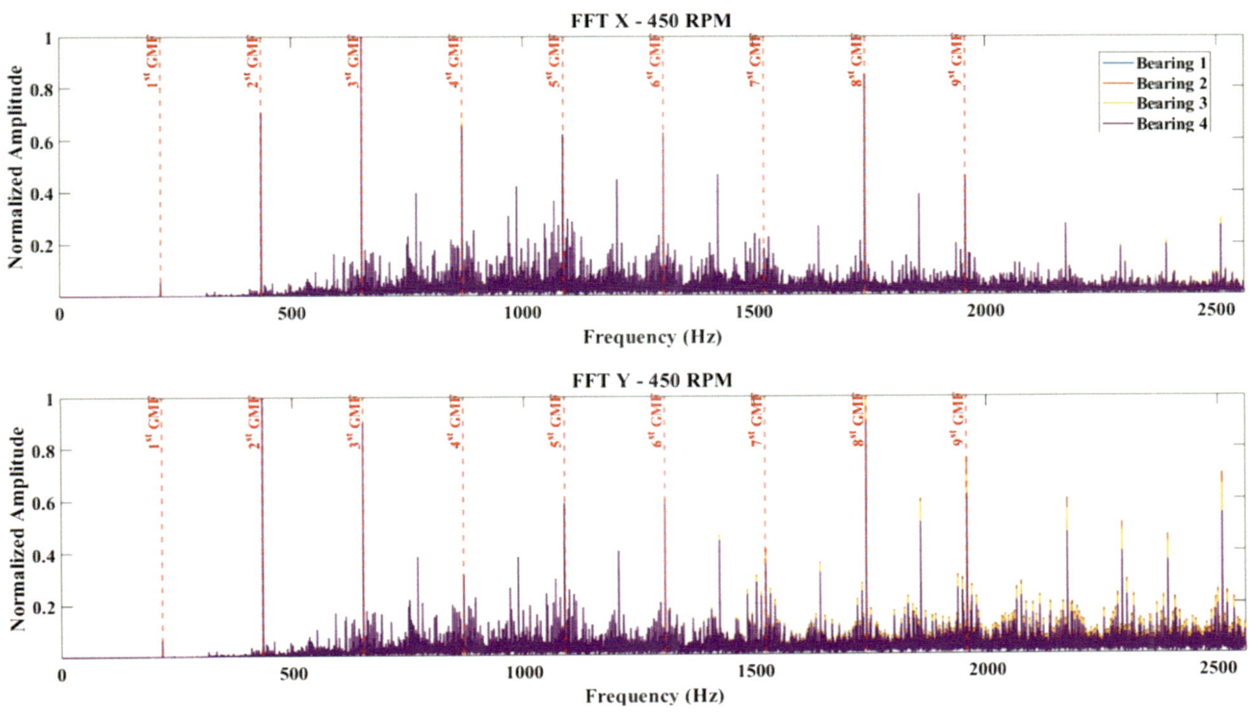

Fig. 6 Frequency response comparison of the optimal MBD system in its healthy state at 450 RPM.

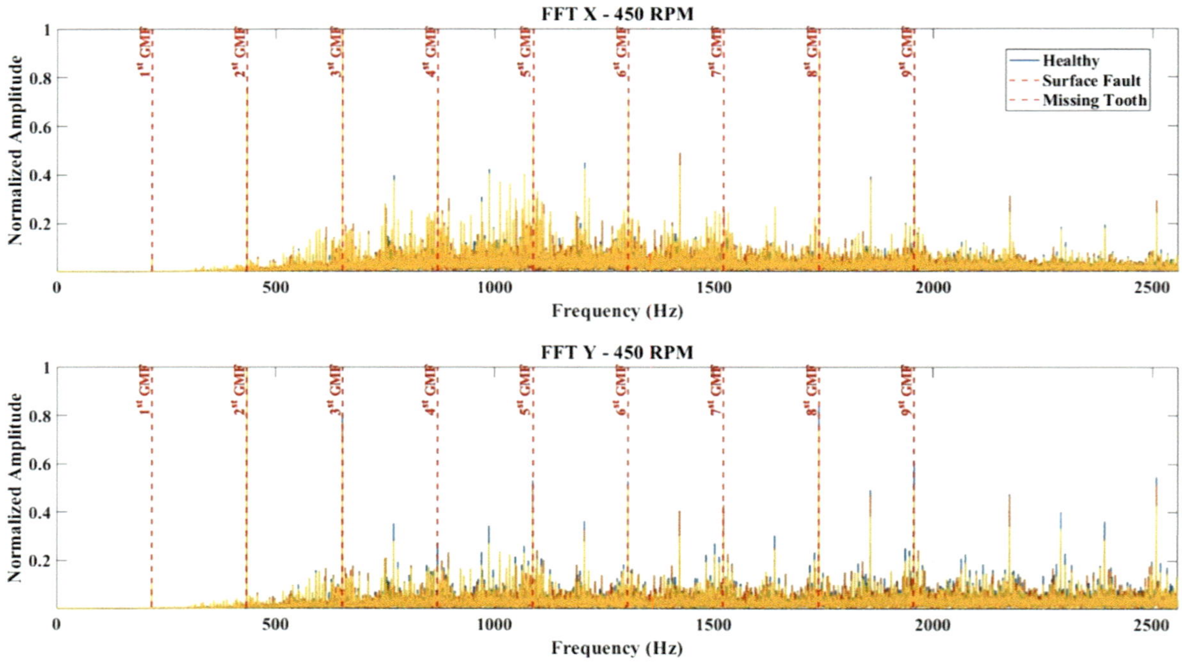

Fig. 7 Frequency response comparison between the healthy and damaged MBD models at 450 RPM.

The training data for this study was generated from optimal healthy and damaged MBD models, comprising 500 examples for the healthy state and 500 samples for each damage scenario, resulting in a total dataset of 1,500 cases. To introduce realism into the models, the optimal hyperparameters (θ) were perturbed by $\pm 3\%$ using a Gaussian distribution. This stochastic variation helps to replicate uncertainties present in experimental scenarios. The computational efficiency of this approach was significant, with the MBD problem solving completed in approximately 20 seconds. Overall, the data generation process was completed in under 30 seconds per example, a marked improvement compared to traditional methods.

The numerical data was organized into labeled datasets corresponding to specific structural health conditions, adhering to guidelines outlined in Background Chapter and forming the training set as defined in Equation (5). Table 4 summarizes the labels used to describe the numerical data. The generated datasets show close proximity among different health states, underscoring the challenge of accurately detecting structural changes within the system.

Table 4 Dataset used labels.

Health State	Healthy	Surface Fault	Missing Tooth
Label Y	0	1	2

The next phase in the machine learning framework involves training the SVM-RBF model for robust classification of the experimental structure's health state using this numerical dataset. Seventy percent of the dataset is allocated for training, allowing the model to learn underlying patterns, while the remaining 30% serves as a validation set for unbiased performance assessment. Prior to training, data scaling standardizes the input features to have zero mean and unit variance, ensuring balanced contributions from all features. Key hyperparameters 'C' and 'gamma' are finely tuned, with 'C' set to 1.2 for balance between decision boundary optimization and error reduction, and 'gamma' assigned the value 'scale' to enhance model performance.

The model's accuracy was thoroughly assessed on the validation set using experimental measurements across the three health states studied, yielding remarkable results: 99.4% accuracy at 450 RPM, 91.8% at 775 RPM, and 98.2% at 1100 RPM. Confusion matrices (Figure 8) provide a comprehensive overview of the model's performance, detailing the rates of true positives, true negatives, false positives, and false negatives for each health state. Overall, the model demonstrates a strong capacity for accurately classifying both healthy and damaged states of the drivetrain, achieving an average efficiency of 95%. Additionally, Figure 9 highlights the model's prediction percentages at various rotating speeds, further underscoring its reliability and effectiveness in real-world applications.

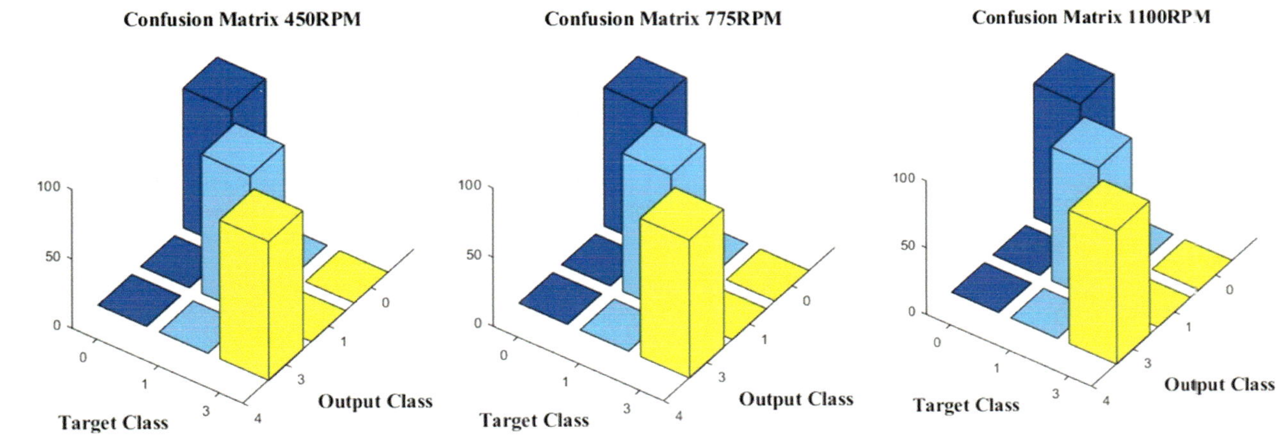

Fig. 8 Confusion matrices for different rotating speeds.

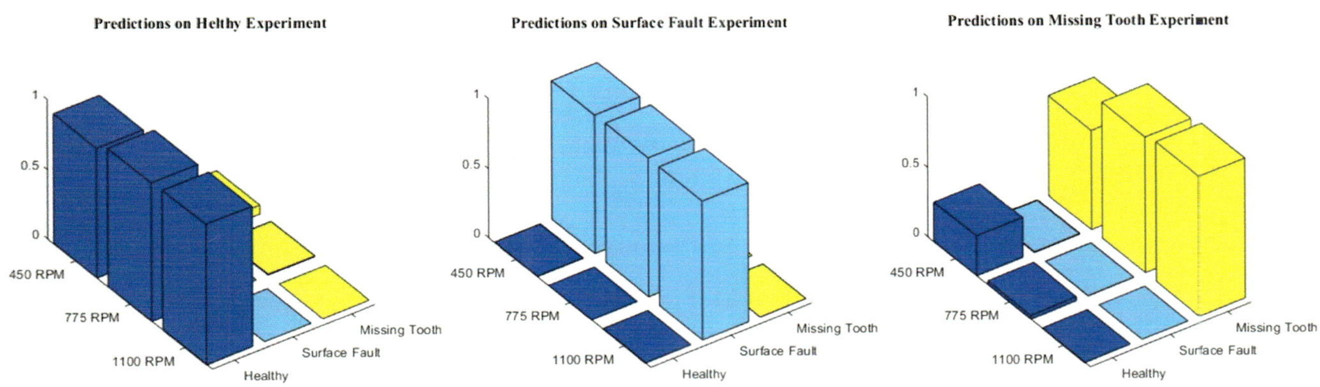

Fig. 9 SVM-RBF prediction percentages on experimental datasets.

Conclusion

This study presents a comprehensive approach to developing a machine learning framework aimed at effectively classifying the health states of a drivetrain system using CFRP gears and shafts. The primary objective was achieved through a combination of advanced simulation techniques and machine learning algorithms, resulting in significant findings and contributions to the field of condition monitoring. First and foremost, the development of the optimal Multibody Dynamics model allowed for the generation of a substantial dataset comprising 1,500 instances, representing various health states of the drivetrain. This dataset was instrumental in training the machine learning model and showcased the effectiveness of simulating different operational conditions, including healthy and damaged states. The use of a Support Vector Machine with a Radial Basis Function kernel demonstrated impressive classification performance, achieving accuracy rates of 99.4% at 450 RPM, 91.8% at 775 RPM, and 98.2% at 1100 RPM on the validation set. This high level of accuracy underscores the potential of the proposed framework for real-time health state classification in practical applications. Furthermore, the integration of Gaussian perturbations into the model's hyperparameters effectively introduced a realistic element of uncertainty, closely mimicking real-world experimental scenarios. This approach not only improved the robustness of the model but also ensured its applicability to varying operating conditions. In conclusion, this study not only demonstrates the efficacy of using advanced simulation techniques and machine learning for health state classification but also provides a valuable framework for future research in the field of condition monitoring and fault detection in mechanical systems. Further investigation into the optimization of the model and expansion of the training dataset will be essential for improving classification performance across all health states, ultimately contributing to more reliable and effective monitoring of drivetrain systems.

Acknowledgments This project is carried out within the framework of the Strengthening the Research Activity of Faculty Members - AUTH Special Account for Research Funds. Project Code: 10627.

References

1. Kawamoto, A., & Ichiro, K. (2018). Advancements in CFRP Technology for Automotive Applications. Journal of Composites in Manufacturing, 24(3), 45-52.
2. Koutsoupakis, J., Seventekidis, P., Giagopoulos, D. (2022). Machine Learning-Based Condition Monitoring with Multibody Dynamics Models for Gear Transmission Faults. Data Science in Engineering, Volume 9 (pp. 51–59). Springer International Publishing.
3. Tandon, N., & Choudhury, A. (2019). Condition Monitoring of Rotating Machinery: A Review. Journal of Sound and Vibration, 208(3), 475-487.
4. Karyofyllas, G., Giagopoulos, D., (2024). Condition Monitoring Framework for Damage Identification in CFRP Rotating Shafts using Model-Driven Machine Learning Techniques. Engineering Failure Analysis 158(11), 108052.
5. Bartelmus, W., & Zimroz, R. (2019). A New Method for Gear Fault Detection and Localization. Mechanical Systems and Signal Processing, 35(1-2), 286–301.
6. Koutsoupakis, J., Seventekidis, P., Giagopoulos, D. (2023). Machine learning based condition monitoring for gear transmission systems using data generated by optimal multibody dynamics models, Mechanical Systems and Signal Processing, 190, 110130.
7. Seventekidis, P., Giagopoulos, D. (2022), Model-based damage identification with simulated transmittance deviations and deep learning classification, Structural Health Monitoring, 21(5):2206–2230.
8. Saito, H., & Tanaka, K. (2020). Machine Learning in Structural Health Monitoring. Journal of Machine Learning Applications, 12(4), 340–350.
9. Harris, S. L., & Cheng, X. (2019). 3D-Printed Gears: Modeling and Fault Detection. Journal of Materials Engineering, 41(3), 227–239.
10. Kuang, K. S. C., & Cantwell, W. J. (2018). The Influence of CFRP Layups on Gear Dynamics. International Journal of Mechanical Sciences, 142, 101–109.
11. Lesh, S. J., & Alkan, B. (2021). Utilizing Machine Learning for Fault Detection in Composite Shafts. Journal of Composites Science, 5(2), 120–132.
12. Wang, Z., & Jia, X. (2020). Supervised Learning Methods for Condition Monitoring in Drivetrains. Journal of Mechanical Systems and Signal Processing, 138, 106554.
13. Macek, W., & Kukla, S. (2022). Application of Multibody Dynamics Models for Gear Fault Detection. Journal of Engineering Simulation, 18(7), 784–799.
14. Liu, Y., & Lee, Y. (2022). Predictive Maintenance for CFRP Structures using Machine Learning. Applied Composite Materials, 29(4), 1245–1260.
15. Zhao, H., & Wu, L. (2022). Simulation-based Fault Detection in Gear Systems Using Data-Driven Methods. Mechanical Systems and Signal Processing, 168, 108585.
16. Alahmadi, S., & Alghamdi, S. (2023). Generalization of Machine Learning Models for Condition Monitoring in Industrial Applications. Journal of Industrial Information Integration, 27, 100–110.
17. Natsiavas, S., Passas, P., Paraskevopoulos, E., (2022), Nonlinear dynamics of constrained multibody systems based on natural ODE formulation, Nonlinear Dynamics, Volume 110, Pages 2951–2977
18. Renqiong Wu, Xiufeng Wang, Zexing Ni, Chun Zeng, (2022)Dual-impulse behavior analysis and quantitative diagnosis of the raceway fault of rolling bearing, Mechanical Systems and Signal Processing, Volume 169
19. Giagopoulos, D. and A. Arailopoulos, Computational framework for model updating of large scale linear and nonlinear finite element models using state of the art evolution strategy. Computers & Structures, 2017. 192: p. 210–232.
20. Karl Thurnhofer-Hemsi, E Karl Thurnhofer-Hemsi, Ezequiel López-Rubio, Miguel A. Molina-Cabello, Kayvan Najarian, (2020), Radial basis function kernel optimization for Support Vector Machine classifiers.

Chapter 12
On the use of Statistical Learning Theory for model selection in Structural Health Monitoring

C. A. Lindley, N. Dervilis, and K. Worden

Abstract Whenever data-based systems are employed in engineering applications, defining an optimal statistical representation is subject to the problem of model selection. This paper focusses on how well models can generalise in Structural Health Monitoring (SHM). Although statistical model validation in this field is often performed heuristically, it is possible to estimate generalisation more rigorously using the bounds provided by Statistical Learning Theory (SLT). Therefore, this paper explores the selection process of a kernel smoother for modelling the impulse response of a linear oscillator from the perspective of SLT. It is demonstrated that incorporating domain knowledge into the regression problem yields a lower guaranteed risk, thereby enhancing generalisation.

Keywords Structural health monitoring · statistical learning theory · structural risk minimisation · kernel smoothers · impulse response

Introduction

The incorporation of intelligent systems in engineering is a subject of increasing popularity in the literature. Of particular interest in the present study is the development of data-based methods tailored to addressing various challenges encountered in *Structural Health Monitoring* (SHM) [1]. Whether these methods are designed to detect, localise or classify damage [2], one aspect that is shared across them is the problem of model selection; namely, of deciding over a set of statistical models, which one can adequately represent the system at hand. The means to determine such a model is by a process of validation during the training phase, which is a crucial step to ensure that the model can genenralise well. Failure to do so can lead to an erroneous representation of the system, and thus inaccurate predictions upon the introduction of new observations. This consideration may arguably be of greater importance in SHM, since poor predictions could be perilous for human safety, and detrimental towards financial projections, in the event of unforeseen failures.

To ensure good generalisation, standard practice is followed, often involving the division of the entire dataset into a *training set* and a *test set*. In short, the training set is used to search for optimal parameters, while the test set simulates unseen data, allowing the evaluation of the prediction error for both sets during the learning process. Some optimal model is chosen that can maintain a low error for the training set while preventing the error to grow large for the test set. This criterion is commonly met heuristically with the use of *cross-validation* methods [3]. The concept of generalisation, however, can be approached in a more rigorous fashion and thus assert the confidence one has about the employed statistical model.

The search for an optimal model is thereby explored here by eliciting the methods found in *Statistical Learning Theory* (SLT) [4]; concretely, in the selection of an optimal kernel smoother for modelling the impulse response of a simple structure. The premise of the following study is to establish a rigorous mathematical framework for the model-selection problem in SHM, ensuring the selection of an optimal model that generalises well when trained with a limited amount of data.

The Model-Selection Problem

To illustrate the model-selection problem, one may first consider the case in which the aim is to fit a function to a set of data. If dealing with a regression problem, then a sensible approach would be to find some weighted combination of inputs that

C. A. Lindley · N. Dervilis · K. Worden
Dynamics Research Group, Department of Mechanical Engineering, University of Sheffield, Mappin Street, Sheffield S1 3JD, UK
e-mail: c.a.lindley@sheffield.ac.uk; n.dervilis@sheffield.ac.uk; k.worden@sheffield.ac.uk

Brian Damiano et al. (eds.), *Structural Health Monitoring & Machine Learning, Vol. 12*, Conference Proceedings of the Society for Experimental Mechanics Series, https://doi.org/10.13052/9788743801573-12

yields values closely approximating their corresponding targets. In other words, to develop a function f that can accurately map a D-dimensional input vector $\mathbf{x}_n \in \mathbb{R}^D$, to a target output scalar $y_n \in \mathbb{R}$, i.e. a predictor $f : \mathbf{x} \to y$. The fit on y can be thought of as an interpolation given by f.

In a statistical sense, the predictor is a function learnt from the data, albeit conditioned on certain assumptions. For example, a linear interpolant may be assumed to fit the data, which will likely result in a poor fit if the true underlying trend is strongly nonlinear. An improved fit can be achieved by increasing the order of the function; that is, a quadratic function will likely provide a better fit than the linear trend, a cubic will be better than the quadratic, and so on. At each step, the fit improves while the function becomes increasingly complex, requiring the addition of more parameters to account for the higher-order terms in the polynomial. Continuing with the inclusion of terms, however, can lead to the point where the function is said to have become too complex, and the model begins to (over)fit noise in the data. Somewhere in this process of adding terms to the predictor, an optimal amount of complexity is attained, whereby the complexity of the data is matched.

Whether the learning problem is of regression or classification, finding some optimal predictor is typically approached by minimising a measure of discrepancy (or *loss*) between the true target values and the corresponding outputs of the predictor. To illustrate, let $\mathrm{z} = (\mathrm{x}, y)$ denote an input-output pair in the training set, and $Q(\mathrm{z}, \theta)$, $\theta \in \Theta$ be the set of loss functions. When given a set of n i.i.d. samples $\mathrm{z}_1, \ldots, \mathrm{z}_n$, the goal of predictive learning is to find a function $Q(\mathrm{z}, \theta^*)$ that minimises the *expected risk*,

$$R(\theta) = \int Q(\mathrm{z}, \theta) p(\mathrm{z}) \mathrm{d}\mathrm{z} \tag{1}$$

where $Q(\mathrm{z}, \theta) = L(\mathrm{y}, f(\mathrm{x}, \theta))$ is some *loss function*, and the integral is evaluated with respect to some (unknown) joint probability distribution $p(\mathrm{z})$. One should note that the set Θ to which θ belongs can be a set of scalar quantities, vectors, or of abstract elements [5]; that is, the function space is not limited to parametric models.

The current framework assumes that the joint distribution is true but unknown, and that the only information that is made available is samples drawn from $p(\mathrm{z})$. In order to minimise the risk functional $R(\theta)$, the following inductive principle is considered,

$$R_{emp}(\theta) = \frac{1}{n} \sum_{i=1}^{n} Q(\mathrm{z_i}, \theta) \tag{2}$$

where $R_{emp}(\theta)$ is referred to as the *empirical risk*, which is evaluated with a finite sample of size n. Given that the empirical risk does not require knowing the underlying generative distribution, the idea is to seek for an estimate providing the minimum empirical risk (2), in hopes that such estimate will also minimise the true risk (1). This approach is called the *Empirical Risk Minimisation inductive principle* (ERM principle) [4].

While minimising the empirical risk (2) promotes learning, a compromise must still be maintained by having a small enough risk without producing an overly complex model. This trade-off is crucial to ensuring good generalisation. A possible solution to this issue is to estimate the expected risk as a function of the empirical risk, penalised by some measure of model complexity [6]; that is,

$$R(\theta) \cong r\left(\frac{h}{n}\right) R_{emp} \tag{3}$$

where the empirical risk is adjusted by a monotonically-increasing function r, defined by the ratio of some *capacity measure* h, over the sample size n [7].

It turns out that the criteria for defining the penalisation function arises naturally in SLT. The foundation of such a criteria derives from demonstrating, in a rigorous mathematical framework, that minimising the empirical risk (2) can in fact yield a small value of the actual risk (1). In short, if one can show that the empirical risk *converges uniformly* to the true expected risk, then one can be (almost) certain that the ERM principle leads to generalised models. This condition is presented in more detail by the following definition:

Definition 1 (Key Theorem of Learning Theory [4]). *For a finite set of bounded loss functions, the ERM inductive principle is consistent if, and only if, the empirical risk converges uniformly to the true risk,*

$$\lim_{n \to \infty} P\left\{ \sup_{\theta \in \Theta} |R(\theta) - R_{emp}(\theta)| > \epsilon \right\} = 0, \quad \forall \epsilon > 0 \tag{4}$$

In the light of this theorem, a bound can be determined on the expected risk, whereby the penalised function is defined. In particular, for regression problems, the implementation of the ERM inductive principle defines the generalisation ability of a learning machine as demonstrated by the following result:

Theorem 1. (Vapnik-Chervonenkis [5]) *For any $\delta \in (0, 1)$, with probability at least $(1 - \delta)$ and $\forall \theta \in \Theta$,*

$$R(\theta) \leq \frac{R_{emp}(\theta)}{(1 - c\sqrt{\eta})_+} \tag{5}$$

where

$$\eta = \eta\left(\frac{n}{h}, \frac{-\ln \delta}{n}\right) = a_1 \frac{h[\ln(a_2 n/h) + 1] - \ln(\delta/4)}{n} \tag{6}$$

when the set of loss functions $Q(z, \theta), \theta \in \Theta$ is nonnegative, unbounded and contains an infinite number of elements. The measure h quantifies the capacity of the function class, and the constants a_1, a_2 and c are adjusted to suit the type of learning problem.

Deriving this bound is, indeed, an involved process, and the final result is presented here without proof. However, a full derivation can be found in [5]. In the interest of the current work, this bound forms the basis for the development of the model-selection strategy followed in the case study below.

Before delving into the uses of the presented theory in SHM, an additional inductive principle must be reviewed. This principle corresponds to the *Structural Risk Minimisation* also formalised by Vapnik and Chervonenkis [4]. It is shown next how SRM sets the stage for a systematic model-selection criteria. Additionally, the concept of complexity is further clarified.

Managing Complexity and Minimisation of Structural Risk

So far, complexity has been implicitly defined by an increasing addition of terms - and thus parameters - in the predictor. At first, this definition seems to make sense, but the definition of complexity in SLT is more elaborate than merely taking the count of parameters in the model. In (5), the *capacity* measure aims to rigorously quantify such complexity. Specifically, h corresponds to a specific type of capacity measure known as the *VC dimension* [4] (abbreviation for Vapnik and Chervonenkis dimension). The VC dimension is formally defined as follows.

Definition 2 (VC dimension [4]). *Let $S_\Theta(n)$ be the number of ways into which a sample of size n can be classified by the function class Θ. Therefore, the VC dimension of a function class Θ is the largest sample size n such that the condition*

$$S_\Theta(n) = 2^n \tag{7}$$

is valid.

In other words, the VC dimension h, corresponds to the size of the largest sample that a given set of indicator functions can *shatter*[1]. If the set of functions under consideration can generate any classification on the sample, regardless of n, then the corresponding VC dimension is infinite. Having an infinite VC dimension translates into having a learner capable of fitting any collection of observations, and thus no valid generalisation is possible; that is, a function in the space exists such that any set of data can be explained, or equivalently, *overfitted*.

Many important generalisation bounds in SLT make use of the VC dimension, included the one presented in Theorem 1. Estimating the VC dimension for different sets of function is, therefore, an essential step in the implementation of error bounds in SLT. However, analytic estimates are often only be determined for simple sets of functions. For example, a set of parametric linear estimators has a fixed complexity (VC dimension) that is equal to the number of free parameters. It is important to note that this is a coincidence and that the estimation of the VC dimension is not always this straightforward.

Once the complexity is defined for given set of functions, estimates of the expected risk no longer depend on the underlying distribution from which the sample is assumed to have been drawn. This implication is advantageous since the problem of density estimation is ill-posed when no prior knowledge of the probability distribution is available [5].

Now, recalling the general problem of model selection, one can leverage on the complexity of the function space to choose an optimal solution for a finite sample. This premise is the basis of the SRM inductive principle for minimisation of the expected risk. Essentially, SRM operates by establishing a structure on some set S of loss functions $Q(\mathbf{z}, \theta)$, $\theta \in \Theta$, consisting of nested subsets (or elements) $S_k = \{Q(\mathbf{z}, \theta), \theta \in \Omega_k\}$ such that,

$$S_1 \subset S_2 \subset \cdots \subset S_k \subset \ldots \tag{8}$$

[1] A function space is said to shatter the observations when a sample of size n exists on which all possible dichotomies can be achieved by the set of indicator functions.

where each element in the structure has a finite VC dimension h_k, and can be ordered according to their respective complexities,

$$h_1 \leq h_2 \leq \cdots \leq h_k \leq \ldots \tag{9}$$

Having defined the structure S, the optimal model selection boils down to two steps:

1. Selecting an element S_k from the structure.
2. Estimating the model from this element.

For each element in the structure (step (1)), the bound (5) is evaluated after estimating the optimal parameters in the element that minimise the empirical risk (step (2)). The penalisation during the learning process is thus established by the denominator in (5), which is computed with respect to the VC dimension h_k corresponding to the element S_k. Therefore, as elements of higher complexity are selected, the empirical risk will likely diminish, but at expense of a higher penalisation as a result of bringing the denominator closer to zero. An optimal element in the structure will be that providing the minimal "guaranteed" risk.

Case Study: Model Selection for Modelling a Sdof Impulse Response

The response of a *Single-Degree-of-Freedom* (SDOF) mass-damper-spring system (Fig. 1) is considered in this simple case study. Here, the dynamical model can be defined by the following equation of motion,

$$m\ddot{x}(t) + c\dot{x}(t) + kx(t) = F(t) \tag{10}$$

where m, c and k are the dynamic coefficients corresponding to the mass, damping and stiffness of the system, $x(t)$ is the response at a given time instance t, and $F(t)$ is the input force. The dots over the variables in equation (10) denote the derivatives of the variable with respect to time. An impulse response, $h(t)$, was simulated here by solving equation (10) for a given selection of coefficients. In particular, the mass, damping and stiffness coefficients were given values of $m = 1$, $c = 20$, and $k = 1 \times 10^6$, respectively.

Using the simulated target function, training samples were generated by the following,

$$\mathbf{y}(t) = \mathbf{h}(t) + \epsilon \tag{11}$$

where ϵ corresponds to additive noise term, which follows a normal distribution $\epsilon \sim \mathcal{N}(0, \sigma^2)$. The noise is defined by a signal-to-noise ratio (SNR) equal to ten. Four training sample sets of varying sizes were created by selecting points at intervals of 16, 12, and 4, whereby the input-training samples t are uniform in $[0, 0.3]$. Therefore, each training set ended up with sample sizes of $n = 63$, $n = 126$ and $n = 251$, respectively.

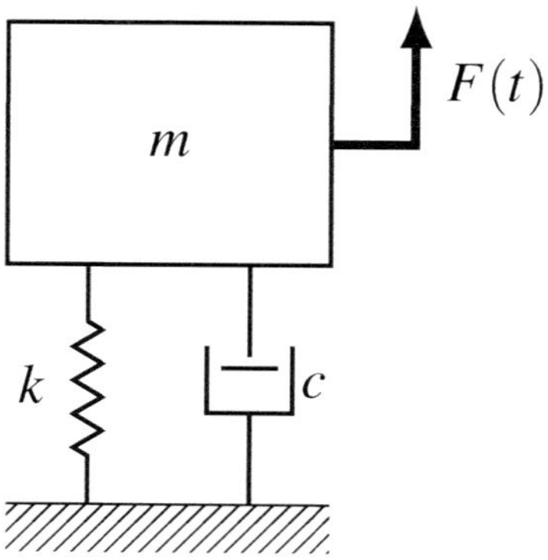

Fig. 1 Mass-spring-damper SDOF system

Predictors for the Regression Problem

In this study, the regression problem is defined by following the kernel smoother representation,

$$f(t_*) = \mathbf{k}(t_*)^T(\mathbf{K} + \sigma_n^2\mathbf{I})^{-1}\mathbf{y} \tag{12}$$

where $\mathbf{k}(t) \in \mathbb{R}^N$ is a vector with elements $k_n = k(t_n, t)$, defined by the *kernel function* $k(\cdot, \cdot)$, and evaluated for a new input t_* with respect to all inputs in the training set. $\mathbf{K} \in \mathbb{R}^{N\times N}$ is the *Gram matrix* with elements $K_{nm} = k(t_n, t_m)$, $\mathbf{I} \in \mathbb{R}^{N\times N}$ is the identity matrix and $\sigma_n^2 \geq 0$.

The ability of the learner to predict the correct output relies mostly on the choice of kernel function. In here, two different kernel functions are compared in the approximation of $\mathbf{h}(\mathbf{t})$. The first of these is the *squared exponential* [8] (SE), which has the form,

$$k_{se}(t, t') = \sigma_{f_{se}}^2 \exp\left(-\frac{||t-t'||}{2l^2}\right) \tag{13}$$

where $\sigma_{f_{se}}$ and l are the adjustable (hyper) parameters that control the characteristic form of the function. The second kernel function corresponds to that derived by Cross in [9], whereby the physics of a linear SDOF system are embedded in the definition of the kernel function.

Definition 3 (SDOF kernel function [9]). *For a single degree-of-freedom linear oscillator with mass m, damping c and stiffness k, the SDOF kernel function is defined as,*

$$k_{sdof}(t, t') = \frac{\sigma_{f_{sdof}}^2}{4m^2\zeta\omega_n^3}\exp(-\zeta\omega_n|t-t'|)\left[\cos(\omega_d|t-t'|) + \frac{\zeta\omega_n}{\omega_d}\sin(\omega_d|t-t'|)\right] \tag{14}$$

where the natural frequency $\omega_n = \sqrt{k/m}$, the damping ratio $\zeta = c/2\sqrt{km}$, and the damped natural frequency $\omega_d = \omega_n\sqrt{1-\zeta^2}$.

Unlike the SE kernel, one may note that the SDOF kernel is defined by parameters that are readily interpretable. In [9], it is shown that the SDOF kernel is better suited at predicting the response of the mass-damper-spring system to a random excitation. More interestingly, however, is its ability to allow the approximating function to extrapolate beyond the limits of the training set. This outcome is a consequence of embedding the relevant physics in the kernel function, and an aspect that models based solely on data lack, such as those in which the SE kernel is employed. Having a model that can extrapolate means better generalisation. One should note that this claim only holds true for this particular scenario. Should the model present nonlinearities, for example, then it may then be unreasonable to expect good accuracy from using the SDOF kernel. Nonetheless, the aim pursued here is to formalise generalisation when employing these kernel functions from the viewpoint of SLT.

Model Selection Strategy

For the model selection process, the SRM induction principle was employed. This approach required the estimation of the upper bound (5), which in turn required the estimation of the VC dimension corresponding to each set of kernel smoothers. Unlike the case of using the parametric representation of (12), the VC dimension of kernel smoothers cannot be determined easily. Some progress can be achieved when translating the kernel representation into an *equivalent basis function expansion* [6], which is done by taking the eigendecomposition $\mathbf{K} = \sum_{i=1}^{n} \lambda_i \mathbf{u}_i \mathbf{u}_i^T$, where λ_i is the ith eigenvalue and $\mathbf{u}_i$ is the corresponding eigenvector. Having the eigenvectors, the number of free parameters - or degrees of freedom - of a kernel can be defined as [10],

$$df = \sum_{i=1}^{n} \frac{\lambda_i}{\lambda_i + \sigma_n^2} \tag{15}$$

and then taken as an estimate of the corresponding VC dimension. This definition roughly counts the number of prevalent eigenvalues, and therefore, if $\sum_{i=1}^{n} \lambda_i/(\lambda_i + \sigma_n^2) << 1$, then the contribution of the components in $\mathbf{y}$ along $\mathbf{u}_i$ are effectively eliminated [8].

As in [6], the general expression for the upper bound (5) can be reduced to,

$$R(\theta) \leq \frac{1}{n}\sum_{i=1}^{n}(y_i - f(\mathrm{x}_i, \theta))^2 \left(1 - \sqrt{p - p\ln p + \frac{\ln n}{2n}}\right)_+^{-1} \tag{16}$$

where the empirical risk is defined by the *mean-squared-error* (MSE) and $p = h/n$. In this expression, the penalisation term is given by setting the constants $c = 1$, $a_1 = 1$, $a_2 = 1$ and $\delta = 4/\sqrt{n}$.

Now, given a kernel function, the model-selection structure can be defined in terms of the smoothing parameters θ. For example, the length-scale parameter in (13) is known to strongly influence the rate at which the smoother varies, assuming the remaining parameters remain constant. A reduction in the length-scale produces functions that appear much more wiggly [8], leading to a slower decay in the corresponding eigenvalues [10] (when sorted in descending order). Consequently, equation (15) would yield a higher estimate of the degrees of freedom, and thus, a higher estimate of the complexity (i.e. VC dimension). Some structure could then be defined on the set of SE kernel smoothers as,

$$S_k = \{f(k_{se}(t, t'; l), \sigma_n), l \geq c_k\}, \quad \text{where } c_1 > c_2 > \dots \tag{17}$$

Each element in the structure is a subset of the next because the length-scale can take smaller values, thereby allowing for smoothers of higher complexity. Finally, the structure can be easily extended to include the effects of the remainder parameters on the complexity of the smoother.

This approach adheres to the SRM inductive principle in the sense that step (1) involves the selection of an element in (17) (i.e. complexity estimation), followed by step (2) on determining the optimal parameters $\theta*$ that minimise the upper bound on the expected risk (16). However, it should be noted that a structure can only be defined for one type of kernel function at a time. Two distinct structures were thus constructed. For each training set size, the fitting experiment was repeated 100 times for a given realisation of the training set (11). At each iteration, the set θ corresponding to each kernel function was found by employing an exhaustive search over a range of values. In the case of the SE kernel, a set of possible values was defined for increasing values of the signal variance $\sigma_{f_{se}}$, and decreasing values of the length-scale l. As for the SDOF kernel, the set of possible values was only defined for the signal variance $\sigma_{f_{sdof}}$, under the assumption that the remaining parameters could be computed analytically from knowing the dynamic coefficients in advance. The noise parameter σ_n was assumed to be known in all cases. The model-comparison strategy finally amounted to choosing the best model from the structure providing the minimum guaranteed risk (16).

Results and Discussion

The results of the regression experiment are shown in Fig. 2. More specifically, for each sample size, the boxplots display the estimated upper bound on the expected risk, and the MSE between the true function and kernel-smoother predictions. Regardless of the sample size, the results show that expected risk was lower in all cases when choosing the SDOF kernel.

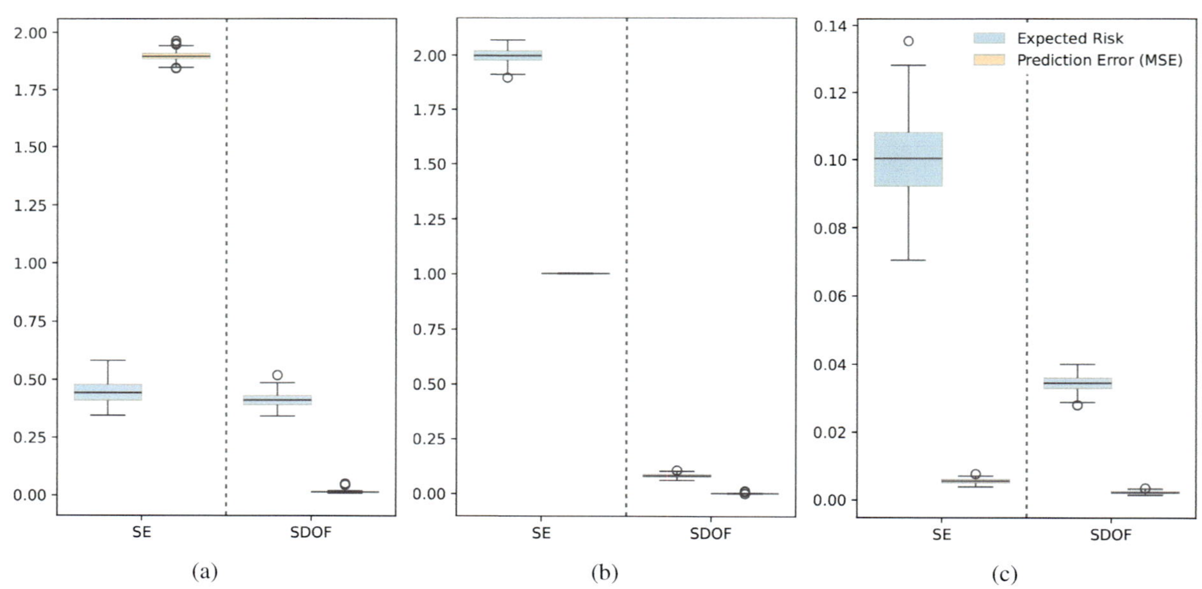

Fig. 2 Expected risk and predition error (MSE) computed for the SE and SDOF kernel function, with training sets of sizes (a) $n = 63$, (b) $n = 126$, and (c) $n = 251$

The SRM inductive principle seems to indicate a preference for the SDOF model even when a handful of samples are available. However, one can note that such a conclusion is not so obvious when looking closer at the estimations obtained for the sample size $n = 63$. In fact, the MSE is much higher than the estimated upper bound, which appears to contradict Theorem 1. Upon closer inspection, a simple explanation to this outcome is explained by having established these bounds to hold with probability of at least $1 - \delta$, where $\delta = 4/\sqrt{n}$. When having a small sample size, such as $n = 63$, the resulting bounds hold with probability of at least 0.49, and likely to yield bounds that may be too "optimistic". In the case of having $n = 126$ and $n = 251$ as in the other two cases, the bounds hold with (higher) probabilities of at least 0.64 and 0.75, respectively. The intuition behind this trend is clear; that is, one can be more confident of the estimates of the risk when the sample size increases. If required, a low value of δ could be enforced to ensure the bounds hold with high probability. While bounds can be made more "pessimistic", these could become too loose to provide any meaningful interpretation. Therefore, determining $\delta(n)$ as a function of the available number of samples is recommended [6, 5].

The kernel-smoother predictions of the true function can be visualised in Fig. 3. Each figure corresponds to the different training sets used in the model selection process, showing the true signal, predictions from employing each kernel function,

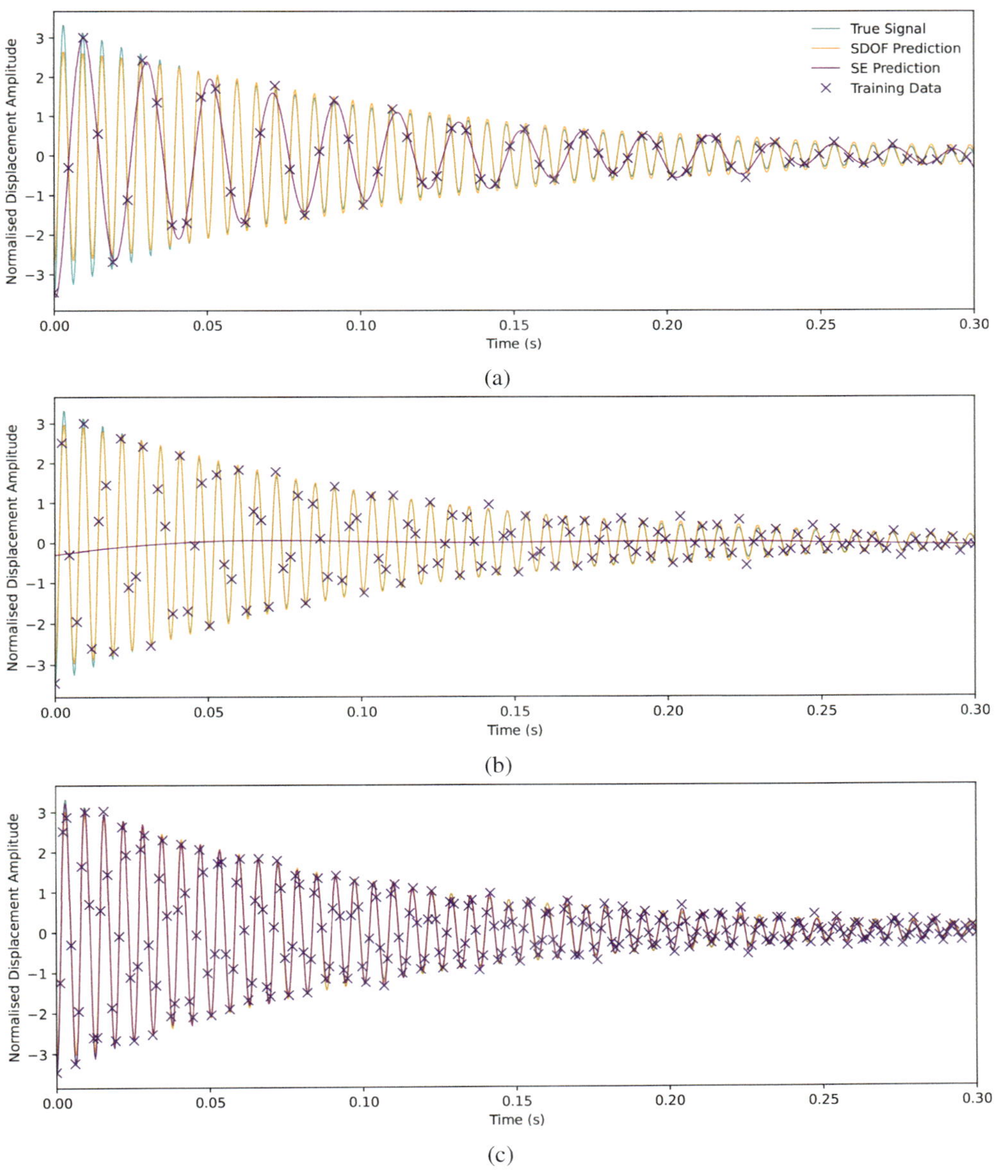

Fig. 3 SE and SDOF kernel-smoother predictions inferred with training sets of sizes (a) $n = 63$, (b) $n = 126$, and (c) $n = 251$. The true underlying signal was included for comparison

and the training data realisation from an arbitrary iteration. As evidenced by the results in Fig. 2, the SDOF kernel smoother tends to generalise better, even when the sample size is small. It is not until $n = 251$ that the SE kernel smoother learns the true underlying function from the data. The increased sample size appears to have relaxed the penalisation term enough to permit higher complexities.

Perhaps of more interest is how the increase in sample size seemed to not only minimise the expected risk, but also bring their estimates closer to the same value regardless of the kernel function used. If enough data samples are thus available, then one may argue the necessity for developing informed kernels (or any approximating function for that matter) to be a superfluous exercise. There are several reason why this claim may not be entirely true. While tighter bounds are, indeed, possible with large datasets, it may not be computationally efficient to have large training sets. Therefore, a model that can represent the system as well as another that requires significantly more data to train should be favoured in the model selection process. Additionally, the availability of labelled data can be very limited in certain applications. For example, in SHM, it is more often the case than not that labelled data are expensive to gather, and the efficacy of statistical models is likely to rely on a reduced dataset. SLT embodies the notion that a lack of data should be compensated with knowledge for better inference, and the results shown here are but a simple demonstration of this notion in SHM.

One final highlight that might be worthy of discussion is on the flexible nature exhibited by the SE-kernel function. Visually, as shown in Fig. 3, the SE smoothing functions displayed varied complexities in all three cases. The rate at which these predictors vary appear to somewhat agree with the respective VC dimensions shown in Fig. 4. These estimates are the optimal complexities provided by the SRM inductive principle. As noted earlier, the complexity of the SE kernel smoother for $n = 63$ was relatively high because of having too optimistic a bound. For the other two cases, however, the models guaranteed better generalisation, even if it may not seem like it (visually) in Fig. 3b. Computing the empirical risk alone for $n = 126$ would have caused the SE-kernel smoother to overfit the data. In such cases the bound exploded to infinity because of the relatively high ratio of complexity to sample size. Conversely, the high VC dimension displayed in Fig. 4 for $n = 251$ was only possible because of having enough sample points to justify such increase in complexity. Unlike the SE kernel function, one may note that the VC dimension estimated from using the SDOF kernel function remained somewhat consistent for all sample sizes.

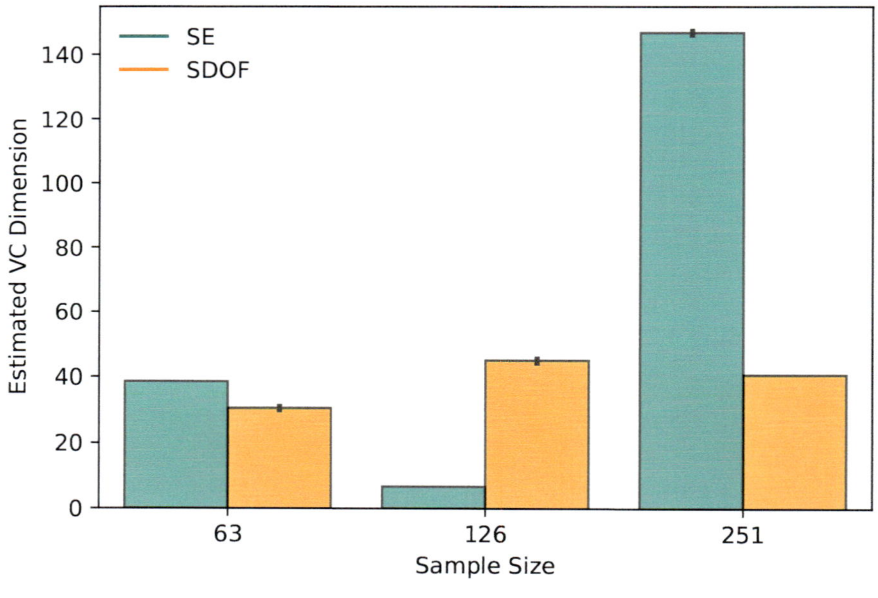

Fig. 4 Estimated complexities corresponding to the SE and SDOF kernel with training sets of sizes (a) $n = 63$, (b) $n = 126$, and (c) $n = 251$

Conclusion

In the present work, the generalisation of kernel smoothers was defined from the viewpoint of SLT. In particular, the model-selection process was simulated in the context of a simple linear oscillator subjected to an impulse response. By employing the SRM inductive principle, the model-selection process involved the elicitation of a kernel smoother that could generalise best when given a reduced dataset. The two kernel functions considered in the experiment differ in their means to characterise neighboring similarities in the data; namely, the SE kernel was compared against the SDOF kernel, with the latter deriving from embedding the physics of the system under consideration. Even though the SDOF kernel function was expected to be a much more suitable model for this application, a mathematical framework to justify the choice of an informed kernel had not been established in this context. The bounds found in SLT offer the possibility to pursue a rigorous and systematic approach to justify the use of an informed kernel over another that is solely driven by data.

However, there are several shortcomings that require further attention to formally validate the results presented in this paper. The first and foremost, is that it is not clear how accurate the number of degrees of freedom of a kernel smoother estimates the VC dimension. Estimating the complexity for nonparametric sets of functions is a subject of ongoing research. The second issue relates to the structure design in the model-selection process. In the study above, to distinct structures were developed, followed by the selection of the minimal risk given by the optimal elements of each. This criterion was based on the idea that each structure may correspond to separate subsections in a vast space of all possible approximating functions. The subsection relating to the SDOF kernel was expected to enclose the true function, and therefore, the true guaranteed risk. Meanwhile, the subsection spanned by the SE kernel function required the extension to parent elements in the structure to approximate closer to the true function. Consequently, the SRM inductive principle accounted for two risk minima corresponding to each structure. Favouring the lowest of the two was then the natural step in selecting the optimal model. The issue here is that the validity of this hypothesis is not one formally addressed in SLT. It may be necessary to refer to the methods found in *decision theory* for this matter. Finally, the last shortcoming that should be acknowledge is on the fact that the dynamic coefficients were provided in the SDOF kernel function. If these coefficients were to be unknown, then their inclusion in the structural minimisation process would be necessary. This issue and the aforementioned ones are certainly worthy of further research, and will be addressed in future work.

Acknowledgments The authors of this paper gratefully acknowledge the support of the UK Alan Turing Institute via funding of the Turing Research and Innovation Cluster on Digital Twins. For the purpose of open access, the authors has applied a Creative Commons Attribution (CC BY) licence to any Author Accepted Manuscript version arising.

References

1. Farrar, C. and Worden, K. *Structural Health Monitoring : a Machine Learning Perspective*. Wiley (2013).
2. Rytter, A. *Vibrational Based Inspection of Civil Engineering Structures*. PhD thesis, Aalborg University (1993).
3. Bishop, C. *Pattern Recognition and Machine Learning*. Information Science and Statistics. Springer (2006).
4. Vapnik, V. *The Nature of Statistical Learning Theory*. Information Science and Statistics. Springer New York (1999).
5. Vapnik, V. and Kotz, S. *Estimation of Dependences Based on Empirical Data*. Information Science and Statistics. Springer New York (2006).
6. Cherkassky, V. and Mulier, F. *Learning from Data: Concepts, Theory, and Methods*. IEEE Press. Wiley (2007).
7. Hardle, W., Hall, P., and Marron, J. "How far are automatically chosen regression smoothing parameters from their optimum?". *Journal of the American Statistical Association*, 83(401):86–95 (1988).
8. Rasmussen, C. and Williams, C. *Gaussian Processes for Machine Learning*. The MIT Press (2005).
9. Cross, E. and Rogers, T. "Physics derived covariance functions for machine learning in structural dynamics". *IFAC*, 54(7):168–173 (2021). 19th IFAC Symposium on System Identification SYSID 2021.
10. Hastie, T. and Tibshirani, R. *Generalized Additive Models*. Chapman & Hall/CRC Monographs on Statistics & Applied Probability. Taylor & Francis (1990).

Chapter 13
Full-field Measurements for Anomaly Detection of Mechanical Systems using Convolutional Neural Networks and LSTM Networks

Carlos Quiterio Gómez Muñoz, Mariano Alberto García Vellisca, Celso T. do Cabo, Yujie Xi, and Zhu Mao

Abstract Structural health monitoring (SHM) of mechanical systems is of great importance for a variety of industries, and an early detection and localization of damage in such situations are often desired. One of the features that can be used for SHM is its dynamic characteristics, which are traditionally obtained by using contact and sparse sensing. In nowadays, technologies that can collect full-field information and perform noncontact sensing have become more advantageous. Among such equipment, laser Doppler vibrometers (LDV) can provide high-quality vibrational data with full-field information. However, damage detection based on vibrational data can also be difficult in complex systems. With the recent advancement of computational power, data-driven approaches have become increasingly popular for complex systems. One of the most known approaches is the convolutional neural network (CNN), which has great capabilities for image processing and classification. Since the LDV measurements can provide full-field information, these data can be converted into 2D matrices and employed in CNN as images. However, CNNs commonly do not keep any temporal dependency between the frames, making it difficult to be employed in vibration analysis where data are all time series. This work proposes combining CNNs with long short-term memory (LSTM) networks, to process video data instead of frames, allowing time-dependent image processing for damage detection. In addition, the results are expected to predict not only if there is damage to the system, but also to classify different types of damage.

Keywords Machine Learning · Convolutional Neural Network · Long Short-Term Memory · Laser Doppler Vibrometer

Introduction

The classification of normal and abnormal vibrations in structure has gained substantial attention due to its implications in Structural Health Monitoring (SHM) and fault detection. Vibrational analysis is critical for identifying potential issues in industrial machinery, infrastructures, and mechanical systems [1–3]. By detecting anomalies early, it is possible to prevent costly repairs and ensure the safety of operations. With the increase interest in machine learning techniques, many studies have been performed in the field of structural vibration for anomaly detection [4, 5]. Specifically, Convolutional Neural Networks (CNNs) have great capabilities for image processing and classification, been employed previously to dynamic systems [6–8]. However, CNN architectures only capture the dependance between pixels in an image. For time-series datasets representing the time dependency of the signal is challenging, leading to the usage of Long Short-Term Memory (LSTM) networks. Such architectures can be combined with CNN to obtain time dependency between frames for video-based sensing [9, 10], or applied into Remaining Useful Life (RUL) applications [11].

This study focuses on analyzing vibrations of a metallic plate subjected to different frequency excitations in both linear and non-linear states. The linear state is characterized by the absence of external disruptions, where the plate vibrates freely. In contrast, the non-linear state introduces rubber bumpers placed at various positions on the plate, altering its vibrational

Carlos Quiterio Gómez Muñoz · Mariano Alberto García Vellisca
HCTLab Research Group, Universidad Autónoma de Madrid, Madrid, Spain
e-mail: carlosq.gomez@uam.es; marianoa.garcia@uam.es

Celso T. do Cabo · Yujie Xi · Zhu Mao
Department of Mechanical and Materials Engineering, Worcester Polytechnic Institute, Worcester, MA, United States
e-mail: ctdocabo@wpi.edu; yxi@wpi.edu; zmao2@wpi.edu

Brian Damiano et al. (eds.), *Structural Health Monitoring & Machine Learning, Vol. 12*, Conference Proceedings of the Society for Experimental Mechanics Series, https://doi.org/10.13052/9788743801573-13

behavior. These bumpers simulate damage or interference, generating abnormal vibration behavior, which can mimic real-world structural irregularities.

By utilizing machine learning techniques, particularly CNNs and LSTM networks, this research aims to distinguish between these vibrational states. The primary objective is to classify the plate's vibrations into their respective states (linear and non-linear) based on the frequency data collected, as well as to compare its efficiency when performing multiclass classification, by differentiating between different locations and number of bumpers in the structure.

The next sections of this papers present the background theory for the proposed approach, including an explanation on CNNs and LSTM networks, the experimental setup and preprocessing of the full-field measurements to obtain the dataset for the machine learning approach. Followed by the results and obtained for both simple nonlinearity detection and multiclass classification and a discussion of the results. Finally, a conclusion will be given with possible directions for future research.

Background

In recent years, machine learning, particularly deep learning techniques, has revolutionized various fields of data analysis and classification. One of the most critical applications is SHM, where machine learning models are employed to detect anomalies in vibrational patterns of structures. This growing field offers the potential to predict failures, optimize maintenance schedules, and improve the reliability of mechanical systems.

Machine learning, especially supervised learning, is widely used to classify vibration data. These models are trained on labeled datasets to predict the state of unseen vibrational data. Deep learning models like CNNs and LSTMs have been particularly effective in handling complex datasets. CNNs are suitable for analyzing time-frequency representations like spectrograms and scalograms, while LSTMs excel in processing temporal dependencies in time-series data.

CNNs process spatial data, making them ideal for analyzing the two-dimensional representations of vibrational signals. By using convolutional and pooling layers, CNNs capture essential patterns in frequency and time, classifying different vibrational states effectively.

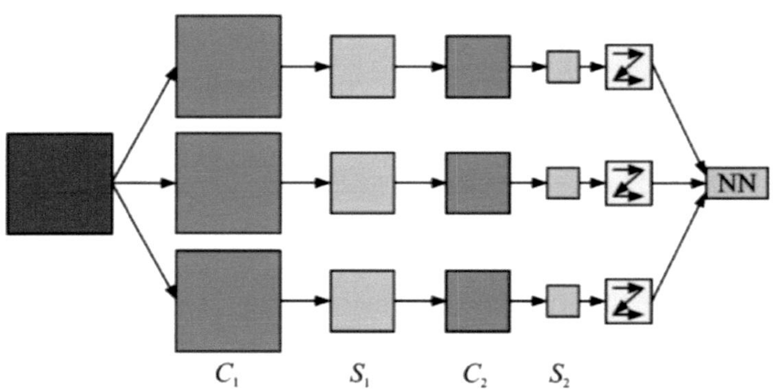

Fig. 1 Flowchart of CNN [12].

Convolution neural network is often designed to analyze two-dimensional data, and it has multi-layer inside the networks. CNNs uses convolution of kernels to learn pattern in 2D data. As shown in Figure 1, a simple convolution neural network structure has convolution layers (e.g. C1, C2) and sub-sampling layers (e.g. S1, S2). In this example, input image is convoluted by three convolution kernels, then three feature maps are generated in the C1 layer, for each feature map, their localized regions are weighted and averaged. Then three new feature maps are generated in S1 layer through nonlinear activation function. After S2, the feature maps will be flattened into a vector which will be used as input for a traditional neural networks (NN) for training [12].

While CNNs are capable of extracting spatial information. LSTMs are designed for sequential data, retaining relevant patterns over time through mechanisms called gates. This makes LSTMs ideal for detecting temporal anomalies in vibration sequences, which is essential in analyzing the vibrational behavior of the metallic plate. The overall layout of an LSTM layer can be seen in Figure 2.

The LSTM layer works by using cell states (C_t) which allows to retain or erase information from previous time-steps, depending on its relevance to predict future states. The states are calculated based on the previous state and with the current time-step information. The terms shown in Figure 2 are presented in Equations (1) to (6).

$$f_t = \sigma \left(W_f \cdot [h_{t-1}, x_t] + b_f \right) \tag{1}$$

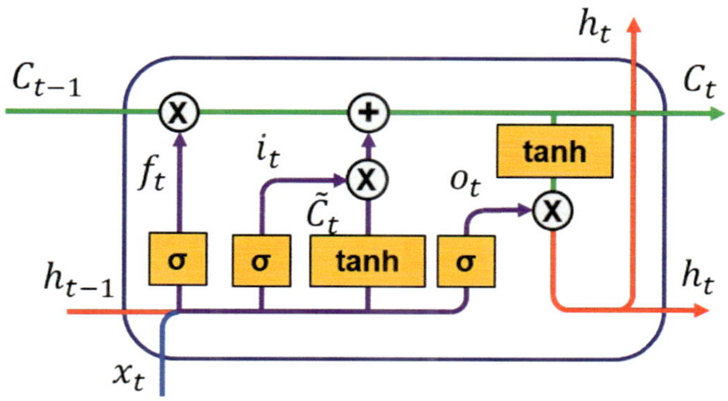

Fig. 2 Flowchart of LSTM cell [9].

$$i_t = \sigma\left(W_i \cdot [h_{t-1}, x_t] + b_i\right) \tag{2}$$

$$\tilde{C}_t = \tanh\left(W_C \cdot [h_{t-1}, x_t] + b_C\right) \tag{3}$$

$$C_t = f_t \odot C_{t-1} + i_t \odot \tilde{C}_t \tag{4}$$

$$o_t = \sigma\left(W_o \cdot [h_{t-1}, x_t] + b_o\right) \tag{5}$$

$$h_t = o_t \odot \tanh\left(C_t\right) \tag{6}$$

Where W represents the weights and b are the biases of the neural network. σ is the sigmoid function and $tahn$ is the hyperbolic tangent used as activation functions for the gates. Meanwhile, $[h_{t-1}, x_t]$ represents a concatenation between the previous time-step output and the current input data.

This work proposes a combination of CNN and LSTM layers in order to extract both spatial and temporal information from the system for abnormal behavior classification, by identifying if there is a nonlinearity in the system and a multiclass classification to predict different locations of nonlinearities.

Experimental Setup

This study examines the classification of normal and abnormal vibrations in a metallic plate subjected to controlled vibrational tests. Both linear (normal) and non-linear (abnormal) states were induced, with data collected at various excitation frequencies.

The testing subject for the experiment consists of a metallic plate, with 6 inches of width, 17 inches height and 0.05 inches thickness, and it was tested using a mechanical shaker. A Laser Doppler Vibrometer (LDV) was used to record the vibrational data for 133 points on the plate's surface. Two states were analyzed:

1. **Linear State**: The plate vibrated freely, representing normal conditions.
2. **Non-Linear State**: Rubber bumpers were placed behind the plate, simulating structural damage and altering the vibrational patterns.

Different frequencies were employed for excitation including 298 Hz, 548 Hz, 1704 Hz, 2118 Hz, 2435 Hz, 2792 Hz, 3907 Hz, 4960 Hz, and 5300 Hz were used to test the plate's response, chosen based on modal analysis. In the non-linear state, bumpers were placed as show Figure 3.

Vibrational signals were recorded at each frequency, capturing the plate's oscillations. The data collected from all 133 points was divided into training and testing subsets, with linear and non-linear data used to train the machine learning models, and testing data to evaluate their classification performance. One sample of the data can be seen in Figure 4.

To optimize the training of the neural network and improve the efficiency of the simulations, exhaustive data preparation was carried out, which included:

- **Capturing Plate Movement:** Each of the 133 mesh points represents the movement at that specific point on the plate. An interpolation of these points was performed to recreate the continuous movement of the plate.

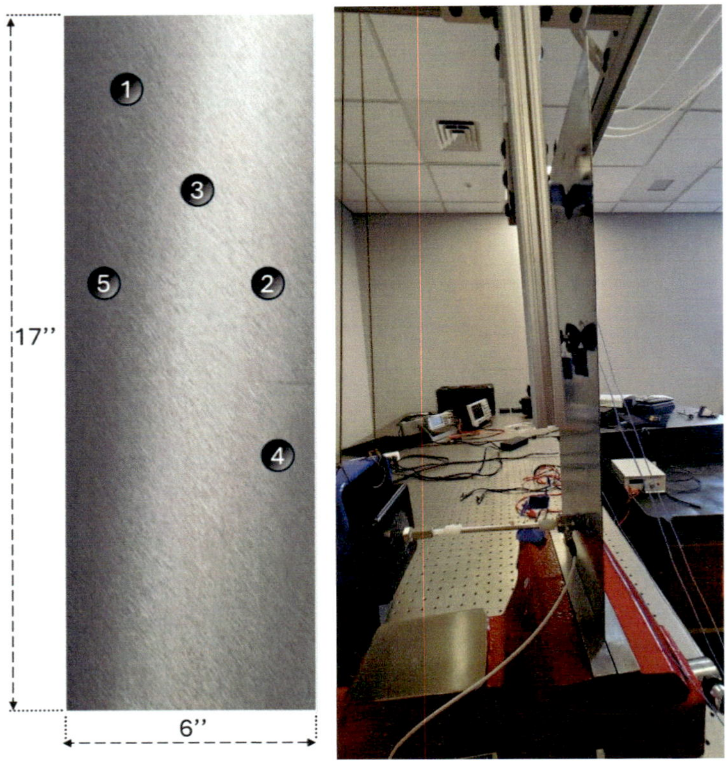

Fig. 3 Location of different bumpers on the plate to generate abnormal vibrations.

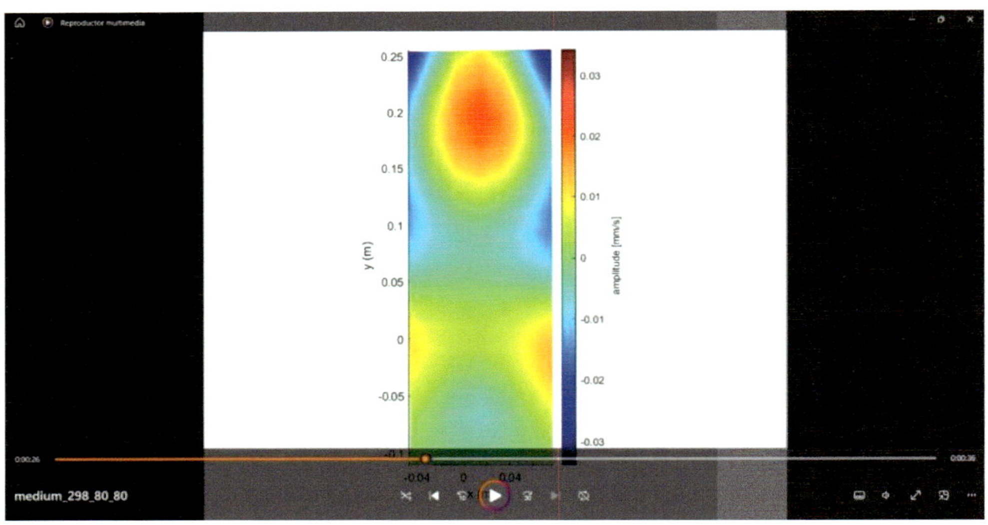

Fig. 4 Video image showing the movement of the place through pseud color representation.

- **Video Generation for Each Case:** Using the interpolated data, a video was generated for each case. This visual representation allowed for a clearer understanding of the plate's dynamics under different conditions.
- **Trimming video duration to 20 seconds**: It was determined that beyond this time, the videos did not provide additional relevant information. By removing segments that did not contribute significantly, processing was streamlined, and unnecessary computational resource consumption was avoided.
- **Balancing the number of videos per frequency and class**: The dataset was unified to have a homogeneous distribution, obtaining one video per frequency for each class (bumper). This allowed for better generalization during training and avoided biases towards classes with more data.

- **Generating copies of the videos**: Each original video was augmented with seven additional copies using data augmentation techniques, increasing the dataset to a total of **560 videos**. This helped improve the neural network's robustness against variations and prevent overfitting.
- **Incorporating and unifying classes**: New classes corresponding to different bumpers were added. After detailed analysis, it was decided to unify some classes to improve representation in the dataset.

The classes assigned to the bumpers were: **Bumper 1, Bumpers 1 and 2, Bumper 3, Bumper 4, Bumper 5 and Linear (no bumpers).**

In addition, the hyperparameters selected for the neural network are presented in Table 1.

Table 1 Hyperparameters of the proposed approach.

Hyperparameter	Value
Batch size	8
Learning rate	10^{-5}
Train/Test split	90% and 10%
Dropout	20%
# of LSTM neurons	2,000

Analysis and Results

The results presented in this section are divided into different cases, starting with Case 1, where the proposed method will do a simple classification of linear and nonlinear behavior. Case 2 will later present the results for the multiclass classification, with the linear response, and 5 different setups with bumpers as shown in Figure 3.

Case 1. Training with Linear and Non-Linear classes.
As a first step, a binary simulation was performed with only two classes: **Linear** and **Non-Linear** (which groups all bumpers). The accuracy was 97.14%.

Case 2. Training with Bumper Classes
Trainings were carried out using the classes corresponding to the different bumpers and with all the frequencies. The accuracy was 94.28%

The results indicate that:

- **Effectiveness of Preprocessing**: The reduction and balancing of the dataset, along with video preprocessing, contributed to improving the efficiency and precision of the simulations. Removing irrelevant segments allowed the network to focus on the most significant information.

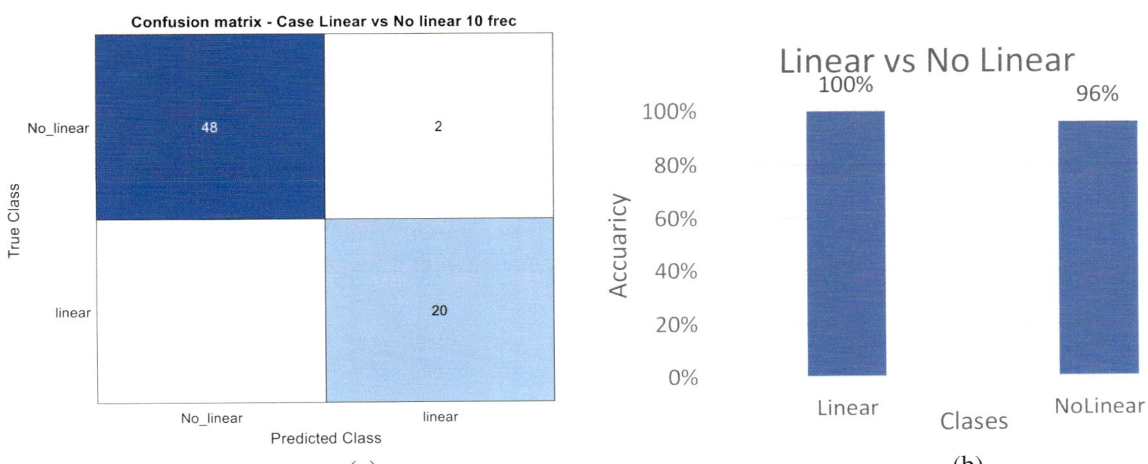

(a) (b)

Fig. 5 Confusion matrix of linear and nonlinear cases (a) and accuracy of each class (b).

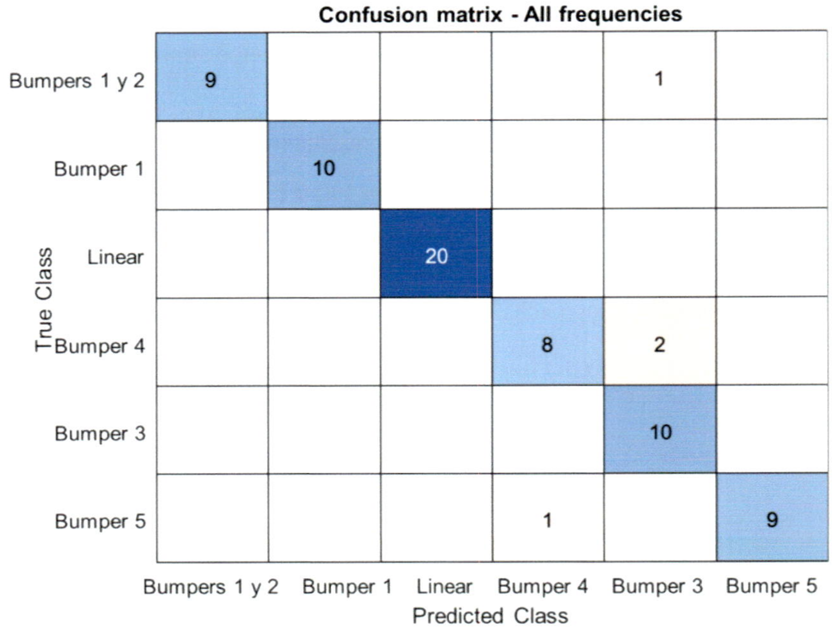

Fig. 6 Confusion matrix of the different bumpers located on the plate.

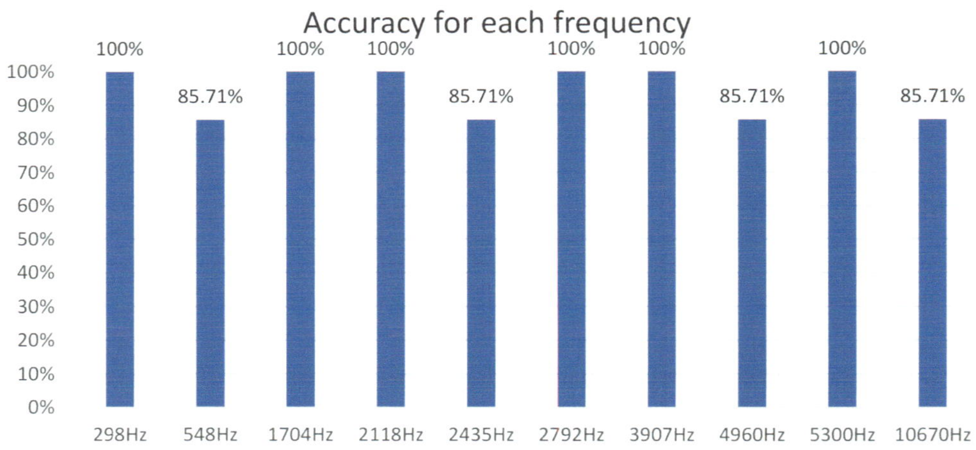

Fig. 7 Accuracy of the classification of all bumpers for each frequency.

- **Importance of Class Balancing**: By unifying the number of videos per class and frequency, bias towards classes with a larger amount of data was avoided, allowing better generalization of the model and a fairer evaluation of its performance.
- **Behavior by Classes (Bumpers)**: It was observed that certain classes presented more errors at specific frequencies. For example, the **Bumper 1** class showed more errors in the simulation with 8 frequencies, while **Bumpers 1 and 2** presented errors at specific frequencies in other simulations.

Conclusion

This study successfully demonstrated the use of LSTM networks for classifying normal and abnormal vibrational states in a metallic plate. By combining these models, it was possible to accurately detect linear and non-linear vibrational behaviors, critical for Structural Health Monitoring.

Key findings include:

1. **Effectiveness of Machine Learning Models**: LSTM networks proved to be highly effective, achieving excellent performance with a peak accuracy of 94.28% in the model. LSTMs excelled at capturing temporal dependencies in time-series data, making them particularly well-suited for tasks involving sequential patterns.
2. **Challenges in Complex Non-Linear States**: The models performed well overall but struggled with more complex non-linear states involving multiple bumpers, which introduced intricate vibrational patterns.
3. **Frequency-Based Performance Variations**: The ability to differentiate between linear and non-linear states depended on the frequency, with the models performing best at natural vibrational frequencies like 2118 Hz and 2792 Hz. However, accuracy declined at higher frequencies, particularly at 4960 Hz, where the distinction between the states became less clear.

The LSTM approach applied to videos generated with laser Doppler vibrometers showed great potential for real-time SHM applications, particularly in complex scenarios and high-frequency performance. This research contributes to the development of machine learning methods for real-time anomaly detection in structural systems.

Acknowledgments This work was supported by the GHAIA (Geometric and Harmonic Analysis with Interdisciplinary Applications) project, under the H2020-MSCA-RISE program of the European Commission. This project has received funding from the European Union's Horizon 2020 research and innovation program under the Marie Skłodowska-Curie grant agreement No 777822.

References

1. M. Arul and A. Kareem, "Data anomaly detection for structural health monitoring of bridges using shapelet transform," arXiv preprint arXiv:2009.00470, 2020.
2. N. D. Boffa, M. Arena, E. Monaco, M. Viscardi, F. Ricci, and T. Kundu, "About the combination of high and low frequency methods for impact detection on aerospace components," Progress in Aerospace Sciences, vol. 129, p. 100789, 2022.
3. D. Caballol, Á. P. Raposo, and F. Gil-Carrillo, "Non-destructive testing of concrete layer adhesion by means of vibration measurement," Construction and Building Materials, vol. 411, p. 134548, 2024.
4. N. M. Kalimullah, A. Shelke, and A. Habib, "A deep learning approach for anomaly identification in PZT sensors using point contact method," Smart Materials and Structures, vol. 32, no. 9, p. 095027, 2023.
5. X. Ye, P. Wu, A. Liu, X. Zhan, Z. Wang, and Y. Zhao, "A deep learning-based method for automatic abnormal data detection: Case study for bridge structural health monitoring," International Journal of Structural Stability and Dynamics, vol. 23, no. 11, p. 2350131, 2023.
6. C. T. do Cabo and Z. Mao, "An Optical Mode Shape-Based Damage Detection Using Convolutional Neural Networks," in Rotating Machinery, Optical Methods & Scanning LDV Methods, Volume 6: Springer, 2022, pp. 157–162.
7. Z. Tang, Z. Chen, Y. Bao, and H. Li, "Convolutional neural network-based data anomaly detection method using multiple information for structural health monitoring," Structural Control and Health Monitoring, vol. 26, no. 1, p. e2296, 2019.
8. S.-Y. Kim and M. Mukhiddinov, "Data Anomaly Detection for Structural Health Monitoring Based on a Convolutional Neural Network," Sensors, vol. 23, no. 20, p. 8525, 2023.
9. C. T. do Cabo and Z. Mao, "An Optical Temporal and Spatial Vibration-Based Damage Detection Using Convolutional Neural Networks and Long Short-Term Memory," in Rotating Machinery, Optical Methods & Scanning LDV Methods, Volume 6: Springer, 2022, pp. 159–165.
10. R. Yang et al., "CNN-LSTM deep learning architecture for computer vision-based modal frequency detection," Mechanical Systems and signal processing, vol. 144, p. 106885, 2020.
11. M. Ma and Z. Mao, "Deep-convolution-based LSTM network for remaining useful life prediction," IEEE Transactions on Industrial Informatics, vol. 17, no. 3, pp. 1658–1667, 2020.
12. A. A. M. Al-Saffar, H. Tao, and M. A. Talab, "Review of deep convolution neural network in image classification," in 2017 International conference on radar, antenna, microwave, electronics, and telecommunications (ICRAMET), 2017: IEEE, pp. 26–31.

Chapter 14
A Generative Modeling Approach for the Translation of Operational Variables to Short-term Vibrations

Arthur Hatstatt and Konstantinos E. Tatsis

Abstract The vibration response assessment of engineering systems using the statistical features of vibration signals is a masked problem, which is limited by the sampling resolution of these statistics. One of the problems falling in this category is the vibration response assessment of wind turbine systems using SCADA data. Despite the fact that the resolution of the latter can be improved by slightly increasing the sampling rate of SCADA systems, which can deliver up to 1-min statistics, a connection is missing between SCADA data and short-term vibrations. Within this context, this paper proposes the use of Gaussian Process Latent Force (GPLF) models in a generative sense for the conversion of one-minute SCADA data to short-term vibration data. To this end, GPLF models are used for the modeling of the generalized modal responses of wind turbines, which are obtained on the basis of sparse acceleration measurements. The parameters of the GPLF models are conditioned on the operational variables of the system, which are available from SCADA data, and the identified model is used to generate short-term vibration signals with the aim of preserving their spectral and statistical properties. The proposed method is tested on a simulated case study and the performance is assessed in terms of the agreement between the generated time series and the ones measured from the simulated model.

Keywords Time series modeling · Gaussian process regression · Structural health monitoring · Latent force model · Generative modeling

Introduction

Vibration based methods are one of the most effective monitoring techniques to assess the structural integrity of engineering systems. Traditionally, vibration-based monitoring methods have relied on installing vibration sensors on critical components in order to capture high-resolution data that allows engineers to evaluate the dynamic behavior of the system under various conditions, offering insights into potential failures or anomalies in the operation. Among others, these methods allow to effectively capture damage accumulation and predict the remaining useful life of systems subjected to cyclic loading. However, there are oftentimes practical limitations to widespread adoption of vibration sensors in certain engineering systems due to installation and maintenance of sensors, which may increase costs and operational downtime. Within this context, various alternatives have been examined in the literature in order to leverage the availability of data from existing systems.

The state-of-the-art Structural Health Monitoring (SHM) methods for engineering systems have seen significant advancements through the use of data-driven approaches. These have been developed and employed either in combination with physics-based models [1–3] and reduced-order system representations [4, 5] for the identification and tracking of system changes or as completely data-driven methods, such as Convolutional Neural Networks (CNNs) [6, 7] for the detection faults using multi-source data or Long Short-Term Memory (LSTM) [8, 9] networks for the identification of damage in time series. Despite these advancements, challenges remain in real-world implementation, particularly in acquiring large, high-quality datasets and accounting for environmental factors [10].

Arthur Hatstatt
Chair of Risk, Safety and Uncertainty Quantification, ETH Zürich, Zürich, Switzerland
e-mail: michael.mcgurk@strath.ac.uk

Konstantinos E. Tatsis
Swiss Data Science Center (SDSC), ETH Zürich, Zürich, Switzerland
e-mail: j.yuan@soton.ac.uk

Brian Damiano et al. (eds.), *Structural Health Monitoring & Machine Learning, Vol. 12*, Conference Proceedings of the Society for Experimental Mechanics Series, https://doi.org/10.13052/9788743801573-14

This contribution is motivated by wind turbine structures, which are oftentimes difficult to instrument and the availability of Supervisory Control and Data Acquisition (SCADA) data has not been leveraged for vibration-based assessment. As such, the methodology proposed in this paper aims at bridging the gap between statistical features of vibration signals, such as the ones offered by SCADA systems, for the generation of vibration signals that can stochastically reproduce the response experienced by the system under various conditions of operation. To this end, a physics-informed Gaussian Process Latent Force (GPLF) [11, 12] is developed for the modeling of the modal response signals, which can be used to compose the entire system response. The model is constructed by leveraging the knowledge of the system structural properties and the features characterising the vibration response signals, such as the energy due to operational harmonics. The aim of the proposed surrogate approach is to served as a generative model that can produce time histories of the vibration response, such that their statistical and spectral information matches the one of the original signals.

This paper is organized into three main sections. The first section outlines the methodology, focusing on the Gaussian Process Latent Force Model as the surrogate model, along with its formulation. The second section presents the application case, detailing the framework used to study the vibrational data of a wind turbine and the analytical approach taken. Finally, the third section showcases the results, offering a comparative analysis of the predictive capabilities of the surrogate model against the ground truth data obtained from simulations.

Methodology

In this section, the formulation of Gaussian Process Latent Force models is described for the representation of vibration response signals obtained from structural or mechanical systems. To this end, the response of the system is decomposed into the modal contributions, whose spectral content is easier to characterise and subsequently represented by a temporal Gaussian Process, whose dynamics are driven by a set of latent forces.

Structural dynamics

Consider an n-degree-of-freedom linear time-invariant dynamic system whose vibration response is governed by the following continuous-time differential equation

$$\mathbf{M}\ddot{\mathbf{u}}(t) + \mathbf{C}\dot{\mathbf{u}}(t) + \mathbf{K}\mathbf{u}(t) = \mathbf{S}_{\mathrm{p}}\mathbf{p}(t) \tag{1}$$

where $\mathbf{u} \in \mathbb{R}^n$ is the vector of displacements, $\mathbf{M}$, $\mathbf{C}$ and $\mathbf{K} \in \mathbb{R}^{n\times n}$ denote the mass, stiffness and damping matrices respectively, $\mathbf{p}(t) \in \mathbb{R}^{n_{\mathrm{p}}}$ is the vector of external forcing terms and $\mathbf{S}_{\mathrm{p}} \in \mathbb{R}^{n\times n_{\mathrm{p}}}$ is a selection matrix that assigns the forcing terms to their corresponding locations. In engineering systems, the dynamics are typically governed by a few vibration modes and as such, the response can be expressed as follows

$$\mathbf{u}(t) = \mathbf{\Phi}\mathbf{q}(t) \tag{2}$$

where $\mathbf{\Phi} \in \mathbb{R}^{n\times n_{\mathrm{m}}}$ is a matrix whose columns contain the mode shapes and $\mathbf{q}(t) \in \mathbb{R}^{n_{\mathrm{m}}}$ denotes the vector of generalized modal coordinates. In view of this expression and under the condition of proportional damping, the initial equation of motion, described by Eq. (1), can be decomposed into m second order differential equations. Therefore, the dynamics of the i-th generalized coordinate $q_i(t)$ are governed by the following equation

$$\ddot{q}_i(t) + 2\xi_i\omega_i\dot{q}_i(t) + \omega_i^2 q_i(t) = f_i(t) \tag{3}$$

which applies for $i = 1, 2, \ldots, n_{\mathrm{m}}$. Moreover, ω_i denotes the natural frequency of the i-th mode, ξ_i the corresponding damping ratio and $f_i(t)$ is the projection of the external loads to the modal space, which is obtained by the following expression

$$f_i(t) = \boldsymbol{\phi}_i^{\mathrm{T}}\mathbf{S}_{\mathrm{p}}\mathbf{p}(t) \tag{4}$$

in which $\boldsymbol{\phi}_i$ denotes the i-th column of the mode shape matrix.

Modal expansion

Under the availability of vibration measurements from a number of sensing points, which are herein denoted by $\mathbf{y}(t) \in \mathbb{R}^{n_{\mathrm{s}}}$, the projection postulated by Eq. (2) can be written selectively for all sensing channels as follows

$$\mathbf{y}(t) = \sum_{i=1}^{n_{\mathrm{m}}} \boldsymbol{\phi}_{\mathrm{s},i}\, q_i(t) \tag{5}$$

where $\boldsymbol{\phi}_{\mathrm{s},i} \in \mathbb{R}^{n_{\mathrm{s}} \times 1}$ denotes the mode shape values of the i-th vibration mode at the locations where measurements are available.

Given that the number of measurements n_{s} is equal to or greater than the number of vibration modes n_{m} that are taken into account for the representation of the system dynamics, the time history of the generalized modal coordinates $q_i(t)$ for $i = 1, 2, \ldots, n_{\mathrm{m}}$ can be retrieved by solving the inverse problem

$$\mathbf{q}(t) = \boldsymbol{\Phi}_{\mathrm{s}}^{\dagger}\, \mathbf{y}(t) \tag{6}$$

where $\boldsymbol{\Phi}_{\mathrm{s}} = \begin{bmatrix} \boldsymbol{\phi}_{\mathrm{s},1} & \ldots & \boldsymbol{\phi}_{\mathrm{s},m} \end{bmatrix} \in \mathbb{R}^{n_{\mathrm{s}} \times n_{\mathrm{m}}}$ is the matrix of mode shapes at the sensing points and $\boldsymbol{\Phi}_{\mathrm{s}}^{\dagger}$ denotes the generalized inverse of $\boldsymbol{\Phi}_{\mathrm{s}}$, which is in this work taken equal to the Moore-Penrose pseudo-inverse $\boldsymbol{\Phi}_{\mathrm{s}}^{\dagger} = (\boldsymbol{\Phi}_{\mathrm{s}}^{\mathrm{T}} \boldsymbol{\Phi}_{\mathrm{s}})^{-1} \boldsymbol{\Phi}_{\mathrm{s}}^{\mathrm{T}}$. It should be noted that Eq. (5) implies the availability of displacement measurements however, a similar expression would apply when acceleration, velocity or strain signals are measured. In this contribution, it will be assumed that the vibration response measurements are obtained from acceleration sensors and therefore Eq. (6) delivers the time history of modal accelerations, which are to be modeled by means of GPLF models.

Gaussian process regression

A temporal Gaussian Process (GP) $h(t) \sim GP(0, \kappa(\tau))$ with stationary covariance function $\kappa(t, t') = \kappa(\tau)$, where $\tau = t - t'$, can be obtained as the output of a linear and constant in parameters differential equation, whose dynamics are driven by white noise $w(t)$ with spectral density $S_w(\omega) = \sigma_\omega$. This results in the following signal representation

$$\frac{d^m h(t)}{dt^m} + a_{m-1} \frac{d^{m-1} h(t)}{dt^{m-1}} + \ldots + a_0 h(t) = w(t) \tag{7}$$

where $a_0, \ldots, a_{m-1}$ are known parameters. The equivalent of Eq. (7) in a compact state-space form is obtained as follows

$$\dot{\mathbf{z}}(t) = \mathbf{F}_{\mathrm{c}}\, \mathbf{z}(t) + \mathbf{L}_{\mathrm{c}} w(t) \tag{8a}$$

$$h(t) = \mathbf{H}_{\mathrm{c}}\, \mathbf{z}(t) + v(t) \tag{8b}$$

where $\mathbf{z} = \begin{bmatrix} h(t) & \frac{dh(t)}{dt} & \ldots & \frac{d^{m-1}h(t)}{dt^{m-1}} \end{bmatrix}^{\mathrm{T}} \in \mathbb{R}^m$ denotes the state vector and $v(t) \in \mathbb{R}$ is the measurement noise, which is assumed to be white Gaussian with variance σ_v. The state matrices are functions of the differential equation parameters and are given by the following expressions

$$\mathbf{F}_{\mathrm{c}} = \begin{bmatrix} 0 & 1 & 0 & \ldots & 0 \\ 0 & 0 & 1 & \ldots & 0 \\ \vdots & \vdots & \vdots & \ddots & \vdots \\ 0 & 0 & 0 & \ldots & 1 \\ -a_0 & -a_1 & -a_2 & \ldots & -a_{m-1} \end{bmatrix}, \quad \mathbf{L}_{\mathrm{c}} = \begin{bmatrix} 0 \\ 0 \\ \vdots \\ 0 \\ 1 \end{bmatrix} \tag{9}$$

while $\mathbf{H}_{\mathrm{c}} \in \mathbb{R}^{1 \times m}$ is a boolean matrix selecting the signal $h(t)$ from the state vector. The continuous-time equations can be transferred to the discrete time domain using a time step $\Delta t = 1/f_{\mathrm{s}}$, where f_{s} denotes the sampling frequency, and converted to the following algebraic equations

$$\mathbf{z}_{k+1} = \mathbf{F}_{\mathrm{d}} \mathbf{z}_k + \mathbf{L}_{\mathrm{d}} w_k \tag{10a}$$

$$h_{k+1} = \mathbf{H}_{\mathrm{d}} \mathbf{z}_k + v_k \tag{10b}$$

where the form of the matrices depends on the assumption regarding the variation of the input. Namely, for a zero-order hold assumption, which implies a constant value of the input between two successive steps, the discrete-time state matrices, which are denoted by the subscript $\square_{\mathrm{d}}$ are $\mathbf{F}_{\mathrm{d}} = e^{\mathbf{F}_{\mathrm{c}} \Delta t}$ and $\mathbf{L}_{\mathrm{d}} = (\mathbf{F}_{\mathrm{d}} - \mathbf{I}) \mathbf{F}_{\mathrm{c}}^{-1} \mathbf{L}_{\mathrm{c}}$, while the output matrix $\mathbf{H}_{\mathrm{d}}$ is identical to $\mathbf{H}_{\mathrm{c}}$. The spectral density of the signal $h(t)$ can be obtained analytically from the state-space matrices and is given by following equation

$$\begin{aligned} S_{\mathrm{h}}(\omega) &= H(i\omega) \sigma_{\mathrm{w}} H(-i\omega) \\ &= \mathbf{H}_{\mathrm{c}} (\mathbf{F}_{\mathrm{c}} + i\omega \mathbf{I})^{-1} \mathbf{L}_{\mathrm{c}}\, \sigma_w\, \mathbf{L}_{\mathrm{c}}^{\mathrm{T}} (\mathbf{F}_{\mathrm{c}} + i\omega \mathbf{I})^{-\mathrm{T}} \mathbf{H}_{\mathrm{c}}^{\mathrm{T}} \end{aligned} \tag{11}$$

where $H(i\omega)$ is the transfer function and i denotes the imaginary unit. It should be noted that when the measurement noise $v(t)$ is additionally considered, the expression of the spectral density of $h(t)$ described above should be slightly adjusted. Due to the fact that the noise term has only an additive effect to the signal $h(t)$, the spectral density of the latter should be added to the one of the measurement noise.

Due to the relation between the spectral density and the covariance function, which under stationary conditions are connected through the Fourier transform, the spectral characteristics of the signal $h(t)$ can be inversely defined by specifying the covariance kernel of the signal, which results in a specific spectral content $S_{\mathrm{h}}(\omega)$. The latter in turn can be converted to a state-space representation, according to the factorization postulated by Eq. (11). It is shown in [11] that such a conversion is possible, when the spectral density of the signal is amenable to a rational form.

Covariance functions

Various classes of covariance kernels exist, each of which can attribute different features to the modeled signal. This work is based on the use of Matern and periodic kernels, whose spectral density has an analytical description and their corresponding state-space matrices are presented below.

Matern kernel

The family of Matern kernels are used to describe stationary covariance functions for different types of random processes, while having only a few tunable hyperparameters. One of the most typically employed kernels belonging to this family is the one for $\nu = 3/2$, whose parameters are l and α. The state-space matrices in this case are obtained as

$$\mathbf{F}_{\mathrm{c}} = \begin{bmatrix} 0 & 1 \\ \lambda^2 & -2\lambda \end{bmatrix}, \quad \mathbf{L}_{\mathrm{c}} = \begin{bmatrix} 0 \\ 1 \end{bmatrix}, \quad \mathbf{H}_{\mathrm{c}} = \begin{bmatrix} 1 & 0 \end{bmatrix}$$

with $\lambda = \frac{\sqrt{3}}{l}$ and $\sigma_w = 12\sqrt{3}\frac{\alpha^2}{l^3}$. Accordingly, the Matern kernel with $\nu = 5/2$, in which case it is again parametrized with respect to l and α, corresponds to the following state-space matrices

$$\mathbf{F}_{\mathrm{c}} = \begin{bmatrix} 0 & 1 & 0 \\ 0 & 0 & 1 \\ -\lambda^3 & -3\lambda^2 & -3\lambda \end{bmatrix}, \quad \mathbf{L}_{\mathrm{c}} = \begin{bmatrix} 0 \\ 0 \\ 1 \end{bmatrix}, \quad \mathbf{H}_{\mathrm{c}} = \begin{bmatrix} 1 & 0 & 0 \end{bmatrix}$$

where $\lambda = \frac{\sqrt{5}}{l}$ and $\sigma_w = 400\sqrt{5}\frac{\alpha^2}{3l^5}$.

Periodic kernel

The periodic kernel enables the modeling of signals which repeat themselves exactly, such as the harmonic signals induced by rotating machines. This type of kernel is entirely deterministic, which implies that the response in time domain does not depend on the noise term. The state-space matrices of a signal whose covariance function is described by a periodic kernel are

$$\mathbf{F}_{\mathrm{c}} = \begin{bmatrix} 0 & -\omega \\ \omega & 0 \end{bmatrix}, \quad \mathbf{L}_{\mathrm{c}} = \begin{bmatrix} 0 \\ 1 \end{bmatrix}, \quad \mathbf{H}_{\mathrm{c}} = \begin{bmatrix} 1 & 0 \end{bmatrix}$$

where ω denotes the eigenfrequency, while $\sigma_w = 0$.

Harmonic oscillator

An extension of the periodic kernel in terms of spectral features is offered by the kernel that represents a harmonic oscillator. This represented by the following matrices

$$\mathbf{F}_{\mathrm{c}} = \begin{bmatrix} 0 & 1 \\ -\omega^2 & -2\xi\omega \end{bmatrix}, \quad \mathbf{L}_{\mathrm{c}} = \begin{bmatrix} 0 \\ 1 \end{bmatrix}, \quad \mathbf{H}_{\mathrm{c}} = \begin{bmatrix} -\omega^2 & -2\xi\omega \end{bmatrix}$$

where ω denotes the eigenfrequency and ξ is the corresponding damping ratio. The dynamics of such a model are driven by a white noise signal with spectrum σ_w.

Gaussian process latent force model

In this section, the GP model is extended in order to accommodate a more expressive structure, which is capable of representing the spectral and statistical characteristics of vibration response signals. Within this context, the aim is to construct a GP model, whose dynamics are driven by a set of latent forces, each of which is modeled as a GP and delivers certain features to the target signal $y(t)$. This is achieved by combining the contributions of latent forces which are characterised by the covariance functions presented in the previous Subsection. The model formulation is described below. where the knowledge of the system dynamics can be incorporated into a GP model that follows the covariance function of a harmonic oscillator. This GP is used to model the dynamics of the decomposed modal signals and is augmented with a number of latent variables $\mathbf{z}_k(t)$, for $k = 1, 2, \ldots, K$. The state-space representation of the augmented system in continuous-time is obtained by defining the state vector $\mathbf{z}^{\mathrm{a}}(t) = \begin{bmatrix} u(t) & \dot{u}(t) & \mathbf{z}_1^{\mathrm{T}}(t) & \ldots & \mathbf{z}_K^{\mathrm{T}}(t) \end{bmatrix}^{\mathrm{T}}$, which contains the state variables that describe the underlying dynamics of the signal, as well as the state variables of the various latent forcing terms $\mathbf{z}_k(t)$.

$$\dot{\mathbf{z}}^{\mathrm{a}}(t) = \mathbf{F}_{\mathrm{c,a}}\mathbf{z}^{\mathrm{a}}(t) + \mathbf{L}_{\mathrm{c,a}}\mathbf{w}^{\mathrm{a}}(t) \tag{12a}$$

$$y(t) = \mathbf{H}_{\mathrm{c,a}}\mathbf{z}^{\mathrm{a}}(t) + v(t) \tag{12b}$$

where $\mathbf{w}^{\mathrm{a}}(t)$ denotes the augmented process noise, consisting of the stacked noise terms for all latent terms. Each one of these noise variables is assumed to be Gaussian and white with spectral density $\sigma_{w,k}$, for $k = 1, 2, \ldots, K$. Lastly, $v(t)$ is the measurement noise, which is also a white process of variance σ_v. The state matrices of the augmented model, which consists of K latent variables are

$$\mathbf{F}_{\mathrm{c,a}} = \begin{bmatrix} \mathbf{A}_{\mathrm{c}} & \mathbf{H}^*_{\mathrm{c},1} & \mathbf{H}^*_{\mathrm{c},2} & \cdots & \mathbf{H}^*_{\mathrm{c},K} \\ \mathbf{0} & \mathbf{F}_{\mathrm{c},1} & \mathbf{0} & \cdots & \mathbf{0} \\ \mathbf{0} & \mathbf{0} & \mathbf{F}_{\mathrm{c},2} & \cdots & \mathbf{0} \\ \vdots & \vdots & \vdots & \ddots & \vdots \\ \mathbf{0} & \mathbf{0} & \mathbf{0} & \cdots & \mathbf{F}_{\mathrm{c},K} \end{bmatrix}, \quad \mathbf{L}_{\mathrm{c,a}} = \begin{bmatrix} \mathbf{0} & \mathbf{0} & \mathbf{0} & \cdots & \mathbf{0} \\ \mathbf{0} & \mathbf{L}_{\mathrm{c},1} & \mathbf{0} & \cdots & \mathbf{0} \\ \mathbf{0} & \mathbf{0} & \mathbf{L}_{\mathrm{c},2} & \cdots & \mathbf{0} \\ \vdots & \vdots & \vdots & \ddots & \vdots \\ \mathbf{0} & \mathbf{0} & \mathbf{0} & \cdots & \mathbf{L}_{\mathrm{c},K} \end{bmatrix} \tag{13}$$

where $\mathbf{H}^*_{\mathrm{c},k} = \begin{bmatrix} \mathbf{0} & \mathbf{H}^{\mathrm{T}}_{\mathrm{c},k} \end{bmatrix}^{\mathrm{T}}$, while the output matrix takes the following form

$$\mathbf{H}_{\mathrm{c,a}} = \begin{bmatrix} -\omega^2 & -2\xi\omega & \mathbf{H}_{\mathrm{c},1} & \ldots & \mathbf{H}_{\mathrm{c},K} \end{bmatrix} \tag{14}$$

which without loss of generality implies the modeling of acceleration signals due to the presence of the harmonic oscillator parameters in the first two entries. These can be adjusted accordingly for the modeling of displacement, velocity or strain signals. Lastly, the state-space representation of the augmented system can be transferred to the discrete-time domain by means of a zero-order hold scheme, similar to the one applied in Section .

Hyperparameter identification

The identification of the hyperprameters can be seen as an optimization problem, whose solution can be obtained by means of the Maximum Likelihood (ML) estimate. In this contribution, a least-squares estimate of the hyperparameters is adopted, which relies on the analytical expression of the spectral density as defined from the Gaussian Process Latent Force model. Similar to Eq. (11), the analytical form of the spectral density is derived using the augmented system matrices, which take into account all different latent forces

$$S_{\mathrm{h}}(\omega) = \mathbf{H}_{\mathrm{c,a}}(\mathbf{F}_{\mathrm{c,a}} + i\omega\mathbf{I})^{-1}\mathbf{L}_{\mathrm{c,a}}\,\mathbf{\Sigma}_w\,\mathbf{L}^{\mathrm{T}}_{\mathrm{c,a}}(\mathbf{F}_{\mathrm{c,a}} + i\omega\mathbf{I})^{-\mathrm{T}}\mathbf{H}^{\mathrm{T}}_{\mathrm{c,a}} \tag{15}$$

where $\mathbf{\Sigma}_w \in \mathbb{R}^{K\times K}$ is the diagonal covariance matrix that contains the variance terms σ_w^k of the noise components that act on the signal $h(t)$ as latent forces and as such, it is the quantity to be identified.

The expression of the spectral density described by Eq. (15) can be reformulated in a vector form with respect to the unknown variance parameters in order to obtain the values using a least squares solution of the form $\tilde{\mathbf{A}}\hat{\boldsymbol{\sigma}}_w = \tilde{\mathbf{b}}$. This is accomplished by evaluating Eq. (15) for a number of sampling frequencies ω_l, for $l = 1, 2, \ldots, L$, thus resulting to a set of L equations for the calculation of the unknown variance terms. The least squares solution is built according to the following equations

$$\tilde{\mathbf{A}}_l = \mathbf{G}_l \otimes \mathbf{G}_l \tag{16a}$$

$$\mathbf{G}_l = \mathbf{H}_{\mathrm{c,a}}(\mathbf{F}_{\mathrm{c,a}} + i\omega_l\mathbf{I})^{-1}\mathbf{L}_{\mathrm{c,a}} \tag{16b}$$

$$\tilde{\mathbf{b}}_l = S_{\mathrm{h,o}}(\omega_l) \tag{16c}$$

where $\tilde{\mathbf{A}}_l$ denotes the l-th row of matrix $\tilde{\mathbf{A}}$ and accordingly, $\tilde{\mathbf{b}}_l$ is the l-th entry of $\tilde{\mathbf{b}}$. Therefore, the vector $\boldsymbol{\sigma}_{\mathrm{w}}$ of unknown variance terms is computed using the generalized inverse of $\tilde{\mathbf{A}}$.

Application

The methodology presented in Section is herein applied for the modeling of vibration response signals obtained from wind turbine systems. To this end, the NREL 5MW onshore wind turbine [13] is simulated using FAST software for various operational and environmental conditions, which are defined by the mean wind speed and the turbulence intensity. For each sample of these conditional variables, a 10 minute period is simulated and the acceleration signals in both x and y directions are extracted from two positions of the tower. The signals are sampled at 50 Hz and are subsequently truncated to 1-minute intervals and transformed into the Fore-Aft (FA) and Side-to-Side (SS) directions. The corresponding SCADA variables are also extracted for the 1-minute intervals. Thereafter, a GPLF model is learned in order to be used as generative model that can translate SCADA variables into 1-min time series, whose spectral characteristics are in accordance with those obtained from simulations. The aim of the generated time series is to emulate the original signal, not only in terms of its spectral content and statistical properties, but also in terms of the loading cycles, which are responsible for the accumulation of fatigue damage. A schematic overview of the workflow followed in this case study is presented in Fig. 1

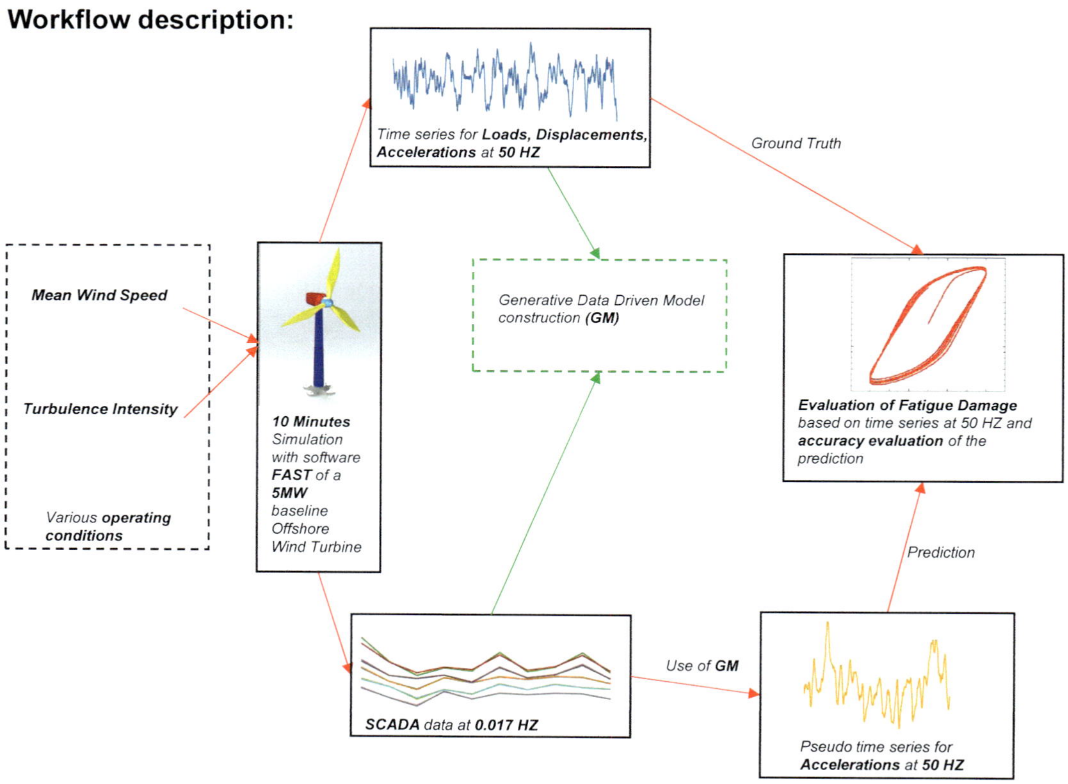

Fig. 1 General workflow description

As underlined in the section of the methodology, the optimization algorithm implies the knowledge of certain hyperparameters, which can be extracted from statistical metric of the signal. In this specific case study, it is assumed that certain characteristics of the response are available from the design, such as the eigenfrequencies and the damping of the system, while some further information can be extracted from the available SCADA data. As such, the dynamics of the acceleration signals of the two modes in each direction, namely FA and SS, are assumed to be governed by a harmonic oscillator kernel, with ω_m and ξ_m being the eigenfrequency and damping ratio of the m-th mode. The dynamics of the modelled signals are driven by a number of latent forces, each of which represents a specific feature of the response. Theses latent forces are mainly driven by the rotation of the wind turbine, and should therefore have frequency components as follows:

- Rotor frequency: $\omega_r = \frac{2\pi}{60} \cdot \text{RPM}$ rad/s
- Blade passage frequencies: $\omega_b^j = 3 \cdot j \cdot \omega_r,\ j \in \mathbb{N}$.

In order to account for the variability of the response, which is induced by the change in environmental and operational conditions, the identified hyperparameters are conditioned on the SCADA variables, which apart from the rotor speed (RPM), contain the following channels:

- **Wind velocity**: The absolute value of wind velocity is computed as the norm of the velocity vector.
- **Turbulence intensity**: The turbulence intensity used for the corresponding simulation.
- **Yaw misalignment**: The misalignment of the yaw position with respect to the wind direction, computed from the difference between the velocity vector and the yaw position angle.

Within this context, a mapping between the aforementioned SCADA variables and the hyperparameters of the GPLF model is identified, which is herein implemented using a Multi-Layer Perceptron (MLP) model, in order to extend the validity of the model to the entire operational spectrum.

Results

In this section the results from the simulated case study, which is described in Section , are presented. Upon simulation of the wind turbine system for different operational conditions, and decomposition of the acceleration response into modal signals in Fore-Aft and Side-to-Side directions, the GPLF model is fitted for each 1-min time series and the identified model is used as a generative surrogate, which aims at preserving the spectral and statistical information of the simulated response.

The performance of the model is assessed in both directions, namely Fore-Aft and Side-to-Side, of the wind turbine and for the first two modes of the structure, which typically contain most of the vibration energy. The comparison is presented in terms of the spectra between the generated and the original time series. In order to avoid having too many hyperparameters for the surrogate model, the damping ratios are considered equal for all cases, namely $\xi^k = 0.01$ for all latent forces. Therefore, the only hyperparameters identified by the algorithm are the measurement noise level σ_v and the spectral densities of the noise driving the latent forces σ_w^k, for $k = 1, 2, \ldots, K$.

The results of the time series generated by the identified models are shown in Figs. 2-3. Concretely, Fig. 2 depicts the spectra and the time series between the original signal and the one generated by the GPLF models for the first FA mode. The corresponding comparison of the signals in SS direction is presented in Fig. 3. For both directions, the generated pseudo time series seem to encapsulate the dynamics of the observations quite well, with a very limited number of hyperparameters. Indeed, as depicted by the power spectra, for both modes and both directions, most of the energy of the signal is concentrated in the frequency range between 0 and 5Hz. Moreover, the energy peaks are concentrated around the physically known

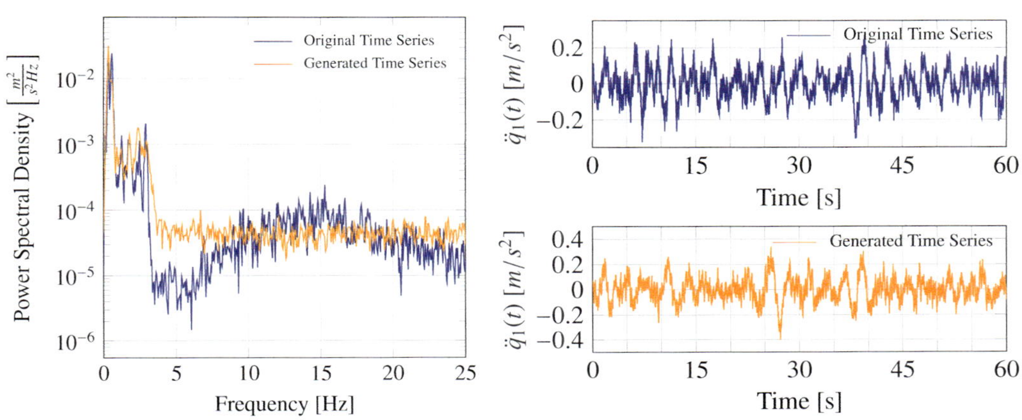

Fig. 2 Comparison of the spectra (left) between the original and the generated time series (right) of the first mode in FA direction

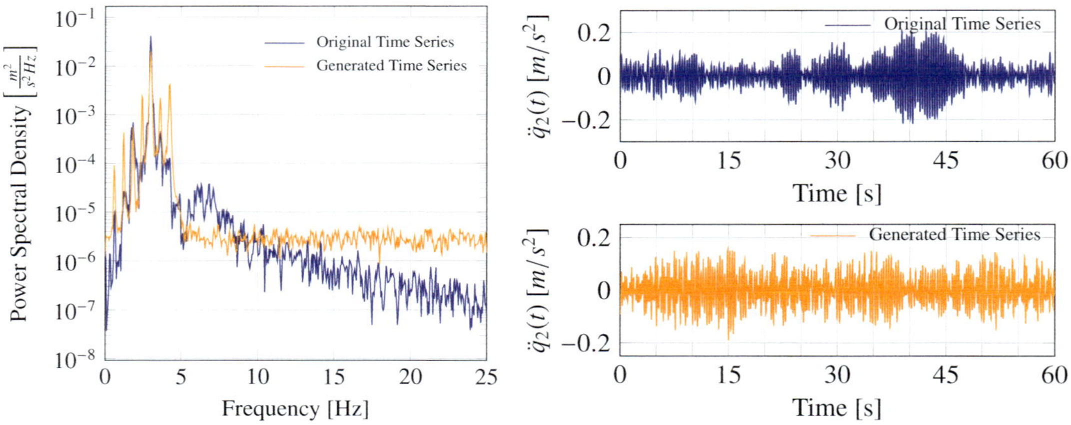

Fig. 3 Comparison of the spectra (left) between the original and the generate time series (right) of the second mode in FA direction

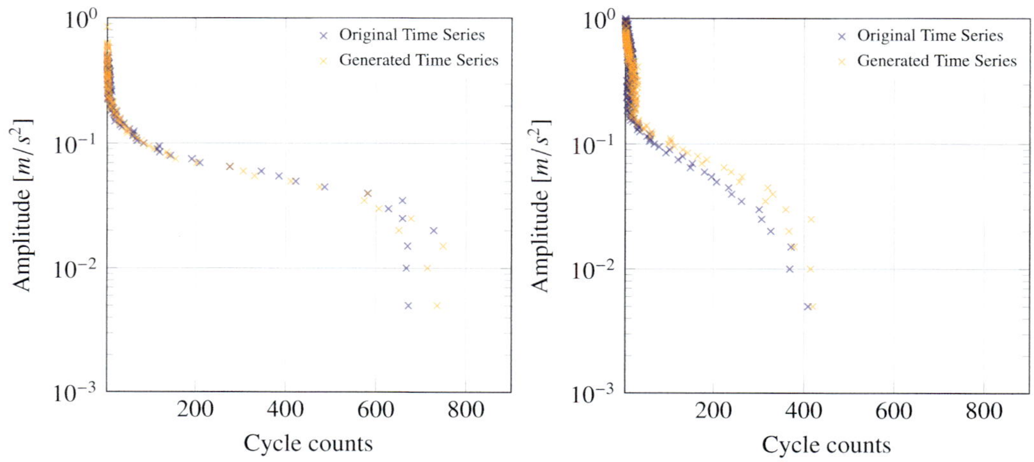

Fig. 4 Comparison of the modal strain cycle counts for the first (left) and second (right) mode in the FA direction

frequencies (eigenfrequencies of the system and multiples of rotational frequency). These two particular characteristics of the physical problem allow the surrogate model to replicate the real-world complex dynamics in a satisfactory manner with a very limited number of hyperparameters. One could argue that more complex models could replicate the dynamics in a better way, which is undeniably the case, however this would overlook the final goal of the surrogate.

The final target being to find a mapping between scarce SCADA data and the hyperparameters of the surrogate model, simpler models are preferred, as fewer parameters usually exhibit higher interpretability and predictabilty. Moreover, the presented approach allows to find analytically the hyperparameters of the model, avoiding the need for optimization algorithms, which, based on the implemented cases, seem to induce a lot more variability in the identified parameters.

Lastly, the quantity of interest is neither the spectra of the obtained signals nor the pseudo time series directly, but their predictive capabilities for structural analysis. A very critical example is the quantification of fatigue accumulation, and the applicability of the generated pseudo time series for this purpose is investigated in the remaining of this section. Fatigue damage is related to the strain cycles history in the tower basis. Following the methodology proposed in [14], the strain history is retrieved from the modal contributions $q(t)$, by initially integrating the modal accelerations in the Laplace domain [15] and subsequently transforming the model displacements to strains through the deformation matrix of the Finite Element model of the system. Once the strain time series are obtained, the number of cycles for each strain level is counted, which is herein performed using the rainflow counting algorithm. The obtained results are presented in Figs. 4, where a satisfactory agreement between the generated and the original time series is achieved.

Conclusions

In this contribution, a generative modeling approach is proposed for the translation of vibration signal statistics to short terms dynamics. The methodology is demonstrated on a simulated wind turbine system, where a Gaussian Process Latent Force (GPLF) model is used to map one-minute SCADA data to the GPLF parameters. With fatigue damage accumulation being a critical phenomenon in wind turbine systems, the generated pseudo time series have a satisfactory predictive capability for the quantification of loading cycles at different amplitudes. The relative simplicity of the surrogate model allows still to have a very decent accuracy compared to a high complexity dynamic model, requiring a lot of computational power and parameters. Moreover, another advantage of the proposed methodology is the connection between the scarce SCADA variables and the short-term dynamics. The major advantage of such a methodology is the generative approach that can be used to estimate the fatigue accumulation in critical parts of the structure based on a relatively general and simple implementation, avoiding the pitfall of data availability encountered by many purely data-driven models.

References

1. Agathos, K., Tatsis, K., Nicoli, S., Bordas, S.P., and Chatzi, E. "Crack detection in mindlin-reissner plates under dynamic loads based on fusion of data and models". *Computers & Structures*, 246:106475 (2021)
2. Gres, S., Döhler, M., Andersen, P., and Mevel, L. "Subspace-based mahalanobis damage detection robust to changes in excitation covariance". *Structural Control and Health Monitoring*, 28(8):e2760 (2021)
3. Tatsis, K.E., Ou, Y., Dertimanis, V.K., Spiridonakos, M.D., and Chatzi, E.N. "Vibration-based monitoring of a small-scale wind turbine blade under varying climate and operational conditions. part ii: A numerical benchmark". *Structural Control and Health Monitoring*, 28(10):e2813 (2021)
4. Tatsis, K., Lourens, E., and Chatzi, E. "A general substructure-based framework for input-state estimation using limited output measurements". *Mechanical Systems and Signal Processing*, 150:107223 (2021)
5. Tatsis, K.E., Agathos, K., and Chatzi, E.N. "A hierarchical output-only bayesian approach for online vibration-based crack detection using parametric reduced-order models". *Mechanical Systems and Signal Processing*, 167:108558 (2022)
6. Zhao, Y., Zhang, Y., Li, Z., Bu, L., and Han, S. "Ai-enabled and multimodal data driven smart health monitoring of wind power systems: A case study". *Advanced Engineering Informatics*, 56:102018 (2023)
7. Gopalakrishnan, S., Laflamme, S., and Hu, C. "Deep cnn-based learning for automated structural damage detection and localization". *Smart Materials and Structures*, 26(5):055027 (2017)
8. Malekjafarian, A. and O'Brien, E.J. "Structural damage detection using long short-term memory networks". *Journal of Civil Structural Health Monitoring*, 11:765–779 (2021)
9. Choe, D.E., Kim, H.C., and Kim, M.H. "Sequence-based modeling of deep learning with lstm and gru networks for structural damage detection of floating offshore wind turbine blades". *Renewable Energy*, 174:218–235 (2021)
10. Azimi, M., Eslamlou, A.D., and Pekcan, G. "Data-driven structural health monitoring and damage detection through deep learning: State-of-the-art review". *Sensors*, 20 (2020)
11. Sarkka, S., Solin, A., and Hartikainen, J. "Spatiotemporal learning via infinite-dimensional bayesian filtering and smoothing: A look at gaussian process regression through kalman filtering". *IEEE Signal Processing Magazine*, 30(4):51 – 61 (2013)
12. Álvarez, M., Luengo, D., and Lawrence, N.D. "Latent force models". *Proceedings of the Twelfth International Conference on Artificial Intelligence and Statistics*, pages 9–16 (2009)
13. J.M. Jonkman, M.B.J. *FAST User's Guide*. National Renewable Energy Laboratory (2005)
14. Mozafari, V.P.R.J., S. and Dykes, K. "Sensitivity of fatigue reliability in wind turbines: effects of design turbulence and the wöhler exponent". *Wind Energ. Sci.*, pages 799–820 (2024)
15. Iliopoulos, A., Weijtjens, W., Van Hemelrijck, D., and Devriendt, C. "Fatigue assessment of offshore wind turbines on monopile foundations using multi-band modal expansion: Fatigue assessment of monopile owts using multi-band modal expansion". *Wind Energy*, 20 (2017)

Chapter 15
Effective Structural Health Monitoring of Rotating Propellers using Asynchronous Neuromorphic Tracking

Guillermo Toledo, Wyatt Saeger, Fernando Moreu, David Mascarenas, Christian Torres, and Jahsyel Rojas

Abstract Structural Health Monitoring (SHM) of rotating propellers has been proved crucial by preventing catastrophic failure, detecting defects early, reducing costs through predictive maintenance and prolonging the lifespan of components. Current techniques for SHM of rotating propellers generally imply high cost, complex installation and configuration or limited effectiveness across different frequency ranges. This study aims to develop and evaluate an effective and efficient Structural Health Monitoring system for rotating propellers using asynchronous neuromorphic tracking. By leveraging advanced neuromorphic cameras and real-time data processing algorithms, the proposed system offers a novel approach to measure the vibrations of the propeller. Elements involved in the displacement data acquisition include Laser Doppler Vibrometer (LDV), scanning galvanometer and Dynamic Vision Sensor (DVS). Out of plane displacement is collected using LDV, which operates through a galvanometer that ensures the laser remains fixed on a specific point on the propeller. Real-time positional data of the propeller is acquired using a neuromorphic camera, which dynamically controls the galvanometer to maintain precision. This research provides a practical and efficient solution for real-time structural health monitoring, offering valuable insights for future engineering applications.

Keywords Neuromorphic camera · Propeller SHM · Tachometer · DVS · Galvanometer · LDV

Introduction

Structural Health Monitoring (SHM) of rotating propellers is a critical component across various industries, including wind energy [1], aerospace [2], and marine [3] applications. Effective SHM plays an important role in preventing failures, detecting defects at early stages, and reducing maintenance costs through predictive strategies. The need for continuous monitoring is fundamental, particularly for high-speed rotating elements, where structural integrity is key to ensure operational safety and efficiency.

Current SHM techniques, such as accelerometers [4], optical methods [5], and motor current analysis [6], present limitations. Accelerometers, while useful for dynamic behavior analysis, have a limited scope for complex or high-frequency vibrations, and their invasive installment can disrupt the dynamics they intent to measure [4]. Optical techniques, including

Guillermo Toledo
Department of Mechanical Engineering, Universidad Carlos III de Madrid, Leganés, Madrid, Spain
e-mail: guille03tnf@unm.edu

Guillermo Toledo · Wyatt Saeger · Fernando Moreu · Christian Torres · Jahsyel Rojas
Department of Civil, Construction and Environmental Engineering, The University of New Mexico, Albuquerque, NM, USA
e-mail: guille03tnf@unm.edu; wsaeger@unm.edu; fmoreu@unm.edu; christian.torres55@upr.edu; jahsyel.rojas@upr.edu

David Mascarenas
Los Alamos National Laboratory, Los Alamos, NM, USA
e-mail: dmascarenas@lanl.gov

Christian Torres
Department of Electrical Engineering, The University of Puerto Rico-Mayagüez, Mayagüez, PR, USA
e-mail: christian.torres55@upr.edu

Jahsyel Rojas
Department of Software Engineering, The University of Puerto Rico-Mayagüez, Mayagüez, PR, USA
e-mail: jahsyel.rojas@upr.edu

Brian Damiano et al. (eds.), *Structural Health Monitoring & Machine Learning, Vol. 12*, Conference Proceedings of the Society for Experimental Mechanics Series, https://doi.org/10.13052/9788743801573-15

laser interferometry and holography, are susceptible to environmental factors such as dust and humidity [7], and they require precise calibration, making them costly and complicated to maintain. Additionally, motor current analysis provides indirect fault detection, usually leading to imprecise diagnostics and limited sensitivity to minor defects.

The development of a novel SHM system utilizing asynchronous neuromorphic cameras aims to address these challenges. Unlike traditional systems that depend on external propeller information for laser positioning [8], the proposed approach leverages the high-frequency tracking capabilities of neuromorphic cameras. This innovation enables instantaneous calculation of the propeller's position, allowing for precise laser orientation that minimizes interference and coordination issues. The ability to measure vibrations remotely without halting machinery represents a significant advancement in SHM technology.

This study aims to develop and evaluate an efficient and effective SHM system for rotating propellers, focusing on the application of neuromorphic tracking for real-time data acquisition. By integrating these advanced technologies, the mentioned system not only enhances measurement precision but also significantly lowers maintenance costs and downtime, thereby extending the lifespan of critical components.

Methodology

This section outlines the methodology developed to create a system capable of monitoring the vibrations of rotating propellers. The scope of this study is ment to track the real-time position of a propeller blade while simultaneously controlling a laser Doppler vibrometer (LDV) for precision measurements. The system combines multiple components including a neuromorphic camera, galvanometer, and data acquisition hardware, all orchestrated to work in sync. The ultimate goal is to demonstrate that the system effectively tracks and measures the dynamic behavior of the propeller in motion, providing accuracy and operational synchronization.

The methodology was built upon the premise of mixing real-time event-based vision with precision laser tracking for vibration analysis. As can be seen in Figure 1, the propeller system was modeled using a small precision lathe, equipped with a plastic propeller approximately 8 inches in diameter. The speed of the propeller was controlled via a mechanism built into the motor, allowing for speeds in between 0 to approximately 2700 RPM. To ensure accurate monitoring of the propeller speed, a tachometer was attached to the lathe with an accuracy of ±5 RPM.

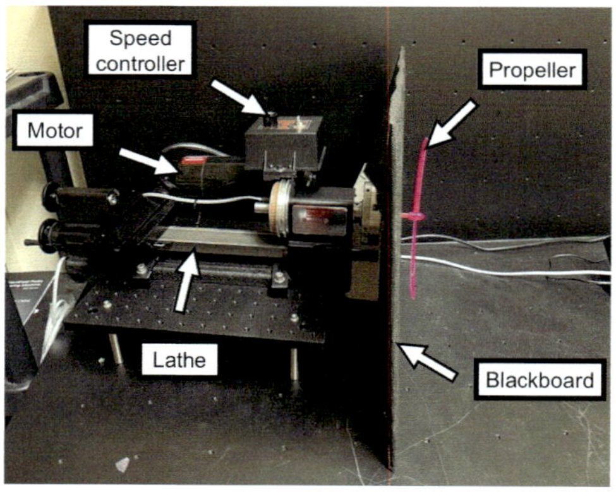

Fig. 1 Propeller set-up

The primary sensing framework incorporated an event-based neuromorphic camera [9], capable of acquiring high-speed changes in the propeller's position. An event-based camera operates by detecting changes in brightness (log intensity) asynchronously at each pixel, unlike traditional cameras that capture full frames at fixed intervals. Each individual pixel in the sensor monitors variation in light intensity and generates an "event" whenever there is a change in brightness that exceeds a previously set threshold detected. Each event contains the pixel's location (x, y), the time (t) of the change, and the polarity, showing whether brightness increased (1) or decreased (0). Events are generated independently, being each one timestamped with microsecond accuracy, allowing event-based cameras to respond rapidly to visual stimuli. Since the output rate depends on the amount of motion or brightness change in the scene, faster movements generate more events per second, making these cameras particularly effective at tracking fast movements without motion blur.

In order to optimize performance, the system was configured to work in a noise-reduced environment. A blackboard was placed behind the propeller to eliminate background noise and ensure that the camera focused exclusively on the movement of the propeller. The camera's output was synchronized with a two-axis galvanometer, that controlled two mirrors responsible for reorienting the laser beam towards the rotating propeller. The galvanometer's movements were driven by analog signals that responded to variations in the propeller's position as detected by the camera. The LDV, a highly sensitive instrument capable of detecting tiny positional variations, was employed to measure the displacement of the propeller on real time. The system was controlled by a Python script executed on a PC, that coordinated the camera, processed the positional data, and converted it into information for the galvanometer.

The tracking system required several key components to function in unison, beginning with the careful integration of the camera, galvanometer, and laser system. The event-based camera constantly provided positional data of the propeller. This data was processed using Principal Component Analysis (PCA) [10] to obtain the angle of the propeller relative to the horizontal plane. Principal component analysis is a linear dimensionality reduction method used to simplify a large data set into a smaller set, while still maintaining significant patterns and trends. Works by finding new axes, or principal components, along which the data shows the most variation. Eigenvalue decomposition is used to find the principal components, which correspond to the axes with the greatest variance.

In event-based applications, Principal Component Analysis (PCA) is an important tool for both reducing noise and obtaining meaningful patterns from large sets of data. In this specific case, PCA plays a vital role in calculating the propeller's angle by analyzing the events generated by the neuromorphic camera. As previously described, the camera creates a cloud of asynchronous events, which, at first glance, appear to have no obvious connection. However, the temporal sequence of these events forms the underlying structure that relates them. By grouping events within small time intervals, it is possible to capture the shape of the propeller. During these intervals, most of the events will cluster along the edge of the rotating propeller, as shown in Figure 2. PCA is applied to these clusters to identify the main direction along which the majority of events align, corresponding to the principal axis of variance. This principal axis represents the dominant direction of the event distribution, which allows the calculation of the angle of the propeller at a given moment.

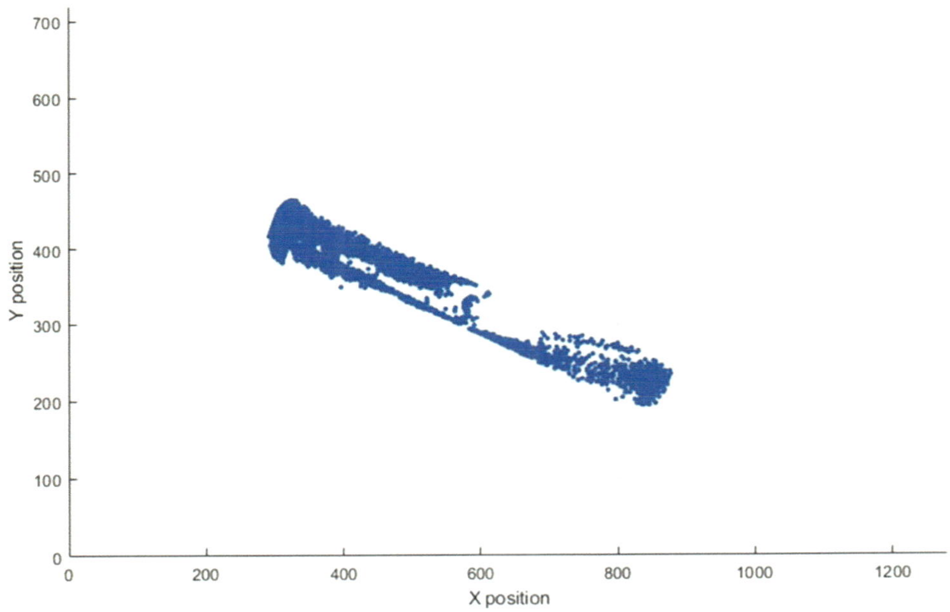

Fig. 2 Events captured during propeller's rotation

The duration of the time intervals chosen for event grouping directly influences the accuracy of the angle estimation. Short intervals result in less events, which leads to higher variability and imprecision in the calculated angle. On the other hand, if the time interval is too long, the propeller will have rotated significantly during the interval, introducing inaccuracy in the angle estimation. Therefore, finding a perfect balance in the interval duration is essential for accurate measurements. Additionally, too short or too large time intervals affect directly the computational load and can reduce significantly the efficiency of the algorithm.

It is also important to note that the effectiveness of PCA in this context is heavily determined by a robust pre-filtering process for the events. Noise captured by the neuromorphic camera can distort the event data and reduce the precision of the PCA-based angle calculation. Hence, adequate filtering to get rid of redundant or noisy events is a crucial step to ensure the accuracy and reliability of this technique.

As the Figure 3a shows, once the angle of the propeller was obtained, it was then used to calculate the sine and cosine of the angle for both the vertical and horizontal axes, providing the necessary input for controlling the galvanometer's mirrors. The galvanometer, which operated through analog signal input, shown in Figure 3b received these values and modified the position of its mirrors to ensure that the laser beam remained fixed on a specific point on the propeller blade. The LDV, reflected by the mirrors, measured the blade's displacement, capturing the small variations that occur during the propeller's rotation.

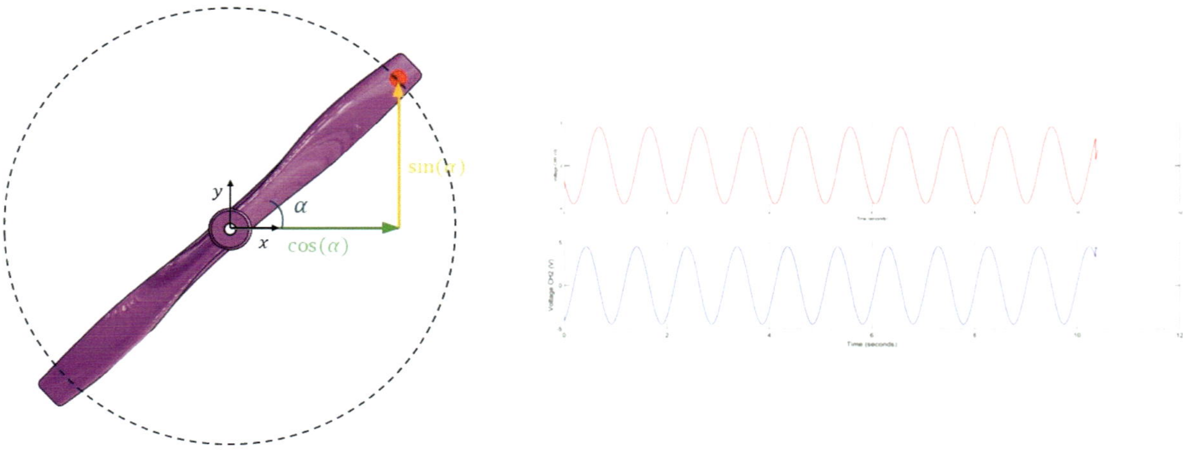

(a) (b)

Fig. 3 Propellers angle transformation into different independent analog signals. (a) Sine and cosine decomposition; (b) Galvanometer 2 axis input

The entire process was iterated at high frequency to ensure smooth tracking of the propeller's motion and to minimize delay between the camera's input and the galvanometer's response. While the system is designed to operate at high speeds, the current experiment was conducted at lower RPMs to mitigate the effects of processing delay, which has not yet been fully optimized.

This initial iteration of the methodology laid the groundwork for integrating the various components, ensuring that data from the camera could be processed in real time, transformed into control signals for the galvanometer, and used to direct the laser towards the moving propeller. Although the system is still in development, these initial results confirm the viability of the approach and demonstrate that the core components function in synchrony to track the propeller's motion accurately.

Analysis

To confirm the functionality of the camera and the program's capability to detect the propeller and obtain its angle, multiple tests were conducted. The results were positive, demonstrating that when using a blackboard as a backdrop, the program reliably detects the propeller consistently, as illustrated in Figure 4. The angle calculations for each time interval were also successfully achieved, as shown in Figure 5.

In order to assess the laser's operation through the galvanometer's small mirrors, a controlled test was conducted. A 'ground truth' test involved pointing the laser directly at the tip of the propeller. Motion was induced and captured by the laser on the opposite side of the propeller, as shown in Figure 6a. This test was then replicated with the propeller, galvanometer, and laser mounted in the setup, directing the laser through the galvanometer's mirrors, as shown in Figure 6b. The results confirmed that while the laser could measure through the galvanometer, tasks such as calibration proved challenging. When using the mirrors, the system lost a significant portion of its reliability, detecting only a small fraction of what would normally be captured under direct conditions, and became sensitive to substantial movements, risking going out of range. So far, the only tests conducted with the laser have been static, collecting data without rotating the propeller; dynamic testing is planned for future iterations. The graph shown in Figure 6b exhibits some variation in between different induced movements due to the low intensity of the return signal captured by the laser, which at times caused a shift in the graph's baseline. This issue is expected to be addressed in future work.

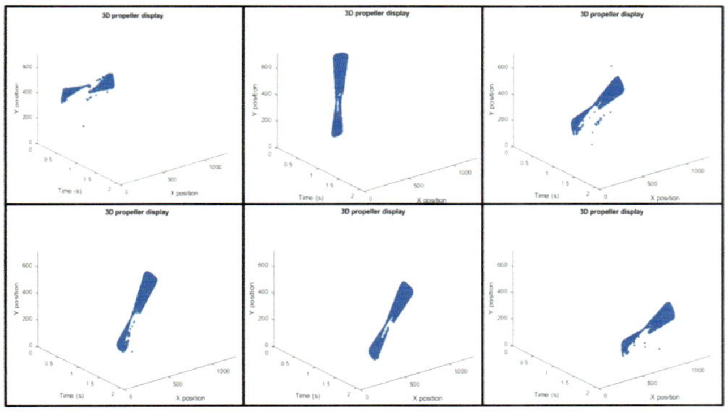

Fig. 4 Detected propeller at different timestamps

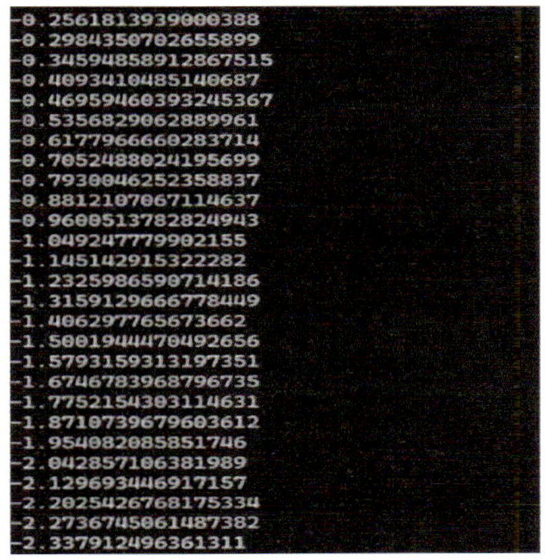

Fig. 5 Angles in radians calculated by the code

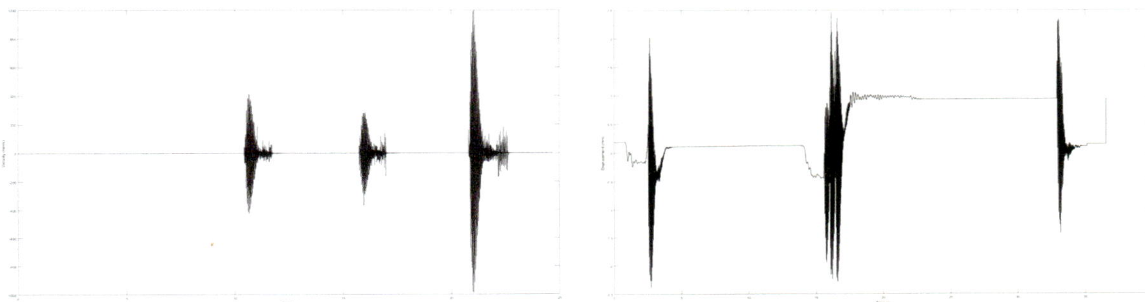

(a) (b)

Fig. 6 Displacement tests conducted. (a) Laser directly pointing at propeller; (b) Laser reflected through galvanometer

Regarding the integrated operation of all system components—namely, the detection of the propeller, angle calculation, information transmission, and mirror position updating—tests were performed where the propeller was spun at varying speeds to observe the mirror movements. The results, shown in Figure 7, indicate that the system can accurately detect the propeller, process information, calculate the angle, and adjust the mirrors accordingly. However, it is important to note that the Python code is not yet optimized, and current hardware limitations create processing delays, causing the laser to move at the same speed as the propeller with a slight lag.

Data acquisition and processing

Initially, the code utilized time intervals to group data, process it, and iterate through the cycle. This approach led to varying data group sizes based on rotational speed, causing slow responses at high speeds and significant delays. To address this issue, the decision was made to implement event-based grouping, maintaining a quasi-constant iteration time regardless of rotational speed.

Furthermore, the original approach involved using two separate Python scripts: one optimized for controlling the camera and processing all data, and the other for operating the data acquisition system (DAQ) and generating the analog signal. It became apparent that communication issues between the scripts increased delays significantly, prompting the integration of both functionalities into a single multifunctional script.

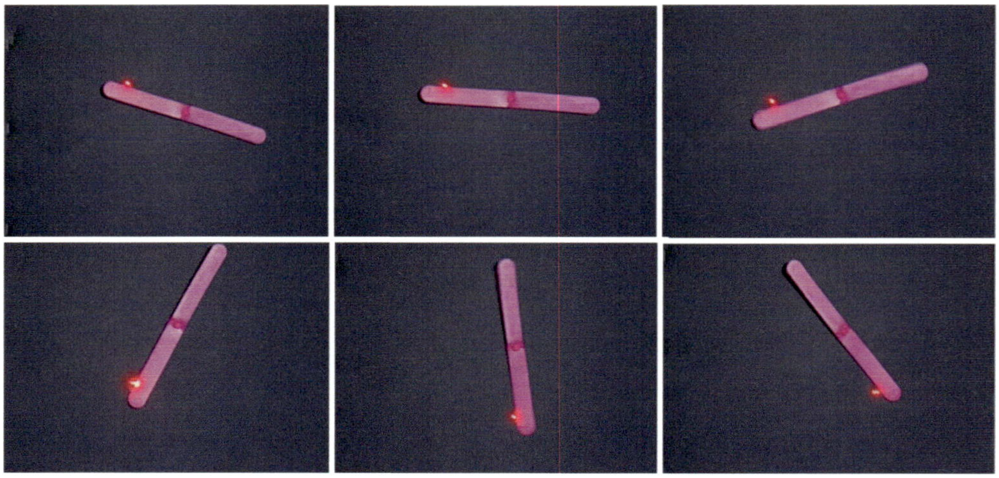

Fig. 7 Laser autonomously following the propeller

Analysis of results

This study establishes a comprehensive framework for monitoring the health of rotating propellers, providing a reliable basis for further research and application. The iterative testing process has validated the core functionality of the system components, ensuring that the camera, laser, and galvanometer can work together effectively. Future refinements, including optimizing code and addressing hardware limitations, will enhance the system's performance and reliability in dynamic conditions. This work not only advances the monitoring capabilities of rotating propellers but also lays the groundwork for implementing predictive maintenance strategies in various engineering applications.

Conclusion

This study has demonstrated the viability of using asynchronous neuromorphic tracking for real-time structural health monitoring (SHM) of rotating propellers. The system proposed offers a positive enhancement over traditional techniques by offering a non-invasive and efficient technique for tracking the position of the propeller and monitoring its structural integrity. The integration of a galvanometer-reflected laser system and a neuromorphic camera allowed to measure propeller displacement in real time, although some challenges stand, particularly in reducing the delay observed in the galvanometer response.

The tests conducted validate the system's capability to detect and track the propeller's movement consistently and accurately. Real-time tracking has been successfully demonstrated, though with a slight processing delay due to hardware limitations and non-optimized code. Further improvements, especially in software optimization and hardware performance, are expected to address this problem, enhancing the system's real-time responsiveness.

Laser measurements through the galvanometer's mirrors have been proven feasible in static conditions, marking an important milestone in the system's development. Although signal loss and sensitivity to substantial movements were observed, these challenges are anticipated to be mitigated in future dynamic tests, which will provide a more comprehensive understanding of the system's robustness under operational conditions.

Ultimately, this study presents a promising alternative to existing SHM techniques. The ability to track propeller motion with high precision and to maintain continuous monitoring without requiring machine stoppages offers clear advantages in terms of maintenance cost reduction and system reliability. Future work will focus on refining the system for dynamic testing and further improving the integration of the neuromorphic camera with the galvanometer, paving the way for even more effective real-time monitoring solutions.

Acknowledgments This research was primarily conducted in the laboratories of the University of New Mexico, specifically within the Department of Civil, Construction, and Environmental Engineering. The authors would like to thank the UNM Center for Advanced Research

Computing, supported in part by the National Science Foundation, for providing the laboratory space and office resources used to conduct this work. Also, authors would like to acknowledge the support of SMILab, which provided invaluable resources and a collaborative environment that facilitated the successful completion of this project. The guidance and contributions of all involved institutions are greatly appreciated.

References

1. Ciang, C.C., Lee, J.R., and Bang, H.J. "Structural health monitoring for a wind turbine system: a review of damage detection methods". *Measurement Science and Technology*, 19:122001 (2008)
2. Misra, P., Kandaswamy, G., Mohapatra, P., Kumar, K., and Balamuralidhar, P. "Structural health monitoring of multi-rotor micro aerial vehicles". *Association for Computing Machinery*, page 21–26 (2018)
3. Huijer, A., Kassapoglou, C., and Pahlavan, L. "Acoustic emission monitoring of composite marine propeller blades using embedded piezo-electric sensors and hydrophones". *e-Journal of Nondestructive Testing*, pages 1–8 (2000)
4. Escriba, C., Fourniols, J.Y., Lastapis, M., Boizard, J.L., Auriol, G., and Andrieu, S. "New real-time structural health monitoring microsystem for aircraft propeller blades". *IEEE Aerospace and Electronic Systems Magazine*, 27(2):29–41 (2012)
5. Abbas, S.H., Jang, J.K., Kim, D.H., and Lee, J.R. "Underwater vibration analysis method for rotating propeller blades using laser doppler vibrometer". *ScienceDirect*, 132:106133 (2020)
6. He, L., Attia, M., Hao, L., Fang, B., Younsi, K., and Wang, H. "Remote monitoring and diagnostics of blade health in commercial mw-scale wind turbines using electrical signature analysis (esa)". *IEEE Xplore*, pages 808–813 (2020)
7. He, Y., Zhu, Y., and Nie, H. "Study on the control of micro-environmental parameters in long distance laser interferometry". *Journal of Physics: Conference Series*, 2002(1):012055 (2021)
8. Johansmann, M., Fritzsche, M., and Schell, J. "A new method for measurement of rotating objects utilizing laser doppler vibrometry combined with an optical derotator with focus on automotive applications". *SAE Technical Paper* (2011)
9. Gallego, G., Delbrück, T., Orchard, G., Bartolozzi, C., Taba, B., Censi, A., Leutenegger, S., Davison, A.J., Conradt, J., Daniilidis, K., and Scaramuzza, D. "Event-based vision: A survey". *IEEE Transactions on Pattern Analysis and Machine Intelligence*, 44(1):154–180 (2022)
10. Khairallah, M.Z., Bonardi, F., Roussel, D., and Bouchafa, S. "Pca event-based optical flow for visual odometry". *arXiv* (2021)

Chapter 16
Estimating Damage Detection of an Aircraft Component with Machine Learning Models

Brandon Jones, Milton Jones, Stephen Keyes, Eamon Mott, and Thomas J. Matarazzo

Abstract Vibration measurements can assist with monitoring and inspecting the condition of aircraft components. This study uses a vibration-based sensor network to assess damage on a specific aircraft component, creating a system that can provide invaluable information to aircraft maintainers. The system implemented in this study used supervised machine learning methods to determine the existence and assess the severity of a specific damage case on an aircraft component. The method was validated experimentally using nondestructive and then destructive testing. Overall, the machine learning model was successful in distinguishing between five levels of damage and was able to predict a loss of mass with an error of 0.5 grams. Overall, the results indicated that the regression model had a strong ability to accurately predict different levels of damage, supporting the use of such a system for aircraft component damage detection.

Keywords Structural Health Monitoring · Damage Detection · Machine Learning

Introduction

Aircraft maintenance is often labor intensive, time consuming, and tedious, but it is an important requirement that must be fulfilled. Furthermore, proper maintenance has become increasingly important as aircraft incorporate advanced technologies with higher expectations in performance. To reduce operational cost and enhance performance of the next generation of aircraft, the development of affordable sensors, powerful algorithms, and stronger data processing technology has made the integration of structural health monitoring (SHM) into aircraft development more feasible [1]. Implementing a system that provides maintainers with valuable information could enhance safety and efficiency in the aviation industry. There are a multitude of techniques that can be used for SHM, which can include using vibration signatures, impedance based technology, limit strain measurement, and fiber optic sensors [2]. The main goal of this study is to develop a damage detection system that accurately and efficiently determines whether maintenance is necessary for an aircraft component. There are key advantages of having a detection system that shows the status of a component, whether it is slightly damaged or on the end of its life cycle. Previously, to standard existing methods for detecting damage on aircraft rely solely on visual inspections. However, structural damage is not always visible to inspectors and maintainers; that is, micro-cracks or internal defects can be difficult to detect during visual inspections.

The overarching method of structural health monitoring used in this study involves completing hypothesis testing to compare a proposed healthy state to a state where damage is introduced. If the means of the "healthy state" is statistically different from the "damaged state" it can be concluded that damage has been introduced, prompting maintenance of the structure [3]. Applying that methodology to the modular effects launcher (MEL), the component of interest, enables comparison of a baseline healthy state with an unknown state and an evaluation of structural condition [4]. The results of previous research illustrate the feasibility of creating a system to monitor the health of various civil and mechanical systems, while highlighting the inefficiencies in current maintenance practices.

Brandon Jones · Milton Jones · Stephen Keyes · Eamon Mott · Thomas J. Matarazzo
Department of Civil and Mechanical Engineering, United States Military Academy, West Point, NY 10997
e-mail: brandon.jones2487@gmail.com; miltonljones4@gmail.com; stephenmckeyes@gmail.com; eamonmorr@gmail.com; thomas.matarazzo@westpoint.edu

Brian Damiano et al. (eds.), *Structural Health Monitoring & Machine Learning, Vol. 12*, Conference Proceedings of the Society for Experimental Mechanics Series, https://doi.org/10.13052/9788743801573-16

Methodology

In order to create a system that meets the requirements set by the sponsors of this study,the computational process for identifying damage had to be determined. This process was narrowed down to three main objectives; determining whether the current state is different from the baseline, the quantity of the difference, and implementing a machine learning model that can predict damage (mass removed from structure). Following these three goals the end product will inform the maintainer about the health of the structure[5].

To find a change of state in the structure it must be excited and its responses recorded in this case acceleration responses were recorded from six sensors placed on locations of interest of the MEL. Once the data is collected from the structure it can be analyzed through damage sensitive features, which are statistical parameters that measure the change in response based on the state of the structure. The damage sensitive features are then trained on the machine learning model. The damage-sensitive features that were utilized prioritized the quantity of transmissibility, which measures the magnitude of frequency response function and relates it to an input-output dynamic [11]. The machine learning model that was used was a linear Support Vector Regression (SVR), which was used because it is simple and yielded the best results for classification problems like this. Once the data was collected and the machine learning model was trained, it can then make a prediction on whether or not the data it is being fed is from a healthy MEL or a MEL with a certain amount of damage. This process is shown in Figure 1 below. In order to quantify and differentiate the states of structure for the model, mass was added (non-destructive) and mass was removed (destructive). The methodology had to be validated through non-destructive techniques before actually damaging the MEL itself, since there was only one undamaged version of the MEL structure. Overall, once the model was validated and coupled with the destructive testing, the model would be able to accurately detect how much mass is removed from the structure based on the response it has received from the excitation.

Fig. 1 Methodology.

Experimental Setup

In designing the experimental setup, there were a couple of key components to consider. The first is how the MEL structure will be placed during testing. The MEL was oriented how it would be hung from an actual aircraft and hung from the lugs by a steel frame, which simulated the MEL's responses to vibrations more accurately to how it would in flight. Next, the sensor type, uniaxial accelerometers were selected as the sensor of choice as they had been proven to be simple and effective, from previous years of conducting similar experiments. These sensors also allowed for immediate testing without the need for the ordering of additional sensors. When considering sensor placement, locations were narrowed down through analysis of the MEL within FEA software, which included seeing the modal shapes and locations of high strain energy. In recording the frequency responses of structures placing sensors at locations of high strain energy and at locations of increased movement in the mode shapes allows for better frequency response.

For the experimental tests, 6 accelerometers were placed around the MEl measuring the response in each direction. When selecting an apparatus to excite the structure, a small piezo buzzer would be ideal for testing due to its low weight and controllable input. However, due to difficulties of manipulating the input signals into said piezo and the additional time needed to understand how to properly employ it, a mini-inertial shaker combined with a small amplifier was used instead to allow for immediate testing and was placed at the bottom of the legs of the MEL. This shaker is connected to a small amplifier, which takes inputs from the DAQ using DewesoftX's function generator. A force sensor is connected to the shaker to measure the input response from the actuator itself. Similarly, the accelerometers are connected to the DAQ as well, providing their response readings throughout testing. The input signal provided by the functions generator itself is also recorded, so that the input signal and the actual input of the actuator can be compared. Throughout testing, the mini shaker would perform a logarithmic sine sweep from a frequency of 10 Hz to 1000 Hz, and then loop back down in the span of 20 seconds. This process allowed for a simple and consistent data collection process due to the input being automated, whilst

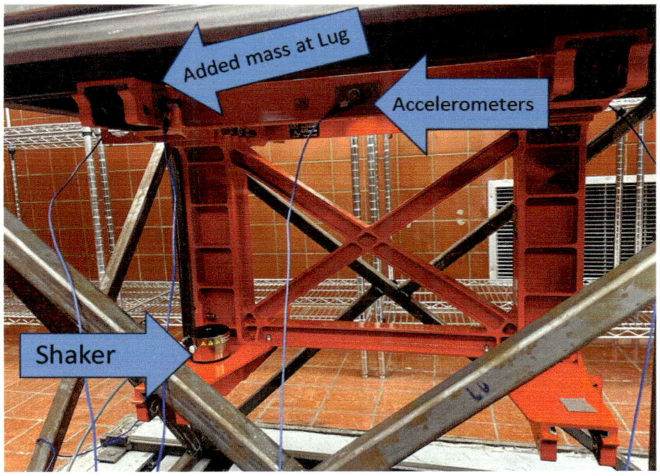

Fig. 2 Experimental Setup.

also being easily repeatable, allowing for the collection of large amounts of data sets at a time. A view of the experimental setup can be seen in Figure 2.

Experimental Results

Non-Destructive Cases

The damages cases for the non-destructive cases include the addition of 5, 7.5,10.15, 22.5, and 30 grams at the base of one lug. Non-destructive testing is a good way to validate our model without having to damage the MEL structure. The data collection process consisted of a sine sweep from the inertial shaker that lasted 20 seconds and accelerometers would record the response. Each testing case included 100 repetitions of acceleration response data. Then 20% of the data was used for training and 80% for evaluation in the SVR machine learning model. If the model is successful it will correctly predict how much damage a particular case has depending on the frequency response. Figure 3 shows that our model had a strong fit and

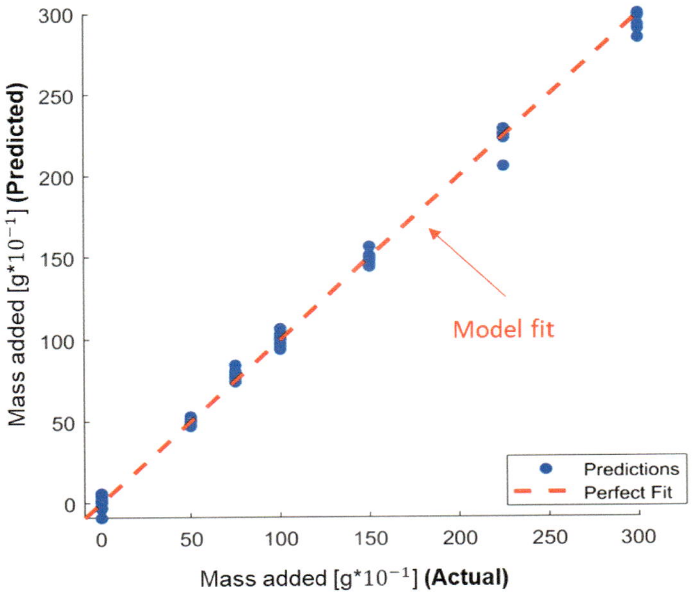

Fig. 3 SVR for Non-destructive Cases.

was able to classify the amount of damage that was present, with a root squared mean error (RSME) of less than 0.5g which means that our model had a high predictive accuracy of how much mass is removed from the MEL.

Destructive Cases

The same methodology and experimental setup was applied for the non-destructive case. The only difference is that the MEL would be damaged by removing mass around the lug. To execute this the MEL was cut by a milling machine, carefully and not excessively damaging the structure. To measure the amount of mass removed from the structure we weighed the MEL before and after it was cut. The first cut removed 1.6 grams and increased to 2.3 grams and ended with 4.1 grams. The cuts that were made on the structure are pictured in Figure 4. Using the same SVR model to see if the machine learning algorithm could predict how much mass was removed from the MEL. In Figure 5, the SVR predictions show a strong correlation in our model identifying how much damage is on the MEL. At this point the model was proven successful and yield promising results.

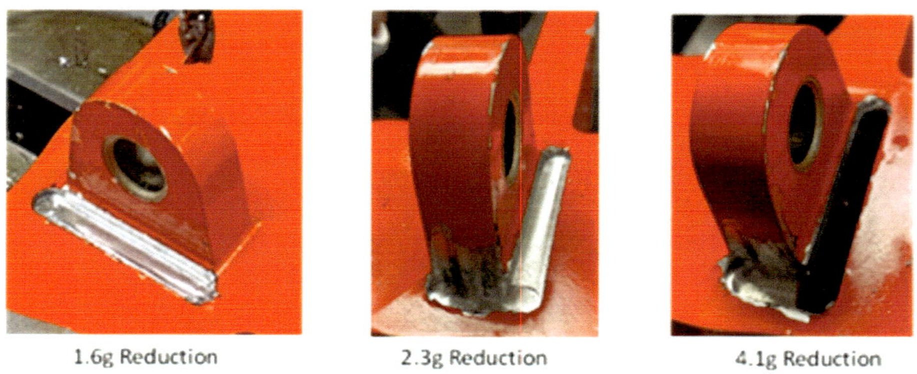

Fig. 4 Damage Test Cases.

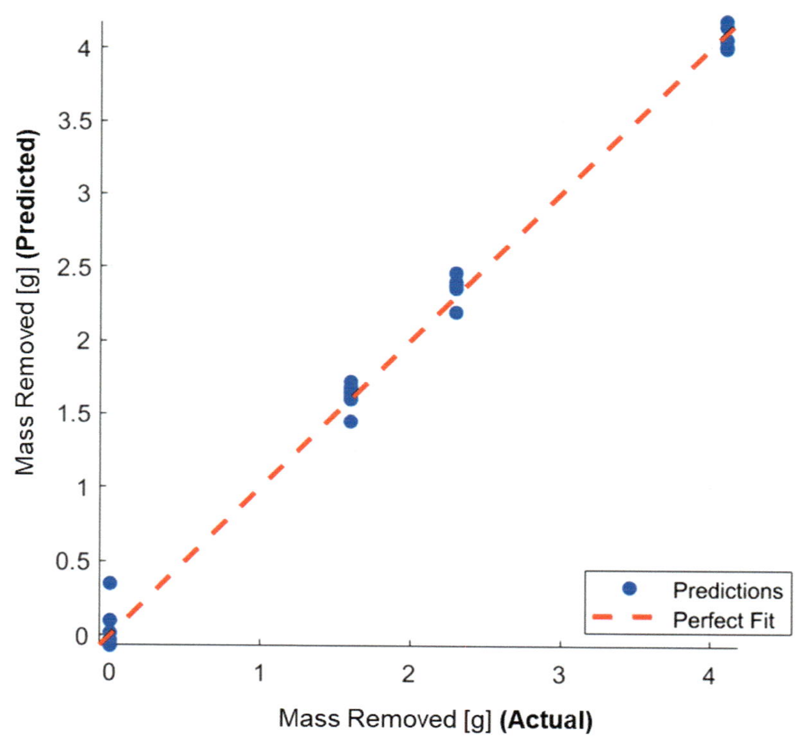

Fig. 5 SVR Results Destructive Case.

Limitations

The regression models developed demonstrated promising results; however it is important to test their robustness. In order to make sure that our model is able to identify if the structure is damaged and not just matching patterns, more analysis is required. One way to examine this, is to to test the performance of the model with regard to unseen data classes. Therefore two scenarios of our destructive cases were tested, damage cases of 1.6 grams and 4.1 grams removed from the structure were removed from the training data. These tests were done separately, not simultaneously, to see if the model could still predict those damage cases, even though they were left out of the training data. In completing this analysis that is shown in figures 6 and 7, the predictions of damage were not accurate. These results can be interpreted that the model will perform well under the circumstance that it has data from every damage case possible. This also indicates that there is a possibility the model was not identifying the physics of the model and rather trying to pattern match and does poorly when it has not seen similar cases in the training data.

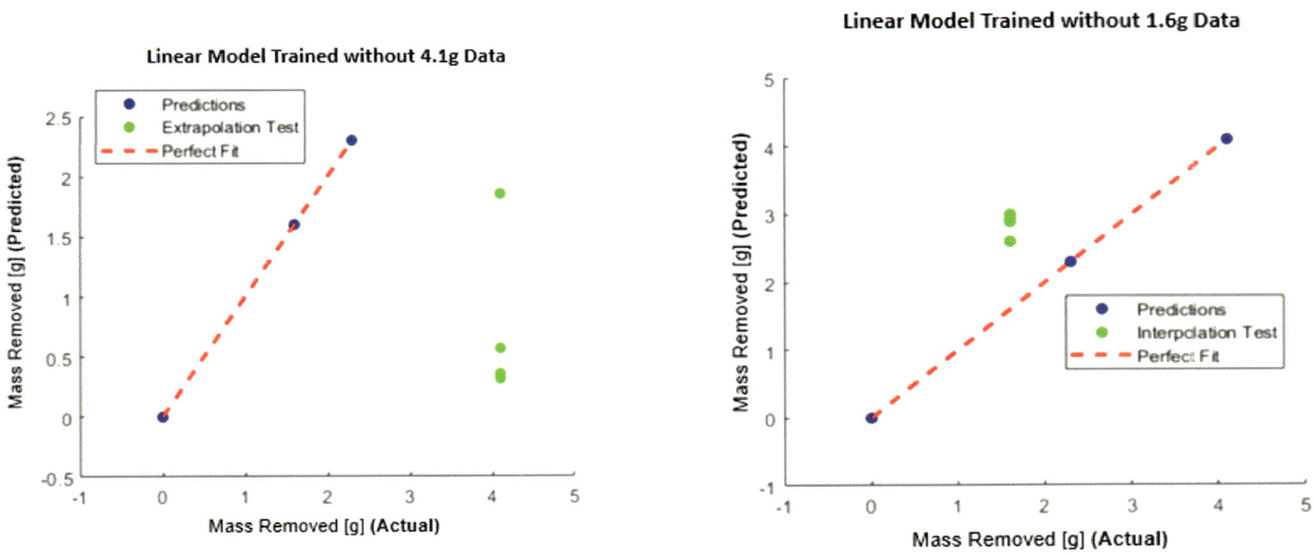

Figs. 6 & 7 SVR INTERPOLATION RESULTS.

Conclusion

The results demonstrate the application of a damage detection system to an aircraft and practicability of utilizing structural health monitoring for damage detection. However, there are still clear limitations of the models used in these experiments, and still have significant room for improvement. Although a regression model can be fit to experimental testing data with a strong correlation, the model fails to accurately predict data it has not seen before. There are a few ways to mitigate the effects of this flaw in the model. The first is to increase the amount of training data. The experimental damage cases only included 3 different test cases, if increased would likely lead to more robust results. Additionally, if there were more cases given as training data for the model, the less the model must interpolate new data. The second method is to change the damage sensitive features implemented in the machine learning model. The purpose of the damage sensitive features is to extract characteristics of the frequency data that are sensitive to damage. The features used in these regression models are not extracting the necessary information from the frequency data and should be changed to ensure stronger results. Aside from improving the accuracy of this system, another area for improvement would be to expand the capabilities of this system to be able to determine the location of damage alongside severity.

Acknowledgments The team would like to acknowledge the support from US Army Program Executive Office - Aviation, PM FARA, and Fulcrum. Specifically, express our gratitude to Dr. Danny Parker, Mr. Kevin McGonigle, Mr. James Hale, Mr. Mike Pollut, Ms. Monna Moser and Mr. Evan Stringer for their advice and support throughout the project. Finally, we would like to acknowledge capstone advisors Dr. Matarazzo and LTC Bellocchio for their unending support for this project and team.

References

1. Boller, C. (2000). Next generation structural health monitoring and its integration into aircraft design. International Journal of Systems Science, 31(11), 1333–1349. https://doi.org/10.1080/00207720050197730
2. Dhakal, D. R., et al. "Different techniques of structural health monitoring." Research and Development (IJCSEIERD) 3.2 (2013): 55–66.
3. N. Doshi, E. Lepp, C. Sowinski, "Evaluating Damage Sensitive Features for Stiffness Loss Detection in an Aircraft Component using ML Classifiers". Pages 2–3.
4. W. Ostachowicz, R. Soman, and P. Malinowski, "Optimization of sensor placement for structural health monitoring: a review," *Struct. Heal. Monit.*, vol. 18, no. 3, pp. 963–988, 2019, doi:10.1177/1475921719825601.
5. M. Rébillat, O. Hmad, F. Kadri, and N. Mechbal, "Peaks Over Threshold-based detector design for structural health monitoring: Application to aerospace structures," *Struct. Heal. Monit.*, vol. 17, no. 1, pp. 91–107, 2018, doi:10.1177/1475921716685039.
6. C. Rainieri, F. Magalhaes, and F. Ubertini, "Editorial Automated Operational Modal Analysis and Its Applications in Structural Health Monitoring," 2019, doi:10.1155/2019/5497065.
7. Y. Bhuiyan, J. Bao, B. Poddar, and V. Giurgiutiu, "Toward identifying crack-length-related resonances in acoustic emission waveforms for structural health monitoring applications," *Struct. Heal. Monit.*, vol. 17, no. 3, pp. 577–585, 2018, doi:10.1177/1475921717707356.
8. J. J. Villacorta *et al.*, "Design and Validation of a Scalable, Reconfigurable and Low-Cost Structural Health Monitoring System," 2021, doi:10.3390/s21020648.
9. K. Krishnan Nair, Anne S. Kiremidjian, Kincho H. Law, Time series-based damage detection and localization algorithm with application to the ASCE benchmark structure, Journal of Sound and Vibration,Volume 291, Issues 1–2, 2006, Pages 349–368,
10. R. Soman, K. Balasubramaniam, A. Golestani, M. Karpiński, and P. Malinowski, "A Two-Step Guided Waves Based Damage Localization Technique Using Optical Fiber Sensors," *Sensors*, vol. 20, no. 20, p. 5804, Oct. 2020, doi:10.3390/s20205804.
11. Reuland Y, Martakis P, Chatzi E. A Comparative Study of Damage-Sensitive Features for Rapid Data-Driven Seismic Structural Health Monitoring. Applied Sciences. 2023; 13(4):2708. https://doi.org/10.3390/app13042708

Chapter 17
Physics-Informed Machine Learning for Advanced Structural Damage Detection and Localization

Zixin Wang, Mohammad R. Jahanshahi, and Shirley J. Dyke

Abstract Structural damage detection and localization are crucial aspects of structural health monitoring. Unsupervised anomaly detection can predict whether the structure is healthy or damaged, but it may face challenges in localizing the damage. In contrast, supervised damage detection can localize damage when the damage diagnosis model is trained with data from a finite element model (FEM) that accurately represents the actual structure. However, mismatches between the FEM and the actual structure are inevitable due to modeling errors, real-world uncertainties, and varying operational conditions. Consequently, a damage diagnosis model trained on the FEM cannot be directly applied to the actual structure because of discrepancies in training and testing data distributions. To bridge this gap, we propose a novel approach using hierarchical physics-informed domain adaptation. Our approach begins by detecting structural anomalies using deep autoencoders and information fusion. If the structure is identified as damaged, physics-informed domain adaptation is then employed to localize the damage. A convolutional neural network (CNN) is pre-trained to predict the frequency response functions of the structure. The weights of this pre-trained CNN model are then used to initialize a domain adaptation neural network, specifically a discriminator-free adversarial learning network (DALN). This modal-based weight initialization imposes physical constraints on the DALN. We evaluate the proposed approach using both numerical and experimental ASCE benchmark setups. The results demonstrate that our approach outperforms existing state-of-the-art methods, even when the damaged state data from the target structure is excluded from training, thereby enhancing the real-world applicability of the proposed solution.

Keywords Structural health monitoring · Structural damage detection · Physics-informed neural networks · Domain adaptation · Deep learning

Introduction

Structural damage detection is critical for ensuring the safety and health of civil infrastructures. Data-driven models based on machine learning have been widely utilized in this field. For example, unsupervised learning uses data in the healthy state of the structure to train a model, which can then be used for structural anomaly detection (i.e., determining whether the structure is damaged). In addition to anomaly detection, damage localization is important for pinpointing the damaged area and retrofitting the structure. Supervised learning requires labeled data in both healthy and damaged states to train a model, which can then be used to predict the damage location. However, collecting massive amounts of data from an actual structure in various damage scenarios is impractical. Therefore, a digital twin, consisting of a physical structure and a corresponding FEM as its virtual representation, can be constructed. The FEM can generate the data needed to train the supervised learning model. It is worth noting that supervised learning relies on the assumption that the training and testing datasets have the

Zixin Wang · Mohammad R. Jahanshahi · Shirley J. Dyke
Lyles School of Civil and Construction Engineering, Purdue University, West Lafayette, IN 47907
e-mail: wang4591@purdue.edu; jahansha@purdue.edu; sdyke@purdue.edu

Mohammad R. Jahanshahi
Elmore Family School of Electrical and Computer Engineering, Purdue University, West Lafayette, IN 47907
e-mail: jahansha@purdue.edu

Shirley J. Dyke
School of Mechanical Engineering, Purdue University, West Lafayette, IN 47907
e-mail: sdyke@purdue.edu

Brian Damiano et al. (eds.), *Structural Health Monitoring & Machine Learning, Vol. 12*, Conference Proceedings of the Society for Experimental Mechanics Series, https://doi.org/10.13052/9788743801573-17

same data distribution, meaning that the FEM must accurately represent the actual structure. However, mismatches between the FEM and the actual structure are inevitable due to modeling errors, real-world uncertainties, and operational conditions. These mismatches can cause the trained model to fail in predicting the damage location on the actual structure.

Domain adaptation, a subset of transfer learning, transfers knowledge from a source domain (e.g., the FEM) to a related target domain (e.g., the actual structure) by learning domain-invariant features through domain-adversarial training. Even though the extracted features from the two domains have close data distributions, the trained model may struggle to extract damage-informative features for damage localization. Additionally, current domain adaptation methods require a large amount of unlabeled data from the target structure to train the model. However, collecting sufficient unlabeled data in various damaged scenarios of the actual structure is infeasible. In this work, we propose a hierarchical physics-informed domain adaptation approach (HierPhyDALN). More specifically, structural anomaly detection is first performed using a deep autoencoder and information fusion, and if the structure is identified as damaged, then physics-informed domain adaptation is employed to localize the damage. Physical constraints are applied to DALN through modal-based weight initialization, which effectively forces DALN to learn damage-informative features. Our approach is rigorously validated using both numerical and experimental ASCE benchmark setups, demonstrating the superior performance of our approach compared to other state-of-the-art methods, even when trained exclusively on data representing the healthy state of the target structure.

Methodology

Intra-class variance evaluates the model's adaptability to a new task, indicating how transferable the model is. Data in damaged states of the structure typically exhibit a larger intra-class variance than data in the healthy state, indicating that the damaged state data is more efficient for domain adaptation. Therefore, hierarchical damage detection is proposed, wherein structural anomaly detection is initially performed using an unsupervised autoencoder and information fusion [1]. If the structure is identified as damaged, physics-informed domain adaptation, which is trained exclusively on the damaged state data, is deployed to predict the damage location. The adversarial paradigm in the form of DALN is adopted for domain adaptation. DALN consists of a feature extractor G and a damage predictor C. The damage predictor C is reused as a discriminator D by incorporating Nuclear-norm Wasserstein discrepancy, which enables feature extractor G to learn domain-invariant features. The loss function used to optimize DALN can be expressed as:

$$\min_{C,G}\left\{\frac{1}{N_s}\sum_{i=1}^{N_s}\mathcal{L}_{ce}\left(C\left(G\left(x_i^s\right)\right),y_i^s\right)+\lambda\max_{C}\left\{\frac{1}{N_s}\sum_{i=1}^{N_s}\|C\left(G\left(x_i^s\right)\right)\|_*-\frac{1}{N_t}\sum_{j=1}^{N_t}\left\|C\left(G\left(x_j^t\right)\right)\right\|_*\right\}\right\} \tag{1}$$

To enforce DALN to learn damage-informative features, we propose a physics-informed neural network using modal-based weight initialization. Specifically, a CNN containing a feature extractor G and a modal predictor M is pre-trained to predict the FRFs of source and target structures. Note that the modal predictor M and the damage predictor C share the same architecture, except for their output layers. The weights from the pre-trained CNN are then utilized to initialize DALN, thereby imposing physical constraints on DALN and enabling it to learn modal-related features such as natural frequencies and mode shapes, which are conducive to damage localization. DALN is fine-tuned using labeled data from the source domain and unlabeled data from the target domain. In this study, the input to the data-driven models is the continuous wavelet transforms of acceleration signals. Fig. 1 provides an overview of the proposed approach.

Numerical Study: ASCE Benchmark Models

The benchmark structure is a four-story, two-bay by two-bay quarter-scale steel frame constructed at the University of British Columbia. A 12-degree-of-freedom (DOF) model and a 120-DOF model, as shown in Fig. 2, are built to generate simulated response data [2]. Though the model parameters of the 12-DOF model are updated using the transitional Markov chain Monte Carlo (TMCMC) approach to match the modal properties of the 120-DOF model, domain discrepancies between the two models still exist. To predict the damage categories on the target structure, domain adaptation is performed between the 12-DOF model (the source structure) and the 120-DOF model (the target structure). Structural damage is emulated by removing the braces on each story, resulting in five categories, including one healthy category and four damaged categories with each story being damaged. A hammer is used to excite each floor and the corresponding vibration responses are calculated. For each damage category, 80 samples are generated with each sample containing 16 sensor signals. Since the

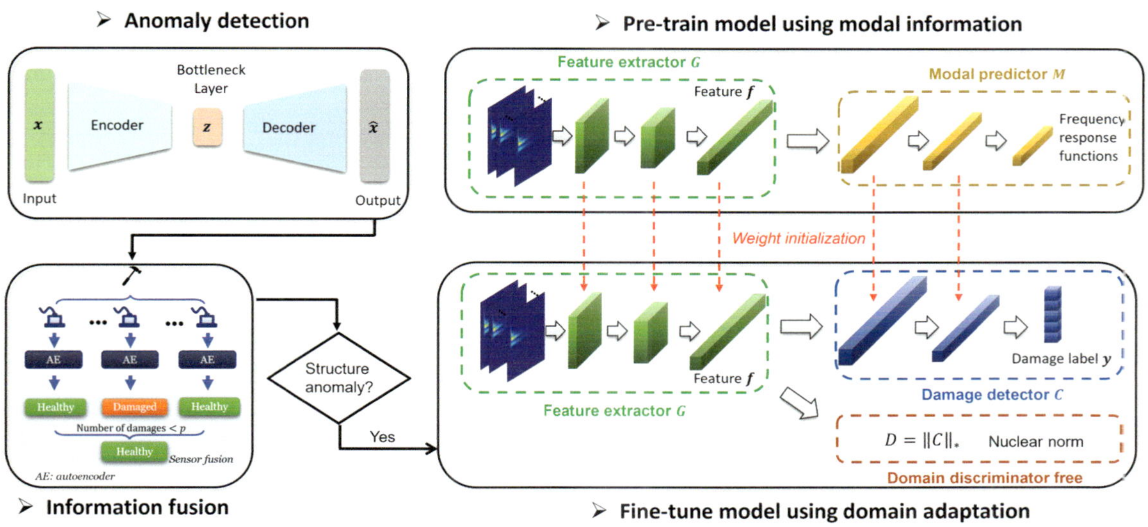

Fig. 1 An overview of the proposed approach.

120-DOF model represents the actual structure, 5% structural uncertainty and 10% measurement noise are introduced to the model.

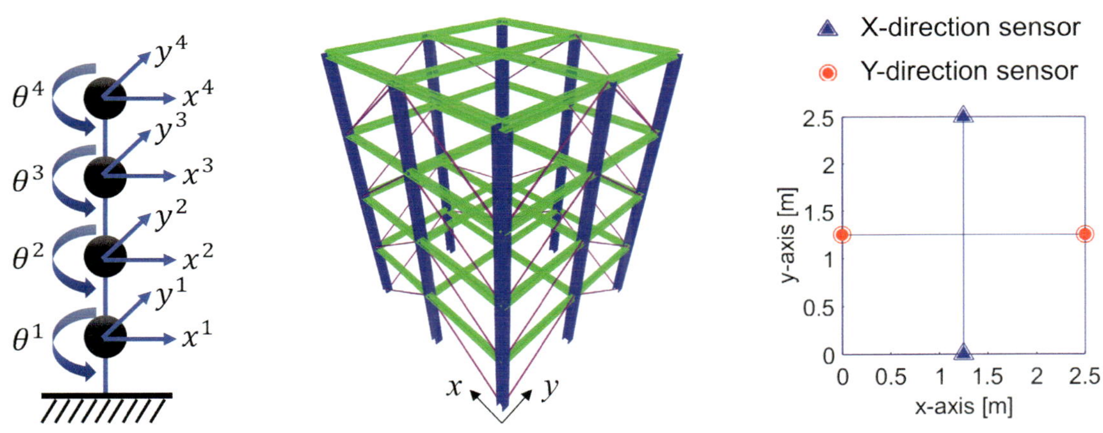

Fig. 2 ASCE benchmark models.

We compared our proposed approach (HierPhyDALN) with other state-of-the-art methods, as summarized in Table 1. Each approach is trained 30 times to consider the randomness of weight initialization during training. Damage detection results on the 120-DOF model using different approaches are presented in Fig. 3. The results demonstrate that hierarchical damage detection, which includes anomaly detection followed by damage localization, can significantly enhance accuracy. This improvement is attributed to the larger intra-class variance of the damaged state data, which enhances the adaptability of the DALN trained exclusively on the damaged state data. Furthermore, the physics-informed DALN outperforms the pure DALN. This is because the modal-based weight initialization constrains DALN from learning damage-informative features, which is conducive to damage localization. It is worth noting that collecting data in different damaged scenarios on the actual structure is impractical. However, our proposed approach can achieve promising performance even when the damaged state data from the target structure is excluded from the training (Fig. 3(b)).

Table 1 State-of-the-art approaches used for structural damage detection and comparison in this study.

Approach	DALN	Physics-informed NN	Hierarchical damage detection
#1: SCNN	×	×	×
#2: DALN	✓	×	×
#3: HierSCNN	×	×	✓
#4: HierDALN	✓	×	✓
#5: HierPhyDALN (ours)	✓	✓	✓
#6: PhyDALN	✓	✓	×

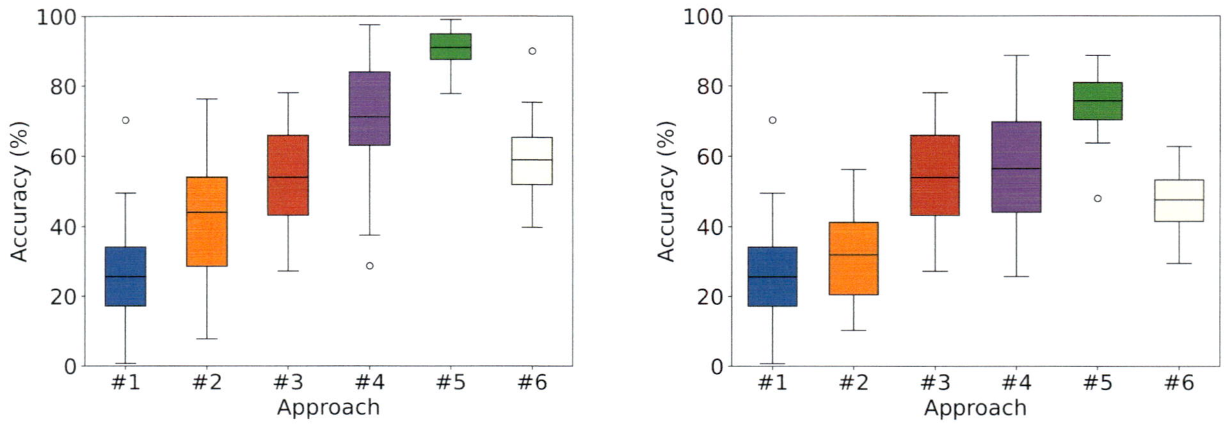

(a) Unlabeled data in damaged states of the 120-DOF model are **included** in the training.

(b) Unlabeled data in damaged states of the 120-DOF model are **excluded** from the training.

Fig. 3 Damage detection results on the 120-DOF model using different approaches.

Experimental Study: ASCE Benchmark Structure

In this section, we validate our approach using the actual benchmark structure (the target structure) and the 120-DOF model (the source structure), as shown in Fig. 4. The model parameters of the 120-DOF model are updated using the TMCMC approach to match the modal properties of the actual structure, yet the source and target domains still exhibit different data distributions. In the target domain, 7 samples for the healthy category are collected from the actual structure subjected to hammer impact, with each sample containing 12 sensor signals. Additionally, three damage categories are implemented on the actual structure: (i) brace damage on the east face; (ii) brace damage on the east and north faces; and (iii) brace damage on all faces, with 24, 6, and 18 samples collected for each damaged category, respectively. In the source domain, 96 samples are generated using the 120-DOF model for the healthy category, and 384, 96, and 288 samples are generated for the three damaged categories, respectively. The damage detection results using different approaches, excluding the damaged state data of the actual structure from training, are shown in Fig. 5. We also perform t-tests on the results obtained by our proposed approach versus other approaches, as listed in Table 2. All p-values are below 0.05, indicating that our approach has statistically significant improvements compared to other state-of-the-art methods, even with limited data from the actual structure.

Table 2 T-test on the results obtained by the proposed approach versus other state-of-the-art methods.

Approach	P-value
#1 vs #5	4.15×10^{-17}
#2 vs #5	2.32×10^{-12}
#3 vs #5	5.18×10^{-12}
#4 vs #5	1.99×10^{-9}
#6 vs #5	4.34×10^{-2}

(a) 120-DOF model (source structure)

(b) Actual benchmark structure (target structure)

(c) Sensor location (top view)

Fig. 4 ASCE benchmark structure.

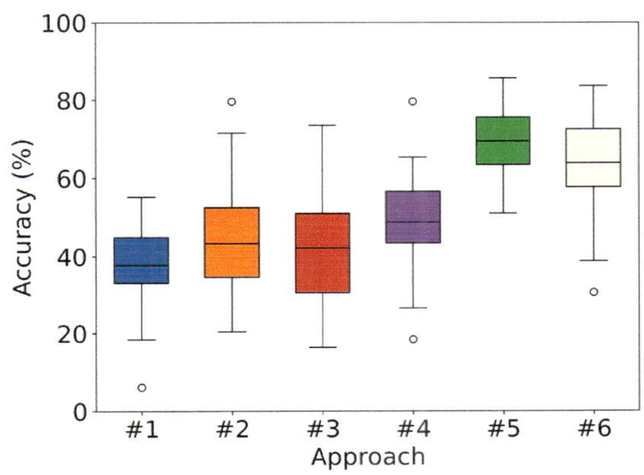

Fig. 5 Damage detection results on the actual structure.

Conclusion

This study proposes a hierarchical physics-informed domain adaptation approach (HierPhyDALN) to address the domain shift between the FEM and the actual structure in supervised damage detection. Hierarchical damage detection leverages the larger intra-class variance of the damaged state data to enhance the adaptability of DALN. The physical constraints through modal-based weight initialization enable DALN to learn damage-informative features. Results from both numerical and experimental ASCE benchmark setups indicate that our approach outperforms other state-of-the-art methods, even when the damaged state data from the target structure is excluded from training, thus enhancing the real-world applicability of the proposed solution.

Acknowledgments This research is funded by the National Aeronautics and Space Administration (NASA) under award number 80NSSC19K1076.

References

1. Wang, Z., Jahanshahi, M.R., Bilionis, I., Fu, Y., Maghareh, A., and Dyke, S.J. Unsupervised Structural Damage Detection on Extraterrestrial Habitats using Information Fusion and Autoencoders. The 14th International Workshop on Structural Health Monitoring (IWSHM), September 12–14, 2023, Standford University, California.
2. Johnson, E.A., Lam, H.F., Katafygiotis, L.S., and Beck, J.L. 2004. "Phase I IASC-ASCE structural health monitoring benchmark problem using simulated data." *Journal of Engineering Mechanics*, 130 (1): 3–15.

Chapter 18
Damage Detection Strategy Based on PCA/Mode-Shapes Developed on a Laboratory Truss Girder Subjected to Environmental Variations

M. Berardengo, F. Lucà, S. Manzoni, S. Pavoni, and M. Vanali

Abstract In recent years, Structural Health Monitoring has become a fundamental area within industrial, aerospace, and civil engineering, offering a wide range of techniques to predict, assess, and manage potential structural damage. Most of the proposed strategies focus on handling and analyzing damage-sensitive features of the system under observation, continuously monitoring and evaluating changes in these characteristics over time. Among the various methods developed recently, vibration analysis has proven to be particularly promising. This work presents an unsupervised learning approach for detecting structural damage using vibration data. The study involves a benchmark test exploiting a custom-designed laboratory truss girder to develop damage detection strategies based on acceleration measurements. The approach employs statistical pattern recognition employing mode-shapes as damage-sensitive features. Distinct attention is given to practical aspects such as sparse sensor layouts, managing long-term monitoring data, and introducing synthetic damage indicators to support maintenance decisions. The algorithm is validated using real data from acceleration measurements on the laboratory truss girder, which has been monitored for several months under varying environmental conditions, including temperature fluctuations and sunlight exposure.

Keywords Structural Health Monitoring · Damage Detection · Principal Component Analysis · Operational Modal Analysis · Environmental Variation

Introduction

Buildings, structures, and mechanical components inevitably deteriorate over time due to environmental exposure and material fatigue, leading to a loss of functionality. Structural Health Monitoring (SHM) plays a fundamental role in the investigation of the conditions of these systems. Indeed, detecting critical conditions or potential damage is essential for both safety and economic reasons, as it allows for planning the maintenance or renovations of determined components most efficiently [1]. In this branch, the interest in vibration-based techniques has grown significantly due to their practical benefit. Indeed, these methods do not require prior knowledge of damage location, and the use of accelerometers (common in these strategies) is non-destructive and can be easily applied to existing structures [2]. Several techniques have been developed to detect damage in real structures or models using modal parameters like natural frequencies [3], damping coefficients [4], and mode shapes [5]. While vibration-based methods appear intuitive, their practical application faces significant challenges due to the impact of environmental and operational conditions [6]. These factors can alter modal parameters to an extent comparable to or greater than possible incoming damage, limiting the effectiveness of these parameters in SHM. Several studies have demonstrated a high correlation between natural frequencies and both daily and seasonal environmental temperature drift

M. Berardengo
Department of Mechanical, Management and Transportation Engineering, Università di Genova, 16145 Genova, Italy
e-mail: marta.berardengo@unige.it

F. Lucà · S. Manzoni
Department of Mechanical Engineering, Politecnico di Milano, 20156 Milan, Italy
e-mail: francescantonio.luca@polimi.it; stefano.manzoni@polimi.it

S. Pavoni · M. Vanali
Department of Engineering for Industrial Systems and Technologies, Università di Parma, 43124 Parma, Italy
e-mail: stefano.pavoni@unipr.it; marcello.vanali@unipr.it

Brian Damiano et al. (eds.), *Structural Health Monitoring & Machine Learning, Vol. 12*, Conference Proceedings of the Society for Experimental Mechanics Series, https://doi.org/10.13052/9788743801573-18

[7]. On the other hand, the influence of thermal gradients on the mode shape evolution is still partially unexplored. Thermal gradients within a structure can affect mode shape estimation, particularly in large structures like bridges and skyscrapers, where uneven sunlight exposure creates non-uniform thermal characteristics. The most common methods for removing the environmental effects rely on the Principal Component Analysis (PCA), which is a powerful tool for detecting structural damage and reducing the ambient and operational impact on measured data [8]. However, this technique requires further exploration in strategies where mode shapes are used as damage-sensitive features. In the literature, mode shapes are commonly evaluated using the Modal Assurance Criterion (MAC), which is an index with a distribution represented by an inverse exponential [9]. Nevertheless, it is often reported that machine learning algorithms are much more effective when input data are characterized with a normal distribution.

This work proposes an unsupervised damage detection strategy using mode shapes as damage-sensitive features. The method employs robust PCA and Mahalanobis Squared Distance (MSD) to filter out outliers and mitigate environmental effects on mode shapes [10]. The method has been validated with real data from a laboratory truss girder structure subjected to environmental variability. Over several months, the structure was monitored under uncontrolled factors such as temperature fluctuations and sunlight exposure, with modal parameters continuously estimated via an automatic Operational Modal Analysis (OMA) algorithm, and environmental parameters tracked using thermocouples. The next section provides an introduction to the truss girder benchmark and data acquisition setup.

Benchmark and Experimental Setup

The benchmark of this work is a laboratory truss girder realized ad-hoc at the University of Parma for SHM purposes. The structure employed as a validation case study is a classic two-dimensional Pratt truss anchored to the floor through rigid support. The structure is secured by Teflon roller connections at both bottom ends through a clamp system. It presents a 4.20-meter span and a height of approximately 80 cm, and it is composed of diagonal and vertical aluminum rods with a 1.2 cm hexagonal cross-section and lengths of 50 cm (vertical) or 70 cm (diagonal). The horizontal members are two steel H-beams, each 430 cm long and 1.1 cm thick. Stability is enhanced by seven 15 kg masses at the base nodes. The structure is held upright by four struts positioned at 1/3 and 2/3 of the span, with stainless steel cylinders functioning as rollers to permit only vertical movement.

Unfortunately, the ambient excitation of the laboratory does not reach an adequate level for a reliable evaluation of the modal parameters. Therefore, an electro-dynamic PCB model 2007E shaker is employed to excite the structure vertically using a band-limited white noise signal up to 200 Hz. The dynamic of the system is measured with 6 Micro Electro Mechanical System (MEMS) accelerometers TE4030 model with a sensitivity of 1 V/g, a measurement range of ± 2 g, and a bandwidth of 0-200 Hz. Ambient conditions are tracked with 4 thermocouples type K placed at different points of the structure. Each test is then performed every 30 minutes to evaluate the evolution of modal and ambient parameters constantly. In Figure 1 the experimental setup layout is presented.

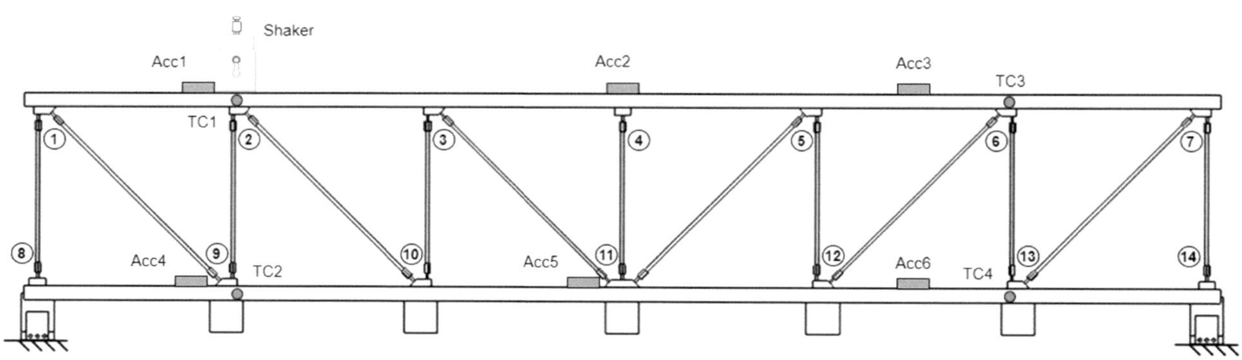

Fig. 1 Truss sketch with node numeration and data acquisition system layout with shaker, accelerometers (grey rectangles) and thermocouples (green circles) location.

Feature Extraction

In this work, the mode shapes of the structure are employed as damage-sensitive features. Modal parameters evaluation is performed employing an automatic OMA algorithm in MATLAB environment, using a poly-reference least-squares complex frequency-domain method [11]. The truss girder presents 5 modes in the frequency range of interest 0-200 Hz. The mode shapes estimated are normalized with respect to the accelerometer 1, which is positioned near the excitation point. Mode shapes experimentally evaluated from the truss girder are presented in Figure 2.

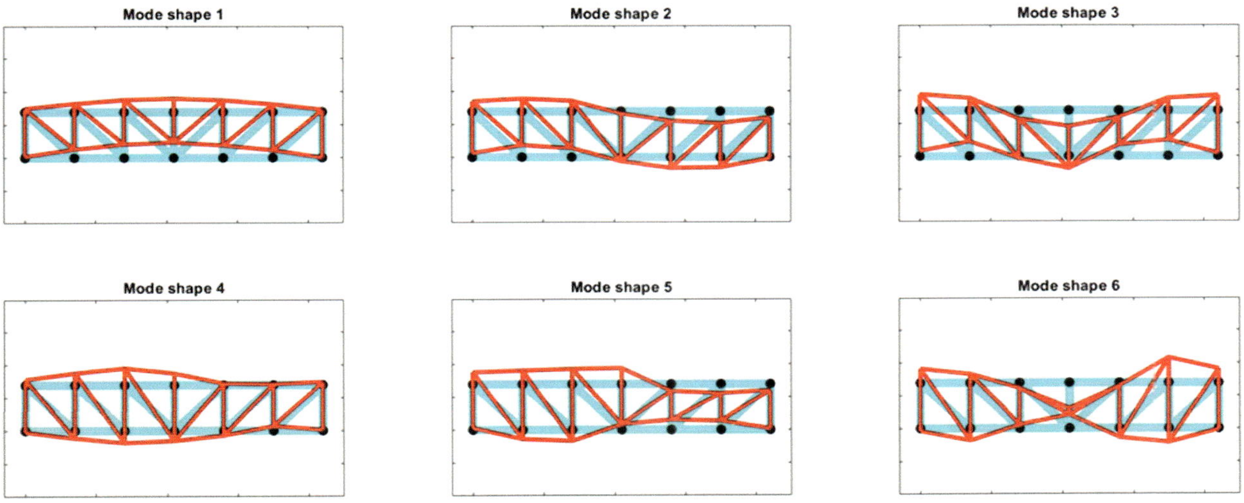

Fig. 2 Truss girder mode shapes experimentally evaluated.

Since the accelerometers employed are 6, for each mode the features available are 5, for a total amount of 25 values for each observation. Therefore, a new observation i obtained for each test results in a vector arranged as follows

$$x_i = [\ \varphi_2^1 \ \ \varphi_3^1 \ \ \varphi_4^1 \ \ \cdots \ \ \varphi_5^5\ ] \tag{1}$$

where φ_j^k is the eigenvector value corresponding to the accelerometer j of the mode k.

Once enough observations to establish a baseline including all ambient variations have been collected while the truss is maintained in healthy condition, PCA has been performed to remove the environmental impact on the data collected. In the case of the study, PCA is used to detect the principal components most sensitive to variations caused by the environmental evolution, in order to remove them and process the remaining principal scores which should represent the real structural state information. Unfortunately, the Pearson's coefficients evaluated between the principal scores and the temperature measurements have not demonstrated a high correlation between the investigated variables. Therefore, the first PCs to be removed have been selected using the Cumulative Variance Contribution Rate (CVCR) adopting a threshold of 99% [12]. The method proposed has shown that the first 11 PCs are representative of the 99% of the variance, as depicted in Figure 3, and, thus are removed from the damage detection strategy.

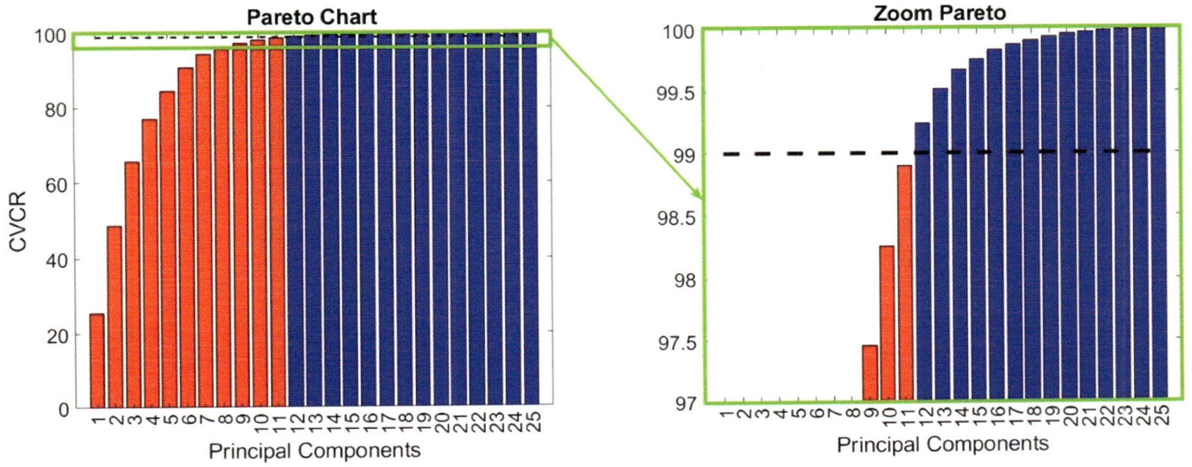

Fig. 3 Pareto chart of the Principal Components with the Cumulative Variance Contribution Rate (CVCR).

Damage Index Evaluation and Results

After the establishment of the baseline dataset and the alert threshold, the following step concerned the development of a synthetic index evaluated from each test performed on the truss girder. Each new damage-sensitive feature observation is standardized by employing the baseline averages and standard deviations. Then, a new vector of principal scores Z_i is achieved by projecting the standardized observation on the orthogonal system obtained from the PCA of the baseline. The first 12 elements are removed obtaining a new vector Z_i^* containing the structure characteristics without the environmental impact. Finally, a synthetic Damage Index (DI) is calculated by exploiting MSD with the following formula:

$$DI_i = \left(Z_i^* - \overline{Z_0^*}\right)^T \Sigma_0^{-1} (Z_i^* - \overline{Z_0^*}) \tag{2}$$

where $\overline{Z_0^*}$ are the baseline principal score averages without the first 12 elements and Σ_0 is the baseline covariance matrix.

Due to different environmental conditions, the baseline dataset has been selected including the period from 6th April to 22nd July. In Figure 4, the thermal gradients monitored during the baseline interval in the structure are shown.

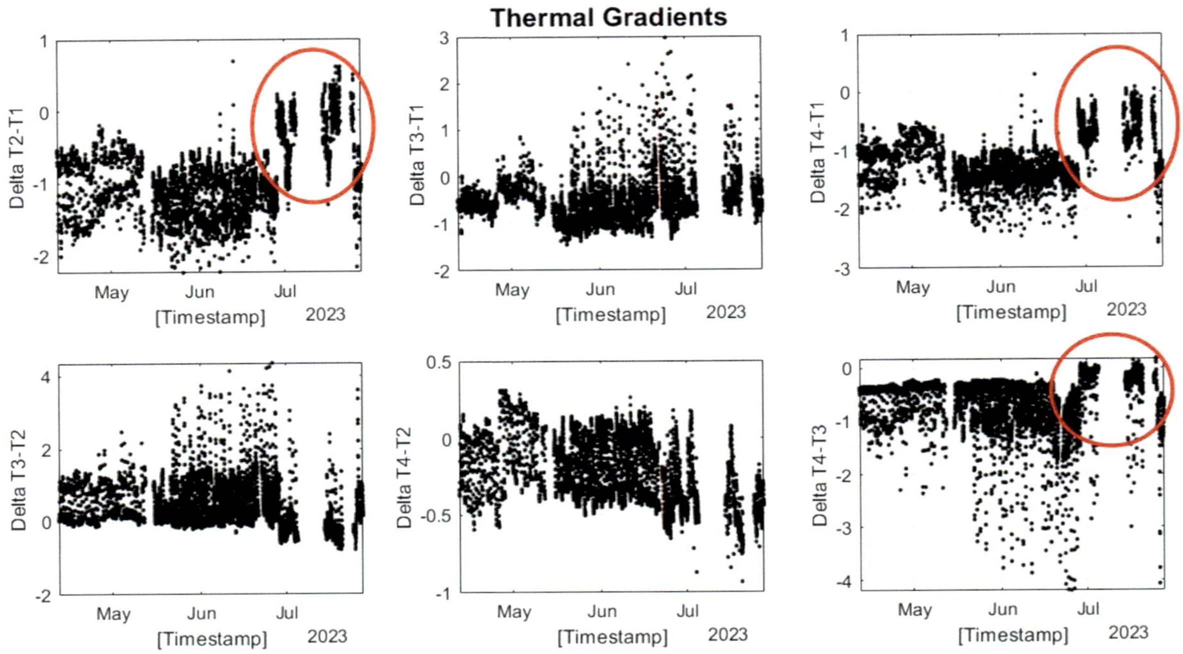

Fig. 4 Thermal gradients measured in the structure during the baseline interval, with different behaviors highlighted with red ellipses.

In the figure above it is possible to understand the extension of the baseline interval to the end of July, due to a completely different behavior of the thermal gradient of the structure.

Then, the strategy proposed has been validated against data measured from the structure, alternating healthy and damaged periods. The damages induced to the structure for the test case are:

- the application of 0.5 and 1 kg masses
- the reduction of the bolts torque in node connection elements.

In Figure 5, damages induced to the structure are presented.

Both scenarios simulate realistic damage typically experienced by a truss girder during its lifespan. The placement of additional masses represents a reduction in stiffness at specific locations of the structure. Given that the total mass of the truss girder is approximately 300 kg, the mass variation induced amounts to 0.17% and 0.33%, respectively. On the other hand, the reduction in bolts torque indicates a decrease in the effectiveness of the connection nodes (bolts or rivets). Initially, all bolts were tightened to a torque of 40 Nm, despite the nominal torque specification being around 12 Nm. The damage has been induced by decreasing it to 30, 20, 10, and 6 Nm.

(a)

(b)

Fig. 5 Damage induced to the structure: a) mass application and b) bolts torque reduction.

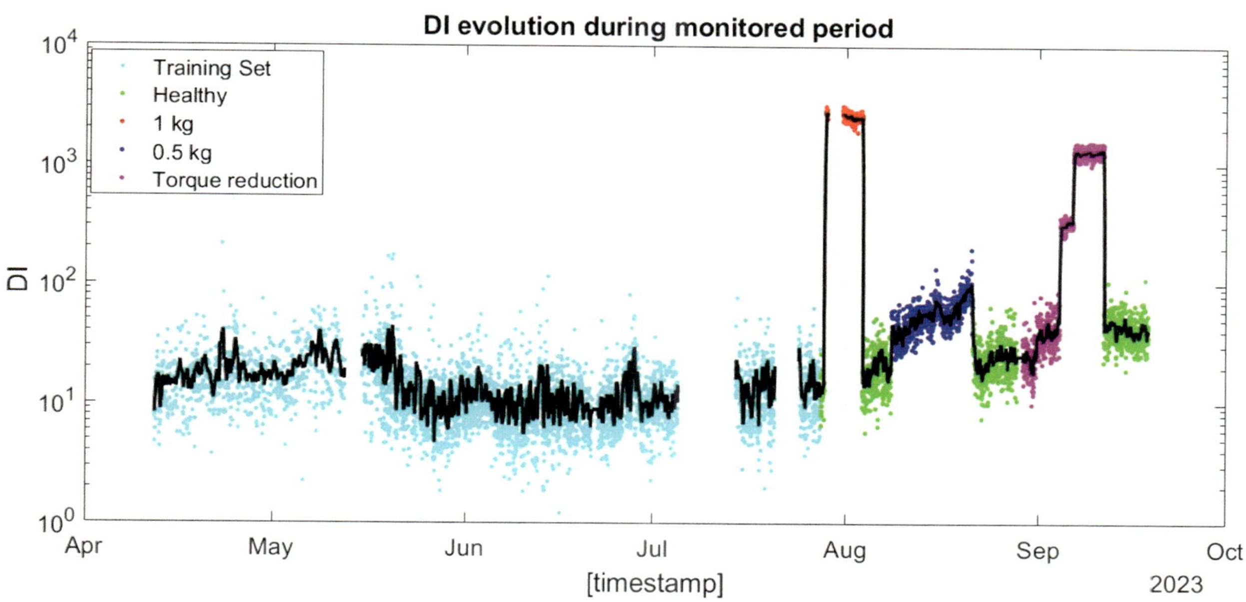

Fig. 6 DI evaluated with the strategy proposed against different damages induced to the structure.

DI results computed during the monitoring period are shown in Figure 6. The index proposed is even evaluated with a traveling mean (black line) to better understand its evolution during the monitored period.

Results show that the DI proposed in this work is not affected by the environmental impact. Furthermore, it is possible to appreciate the incredible increase in DI when the structure is affected by damage, while it returns to the baseline range when the structure is recovered to healthy conditions.

Conclusion

This paper proposes a new damage detection strategy with a strong immunity to environmental variations. A synthetic index DI is evaluated by analyzing the mode shapes of the structure in healthy conditions to establish a reference baseline. Then, mode shapes are processed using the PCA, excluding the first principal components (first eleven) affected by environmental factors by exploiting the CVCR method. The remaining principal scores, which are immune to ambient influences, are analyzed using statistical tools such as the MSD. Outliers in the proposed DI are interpreted as changes in the dynamic behavior of the structure caused by potential damage incoming. In order to validate the strategy proposed, two different damages have been induced to the structure: the positioning of different masses and the reduction of the tightening torque of the bolts in the connection elements between rods. Results obtained from the DI proposed demonstrate that the synthetic index effectively detects structural damage while remaining highly resistant to ambient variations.

References

1. C. R. Farrar and K. Worden, *Structural Health Monitoring*. Wiley, 2012. doi:10.1002/9781118443118.
2. Wei Fan and Pizhong Qiao, "Vibration-based Damage Identification Methods: A Review and Comparative Study," *Struct Health Monit*, vol. 10, no. 1, pp. 83–111, Jan. 2011, doi:10.1177/1475921710365419.
3. M. Radzieński, M. Krawczuk, and M. Palacz, "Improvement of damage detection methods based on experimental modal parameters," *Mech Syst Signal Process*, vol. 25, no. 6, pp. 2169–2190, Aug. 2011, doi:10.1016/j.ymssp.2011.01.007.
4. M. S. Cao, G. G. Sha, Y. F. Gao, and W. Ostachowicz, "Structural damage identification using damping: a compendium of uses and features," *Smart Mater Struct*, vol. 26, no. 4, p. 043001, Apr. 2017, doi:10.1088/1361-665X/aa550a.
5. A. K. Pandey, M. Biswas, and M. M. Samman, "Damage detection from changes in curvature mode shapes," *J Sound Vib*, vol. 145, no. 2, pp. 321–332, Mar. 1991, doi:10.1016/0022-460X(91)90595-B.
6. C. R. Farrar, S. W. Doebling, and D. A. Nix, "Vibration–based structural damage identification," *Philosophical Transactions of the Royal Society of London. Series A: Mathematical, Physical and Engineering Sciences*, vol. 359, no. 1778, pp. 131–149, Jan. 2001, doi:10.1098/rsta.2000.0717.
7. S. W. , and C. R. F. Doebling, "Using statistical analysis to enhance modal-based damage identification," *DAMAS. Vol. 97.*, 1997.
8. N. P. Raut, A. B. Kolekar, and S. L. Gombi, "Optimization techniques for damage detection of composite structure: A review," *Mater Today Proc*, vol. 45, pp. 4830–4834, 2021, doi:10.1016/j.matpr.2021.01.295.
9. S. Greś, M. Döhler, and L. Mevel, "Uncertainty quantification of the Modal Assurance Criterion in operational modal analysis," *Mech Syst Signal Process*, vol. 152, p. 107457, May 2021, doi:10.1016/j.ymssp.2020.107457.
10. A. Deraemaeker and K. Worden, "On the use of the Mahalanobis squared-distance to filter out environmental effects in structural health monitoring," *MATEC Web of Conferences*, vol. 16, p. 02004, Sep. 2014, doi:10.1051/matecconf/20141602004.
11. B. Peeters, H. Van der Auweraer, P. Guillaume, and J. Leuridan, "The PolyMAX Frequency-Domain Method: A New Standard for Modal Parameter Estimation?," *Shock and Vibration*, vol. 11, no. 3–4, pp. 395–409, 2004, doi:10.1155/2004/523692.
12. K. Pearson, "LIII. On lines and planes of closest fit to systems of points in space.," *The London, Edinburgh, and Dublin Philosophical Magazine and Journal of Science*, vol. 2, no. 11, pp. 559–572, Nov. 1901, doi:10.1080/14786440109462720.